DICTIONARY
of
BRITISH EDUCATION

PETER GORDON
DENIS LAWTON

WOBURN PRESS
LONDON • PORTLAND, OR

First published in 2003 in Great Britain by
WOBURN PRESS
Crown House, 47 Chase Side, Southgate
London N14 5BP

and in the United States of America by
WOBURN PRESS
c/o ISBS, 5824 N.E. Hassalo Street
Portland, Oregon, 97213-3644

Website: www.woburnpress.com

British Library Cataloguing in Publication Data

Gordon, Peter, 1927–
  Dictionary of British education
  1. Education – Great Britain – Dictionaries
  I. Title II. Lawton, Denis, 1931–
  379.4′1′03

        ISBN 0-7130-0237-9 (cloth)
        ISSN 0-7130-4051-3 (paper)

Library of Congress Cataloging-in-Publication Data

Gordon, Peter.
  Dictionary of British education/by Peter Gordon and Denis Lawton.
     p. cm.
  Includes bibliographical references and index.
  ISBN 0-7130-0237-9 (cloth) – ISBN 0-7130-4051-3 (pbk.)
    1. Education–Great Britain–Dictionaries. I. Gordon, Peter, 1927– II. Title.

LA632.L35 2003
370′.941′03–dc21

                                                    2002032766

Typeset in 11/13 Times by Cambridge Photosetting Services
Printed in Great Britain by MPG Books, Bodmin, Cornwall

CONTENTS

Introduction

Section 1 describes, in brief outline, the education differences between England, Northern Ireland, Scotland and Wales. Some distinctions have tended to develop since devolution in 1999–2000.

It was not easy to find a title for this book that would adequately describe what we have tried to do. We thought that we should provide a dictionary, but more than a simple set of definitions. Many words in education have to be put into some kind of historical or political context to become fully meaningful. For some items we have added whatever background we felt necessary.

Section 2, by far the longest section of the book, consists of an alphabetical list of items, with cross-references to other dictionary items in **bold** print to indicate any related items in the dictionary.

Section 3 of the book provides some historical background of events since 1800. We have limited what might have been a very long list by quoting only important landmarks.

Section 4 provides a list of Secretaries of State for Education, and of the Ministers, Presidents of the Board and Vice-Presidents of the Council who preceded the Secretaries of State.

Finally, Section 5 attempts to provide an up-to-date list of acronyms and abbreviations. There are too many of these in education and they have multiplied considerably in recent years. We have tried to include those we consider important and likely to last.

We hope that the book will enable parents, governors and others – as well as teachers and students – to find their way about the complex world of education. We would welcome any comments and corrections for later editions.

SECTION ONE

British Education

An Introduction to Four Systems

British Education: An Introduction to Four Systems

It is a mistake to assume that the four countries in the UK share the same education system. There are many similarities with some very important differences: for example, education is compulsory in all four countries, the compulsory period being 5–16 in England, Wales and Scotland, but 4–16 in Northern Ireland; all four systems have primary schools leading to post-primary or secondary schools but the age of transfer is 12 in Scotland, whereas it is 11 in the other three; in Scotland and Wales all secondary schools are comprehensive, whilst that is not true of England and Northern Ireland.

Attempts have sometimes been made to keep the systems close together; however, devolution in 2000 has encouraged Wales and Northern Ireland to develop distinctive differences, since most aspects of education policy have become the responsibility of the National Assembly of Wales and the Assembly of Northern Ireland; Scotland has always had an education system separate from that of England.

ENGLAND

In England education is the responsibility of the Department for Education and Skills (DfES) and the Secretary of State is a member of the Cabinet. It is by far the largest of the four systems, having about eight million children in more than 30,000 maintained schools. All children must begin attending full-time primary schooling at age five (unless parents make other satisfactory arrangements), but most children start much earlier: over half of the 3–4-year-olds attend nursery schools. The great majority of pupils transfer to secondary school at age 11, but a few local education authorities (LEAs) still have some middle schools for the 8–12 age group, or 9–13. Most secondary schools in England are comprehensive, but some LEAs have retained grammar schools and a selection system at age 11 plus based on performance in tests designed to assess academic ability.

Since the School Standards and Framework Act (1998) there have been three categories of school: community, foundation, and voluntary (divided into controlled and aided). Community schools (formerly county schools) are under greater control from the LEA which employs the staff, owns the land and buildings and has responsibility for deciding the arrangements for admissions. At foundation schools, the governing body employ the staff and have primary responsibility for admissions. Land and buildings are owned by the governing body or by a charitable foundation. Many voluntary aided schools are church schools (mostly Church of England or Roman Catholic but there are other schools linked to faith groups, including a few Islamic schools); the governing body employs the staff and decides admission arrangements. Land and buildings are normally owned by a charitable foundation. The governing body contributes towards capital costs. Voluntary controlled schools are nearly always church schools, with the land and buildings owned by a charitable foundation. However, the LEA employs the staff and makes arrangements for admissions.

To complicate the categorisation still further, any maintained secondary school can apply to be designated as a specialist school in one of four subject areas: technology (which would include science and mathematics), languages, sports (including physical education), and arts (fine, performing and media arts). From 2002, three new specialisms have been proposed: science, engineering, and business and enterprise. (*See* city technology colleges and city academies, which are technically independent schools but often in receipt of public funds.)

Since the Education Reform Act (1988) there has been a national curriculum with statutory requirements and assessment at four Key Stages (KS): KS1 (5–7 year-olds); KS2 (8–11-year-olds); KS3 (11–14-year-olds); and KS4 (14–16-year-olds). At KS4 most pupils will prepare for the General Certificate of Secondary Education, originally thought of as a school-leaving examination, although now most pupils remain in full-time education beyond 16. At the age of 16, there will probably be a choice of a school from 16 to 18, a sixth form college or a college of further education. At the age of 18 there is a choice of examinations, including General Certificate of Education A Level, and the Government's aim is for 50 per cent to move on to some kind of higher education.

The inspection of educational institutions and local education authorities is the responsibility of the Office of the Chief Inspector for Education – the Office for Standards in Education (OFSTED).

WALES

It used to be possible to talk of the education system of England and Wales, but since devolution in 2000 it would be misleading (and probably offensive) to do so; even before devolution there were, especially since the introduction of the national curriculum in 1988, important differences in the curriculum for schools in Wales, because the Welsh language and Welsh ethos were accepted as legitimate areas for distinctiveness.

Since 2000 the National Assembly for Wales has established a National Council for Education and Training for Wales which operates in tandem with the Higher Education Funding Council for Wales under the joint title of ELWa (Education and Learning Wales). Apart from important differences in the school curriculum and teacher education, education in Wales remains fairly close, but not identical, to the English system. Perhaps the most important difference is that secondary education is entirely comprehensive: there is no selection at age 11.

HM Inspectorate in Wales is quite separate from that of England: it has its own Chief Inspector and is known as ESTYN. It is independent of, but funded by, the National Assembly for Wales under Section 104 of the Government of Wales Act.

SCOTLAND

In Scotland there are over 830,000 pupils in more than 5,000 pre-school centres, and primary, secondary and other schools. Education is the responsibility of the Scottish Executive Education Department (SEED) working in partnership with 32 unitary local authorities. There are two executive agencies linked to SEED: HM Inspectorate of Education (HMIE) and Historic Scotland. In addition, Learning and Teaching Scotland (LTS) is a national public body sponsored by SEED. LTS provides advice, support, resources and staff development. Its remit is to keep education under review, and provide independent advice to Ministers and the Scottish Parliament on all matters relating to the school and pre-school curriculum, including the use of information and communications technology (ICT) to support the delivery of that curriculum; to keep under review, and provide independent advice to Scottish Ministers and Funding Councils, on all matters relating to the use of ICT in Scottish education and lifelong learning. There is no statutory (national) curriculum in Scotland, but non-statutory guidelines are available from SEED. There is no restriction to secondary education (i.e. no selection): the first two years (S1 and S2) are concerned with general education; S3 and S4 (from about age 14 onwards) education may become more specialist and vocational. Between the age of 14 and 16 pupils are preparing for Standard Grade courses, for which assessments are marked and regulated by the Scottish Qualifications Authority (SQA), at three levels (general, credit and foundation). S5 and S6 students take Higher and Advanced Higher examinations at five levels: access, intermediate (1 and 2), Higher and Advanced Higher (all operated by the SQA).

Scotland was also considerably ahead of the other three countries in establishing a General Teaching Council (the GTC (S) Act, 1965). GTC (S) also has more powers that the other three.

NORTHERN IRELAND

In Northern Ireland, since devolution in 2000, responsibility for education is shared between two departments, each with its own Minister: the Department for Education, mainly concerned with schools, and the Department for Employment and Learning (concerned with further education and higher education).

Every child is required to receive 12 years full-time education from age 4 to 16. The majority of pupils transfer from primary to 'post-primary' schools at age 11. There are two kinds of post-primary school: secondary schools for the majority of pupils (at 11–16), with more academic grammar schools for about 40 per cent of pupils (at 11–19). At the age of 11 pupils have the opportunity of applying to a grammar school, and taking an entry test, officially called the 'Transfer Procedure' test. In 2001 the idea of selection at 11 had been challenged by the Burns Report and consultations were taking place exploring alternative methods of organisation at 11–16 which would avoid the disadvantages of selection at 11.

Schooling is divided, as in England, into four Key Stages and pupils take the General Certificate of Secondary Education examination at about 16 and Advanced Levels at 18–19 as in England. The statutory curriculum is close to but not identical to the English national curriculum. Like Wales and Scotland, the Northern Ireland system is small: five higher education institutions, five area boards, one regional training unit, and a single inspectorate, the Education and Training Inspectorate (ETI). The Inspectorate has avoided following the English example of OFSTED, and has retained a more supportive role.

In terms of public examinations, England, Wales and Northern Ireland have kept fairly close to each other with General Certificate of Secondary Education, A Levels and Vocational Qualifications. However, Scotland has preferred to remain separate (*see* Scottish Qualifications Authority).

SECTION TWO

The Dictionary

An Alphabetical List of Definitions in Education and Training

A

A Level (See **Advanced Level**)

ability The 1944 Education Act stated that children should be educated according to age, **aptitude** and ability. Age caused little difficulty, but it was never clear what precisely was meant by aptitude and ability, although the phrase was occasionally used to justify selection for different kinds of **secondary school**. It may have been the intention to link ability with **academic** ability, and aptitude with a more specific aptitude for a technical **curriculum**. There is now a tendency to use ability in a more general way and to confine aptitude to more specific kinds of ability; both words are closer to 'capacity' than to '**attainment**' – it is quite possible to have high ability but low **attainment**, **achievement** or performance.

ability groupings Most education systems group children mainly according to their age. Some countries, e.g. Japan, make the assumption that it is reasonable to expect uniform achievements; other countries, including the UK, expect differences. (See also **mixed-ability grouping**, **setting**, **streaming**, **unstreaming**)

Abitur The German examination for 18- to 19-year-old school leavers. Like the **GCE A Level** in England, it is a university entrance qualification as well as being recognised as a general educational qualification for entry into some kinds of employment. Unlike the A Level it is a broadly based examination, more like the French **Baccalauréat**.

academic (1) A teacher or researcher in higher education. (2) An adjective applied to scholarly activities, sometimes as a term of abuse.

Academic Audit Unit (AAU) Responding to demands for greater accountability in United Kingdom universities, the **Committee of Vice-Chancellors and Principals** (CVCP) set up the Academic Audit Unit (AAU) in 1989. The purpose of the AAU was to look at methods for monitoring academic standards, to spread good practice and to keep the system under review. The AAU, together with the **Council for National Academic Awards** (CNAA), were replaced by a single quality audit unit as a result of the Further and Higher Education Act (1992), and by the **Higher Education Quality Council** (HEQC) and the quality assessment divisions of the Higher Education Funding Councils, the functions of which were transferred in 1997 to the **Quality Assurance Agency for Higher Education** (QAA).

academic board   A group of academic staff in a college or university normally elected in order to regulate academic affairs; usually one of the most senior committees, possibly responsible only to the senior governing body of the institution. Academic boards rarely exist in schools, but it is sometimes suggested that such an organisation would be highly desirable.

academic disciplines   (See **disciplines**, **academic**)

access course   Many universities are prepared to accept **mature students** without standard qualifications (i.e. a minimum of two **A Levels**), provided that they can be satisfied that the students have reached appropriate standards by other means. One of the alternative routes is an access course, run either by the higher education institution itself or by another approved college. This may lead to a **General Certificate of Secondary Education** and **A Level** examinations. Those wishing to be considered for **initial teacher training** degree entry would normally offer GCSE mathematics, English, science and appropriate **A Levels**.

Access Course Recognition Group (ACRG)   The ACRG was set up by the **Committee of Vice-Chancellors and Principals** and the **Council for National Academic Awards** to provide a framework of national recognition of access courses to higher education. The ACRG allowed certain higher education institutions to be Authorised Validating Agencies (AVA) which could approve access courses regarded as appropriate. This function was later transferred to the **Quality Assurance Agency for Higher Education**.

access funds   Access funds are used to make small payments on a one-off basis to young people, aged 16 or over, in full-time education, with particular financial needs. They are intended as a safety net for short-term emergencies. Access funds are administered on a discretionary basis by schools, colleges and universities in order to help students continue on their courses. (See also **education maintenance awards**)

access to higher education   In 1998 when the **Secretary of State for Education** announced additional funding for higher education from 1999, he said that he expected resolute action to broaden access to universities from under-represented social groups. The higher education access fund was increased for that purpose as well as to encourage such schemes as Access Advisory Partnerships, which deliberately set out to encourage applications to prestigious universities from those living in deprived areas. The Education Select Committee Report on access was published in March 2001. In the process of reviewing the proportion of applicants from **comprehensive schools** to Oxford and Cambridge, both universities were concerned at the under-representation of working-class, comprehensive school pupils, both in terms of applications and admissions. Oxford and Cambridge both attempted to improve that aspect of access and they were urged by the Labour Government to ensure that the situation improved in 2000–1. In March 2001 the Foyer Federation launched a guide, funded by the Nuffield Foundation, to help encourage young homeless people into higher education.

accountability   A word imported from business and commerce into education during the 1960s, initially in the USA. Despite various academic attacks on the concept of accountability on grounds of lack of clarity, and the fact that education is more complex than the world of business, the use of the term has continued. (See also **performance indicators**)

accreditation   A process by which one academic institution, perhaps a university, officially approves the awards of another institution and guarantees that they are of a certain standard.

achievement   This term indicates actual **attainment** or performance and is to be distinguished from other words such as **ability** and **competence**.

achievement test   A test that measures **achievement (attainment)** in a particular subject or occupation rather than potential.

action research   A study of a particular social situation (which might or might not be concerned with education) in which the intention is not simply to understand and report, but to bring about certain improvements. A well-known educational example concerned the study of educational priority areas (EPAs). (See also **research and development**)

active learning   Learning that encourages the student to do more than receive information from a teacher or textbook, memorise the information and reproduce it. Active learning would require the student to make something, be involved in a **project** or experiment. When revising, for example, students are often advised to 'do' something such as construct their own notes, rather than just read. (See also **experiential learning, passive learning**)

active vocabulary   The words that a child (or adult) is able to *use* in speech or writing (or both), not just recognise and understand. (See also **passive vocabulary**)

Adam Smith Institute   A right-wing pressure group/think tank founded in 1978 by Madsen Pirie and Eamonn Butler to promote free market ideas – in particular the work of the economist, F. A. Hayek.

admission appeals   Parents may appeal against a decision not to admit their child to a particular school. For this purpose, governing bodies are required to set up independent appeal panels excluding the school's governing body and the local education authority from their membership but including lay people. **School adjudicators** also deal with issues relating to maintained schools admissions. Decisions are binding on the admission authority.

admission to school   (See '**rising fives**')

admissions   **Governors**, unless given delegated responsibility, have a duty to admit pupils who have been offered places by the **local education authority**. In the case of a refusal, the local education authority can refer to the **Secretary of State** for a direction under Sections 496 or 497 of the 1996 Education Act. However, **foundation** and **voluntary aided schools** are responsible for their own admission policies. Governing bodies are empowered to delegate their functions to an admissions committee which must include the **headteacher** as one of its members. One aspect of admissions that attracts much criticism concerns the parents' right to 'express a preference' for the school at which they wish their child to be educated. This arises from the differing admission requirements of schools, variations in popularity, and the exemption of foundation and voluntary aided schools from normal requirements. Between 1995 and 1998, the number of appeals by parents in England who were unsuccessful in obtaining a place for their child at their first choice of secondary school had doubled. Nevertheless, in 2002, 92 per cent of pupils secured their first- or second-choice primary or secondary school. (See also **admission appeals**)

adult education   Courses of an informal character provided for adults in a range of interests: these are usually held in institutions different from colleges and universities attended by school leavers. They range from leisure pursuits to higher degree qualifications. (See also **community college**, **continuing education**, **recurrent education**, **U3A**, **village college**)

Adult Learning Inspectorate (ALI)   Until **Her Majesty's Inspectorate** (HMI) was reorganised following the Education (Schools) Act (1992), HMI were responsible for inspecting all spheres of education except universities. After the 1992 Act the **Office for Standards in Education** (OFSTED) was concerned mainly with schools and **initial teacher training**, and other specialist inspectorates were developed, including the ALI, each with its own Chief Inspector. The ALI was set up in August 2000 to become operational in April 2001, taking over responsibility for: adult education, all work-based learning 16-18 (both public and private), and training under the **new deal**. In some cases where there is an overlap of responsibility, e.g. some **tertiary colleges**, ALI and OFSTED inspect jointly. The ALI grades courses and aspects of management on a 1 to 5 scale from outstanding (1), to very weak (5). (See also **Learning and Skills Council**)

adult literacy   The setting up of an Adult Literacy Research Agency in 1975 was the first official recognition of the large proportion of the adult population in need of literacy skills. A national campaign was mounted and local authorities and voluntary agencies were given short-term financial assistance in starting their schemes. In 1978, an Adult Literacy Unit was established but was replaced in 1980 by an **Adult Literacy and Basic Skills Unit** (ALBSU), which covered other areas such as English as a second language and numeracy. It became the **Basic Skills Agency** in 1995. The Kennedy Report, *Learning Works*, the deliberations of a committee appointed by the **Further Education Funding Council**, dealt with aspects of this problem, particularly the under-participation of young adults from deprived areas. (See also **Basic Skills Agency**, **Moser Report**, **National Institute of Adult Continuing Education**)

Adult Literacy and Basic Skills Unit (ALBSU)   See **Basic Skills Agency (BSA)**

Advanced Extension Awards (AEA) Curriculum 2000   included plans for Advanced Extension Awards, starting in the summer of 2002. They were intended to stretch the most able **A Level** students by requiring greater depth of understanding. The award is based on a paper taken in addition to the usual A Level examinations but covering the same subject matter. AEA has two grades, merit and distinction. (See also **Matriculation Diploma**)

Advanced Level (A Level)   The advanced level of the **General Certificate of Education** (GCE) is an examination taken by more able pupils, usually after a two-year period of study following the **General Certificate of Secondary Education** (GCSE). It is closely associated with the traditional sixth form of a school. A wide range of subjects is available at A Level, though candidates normally choose two or three to study. This specialisation and narrowness has been criticised, but attempts at its reform have not been successful. Passes in at least two A Level subjects are normally required for admission to university. In 1993 an alternative '**Vocational A Level**' was introduced on an experimental basis. From 2000, the A Level structure was modified. Students were encouraged to begin their A Level course by taking four or five **Advanced Subsidiary** (AS) **Level** subjects in their first year, and to proceed to full A Levels in fewer subjects in their second year. Unfortunately, in 2002, when the new pattern of A Level examinations was marked for the first time, there was some confusion among the Boards and examiners about the required level for AS examinations. Some re-marking was needed, and the whole process was investigated, at the request of the Secretary of State for Education, by the recently retired Chief Inspector for

Schools, Mike Tomlinson. In his Report, it was clear that the increased number of examinations, combined with growing numbers of candidates, was putting pressure on Boards and examiners and making errors more likely. Tomlinson and others doubted the wisdom of the fact that England, unlike most other countries, did not make much use of internal assessment by the teachers themselves. (See also **Curriculum 2000, GNVQ**)

advanced skills teacher (AST)   The grade of advanced skills teacher was introduced by the **Department for Education and Employment** (DfEE) in 1998 to meet the criticism that if a teacher wished to secure promotion, she/he had to do less teaching and more administration. Teachers who achieve very high standards of classroom practice can apply to the Department for the grade which carries with it extra pay of between £3,000 and £5,000 a year. Successful candidates are expected to share their skills with teachers within their own schools and in others. An **Office for Standards in Education** (OFSTED) survey published in June 2001 showed that ASTs in secondary schools were often successful heads of year or departments. Eighty per cent of their time should be spent teaching in their own school, and the other 20 per cent in working with teachers in other schools.

Advanced Subsidiary (AS) Level   The **Dearing Report**, *Review of Qualifications for 16–19 Year Olds* (1996), recommended that the title AS should be changed from Advanced Supplementary to Advanced Subsidiary. The new AS Level is based on about half an **A Level** syllabus but with lower achievement expectations. (See also **Curriculum 2000)**

Advanced Supplementary (GCE) (AS)   In 1984 the Department of Education and Science proposed a new kind of GCE examination – Advanced Supplementary or AS. AS courses were designed to be at **A Level** standard but covering only 50 per cent of the content. The intention was to broaden the typical student's curriculum by encouraging a programme of two A plus two AS subjects in place of the traditional three A programme. Originally two kinds of AS were envisaged: complementary and contrasting, but that distinction did not survive the test of time. The Advanced Supplementary examination was replaced by the **Advanced Subsidiary Level** in 2000.

advisers   Experienced professionals, often former headteachers or senior members of staff, employed by **local education authorities** to carry out a variety of functions, including monitoring and supporting schools, target setting, and providing advice to governors in interviewing for new heads. Many LEAs have reduced the size of their advisory teams in recent years. (See also **advisory teachers**)

Advisory Centre for Education (ACE)   Founded in 1960, ACE is a non-profit making organisation, stemming from the Consumers' Association, which disseminates information on many aspects of schooling. It mainly helps parents to understand the school system and produces many guides for parents, schools and governors. It has mounted campaigns on issues such as corporal punishment, secrecy in school records and the rights of excluded children. The Centre also provides educational advice to community workers.

advisory teachers   Experienced teachers who are appointed or seconded for a short term by a **local education authority** to advise school staff. They work closely with **advisers** but have the advantage of recent classroom experience.

aesthetic   A term increasingly used in discussions of a balanced curriculum to indicate those subjects or areas of experience by means of which a pupil is introduced to the world of beauty (e.g. art, music, literature). The basis for this distinction dates back to the German philosopher, Immanuel Kant (1724–1804). An opposite point of view was taken in England by William Morris and John Ruskin, who did not wish to accept the separation of art and morality.

affective   In Benjamin Bloom's *Taxonomy of Education Objectives* (1956) a distinction is made between the **cognitive**, the psychomotor and the affective domains; the affective being concerned with emotions, feelings and attitudes rather than with cognitive processes or physical skills.

after-school activities   Extra-curricular activities which often take the form of clubs, societies and groups, and form an important addition to the normal school day. The range is very wide and can include music, drama and sports, as well as homework clubs. Teachers play a leading role in this work.

age: chronological and mental   Chronological age is the everyday usage of an individual's age defined in terms of time since date of birth. For educational purposes, it is sometimes useful to compare chronological age with mental age or **reading age**. Mental age is calculated by comparing a child's score on an **intelligence test** with the average scores of children. For example, a child might have a chronological age of eight and a mental age of ten, that is, she/he is mentally advanced for her/his years and is capable of reasoning at the same level as the average ten-year-old – she/he would thus have an above-average **IQ**. (See also **intelligence**)

age of transfer   Up to 1964, the age of transfer from primary to secondary schools was between 10½ and 12 years of age. The **Secretary of State** in 1964 encouraged experiments in different sorts of schools, especially the **middle school**, which recruits pupils of between 8 and 12 or 13. The present situation is very confused: throughout the country, transfer occurs at many different ages according to the educational planning of **local education authorities**. The problem has been mitigated, to some extent, by the **national curriculum** (1988) structure which introduces the concept of **Key Stage**: Key Stage 2 finishes at age 11 and Key Stage 3 (age 11–14) prescribes a 'secondary curriculum' for all pupils.

age participation rate (APR)   A term used in calculating demand for higher education (and sometimes further education). The age participation rate for higher education is calculated by showing the number of 18-year-olds who enter higher education as a proportion of the whole group.

aggregation   The process of combining the marks of small units of credit awarded through an assessment scheme. Aggregation methods used for **national curriculum** testing were at first criticised for being unnecessarily complicated and time-consuming for teachers.

agreed syllabus   The **Butler Education Act** (1944) stipulated that local education authorities, together with Church and teacher representatives, should draw up an agreed non-denominational syllabus in religious education. Authorities were not restricted to using their own syllabus: they could borrow a syllabus developed by another authority. (See also **Standing Advisory Council on Religious Education** (SACRE))

agreement trial   A meeting to help ensure teachers apply the same standards in assessing their pupils.

aims   Statement of educational intentions or purposes of a more general nature than **objectives**. Although all three terms (aims, goals and objectives) are sometimes used synonymously, they are increasingly used distinctively to represent three levels of intention from the most general aims to more specific objectives. 'Aims' became unfashionable with educational theorists in the 1960s and were avoided in the **Plowden Report**, but in the 1980s philosophers returned to the concept.

Albemarle Report   A Departmental Committee on the Youth Service in England and Wales, under the chairmanship of Lady Albemarle, reported in 1960. It recommended that the Government should establish an emergency training college for youth leaders and also a Youth Service Development Council to superintend a national building programme. The Report was accepted by the Government: a training college was set up at Leicester, a Council was formed, and a small building programme was approved. (See also **McNair Report, Thompson Report, Youth Service**)

all-age school   A school in which pupils spent the whole of their school life from the age of five. This pattern had been universal in elementary education in the nineteenth century, but separate infant schools were common by the 1920s. The **Hadow Report** (1926) recommended a break at 11, but over a third of 13-year-olds were in all-age schools in 1949. All-age schools no longer exist in the maintained system.

alternative schooling   A general term used to indicate a form of schooling which is different from that offered by the State or other traditional agencies. Alternative schools are usually, but not necessarily, associated with radical and progressive views of education, such as the avoidance of a formal curriculum and formal teaching methods. (See also **deschooling**, **Education Otherwise**, **free school**, **home education**)

ancillary staff   Non-teaching staff (NTS) of an institution who assist in its everyday running, for instance, media resources officers and laboratory technicians or **information and communications technology** (ICT) officers.

annual maintenance grant (AMG)   The annual sum provided to **grant maintained schools** for running costs. The direct AMG was equivalent to what a school would have received from its **local education authority** under local management; to this was added the central AMG to pay for the services previously provided by the local education authority before the school opted out. From 1 April 1999, grant maintained schools were treated on the same terms as other schools maintained by the local education authority. In 1998–99, the great majority of these schools received as AMG the amount they would have received under the **local management of schools** scheme, as well as a sum of money held back centrally by local educational authorities for services to its schools. Grant maintained schools were replaced by **foundation schools** from 2000.

annual parents' meeting   Since the School Standards and Framework Act (1998), a governing body of a school has been obliged to hold an annual meeting with parents to report on progress made by pupils in the past year and to discuss plans for the future, as well as such matters of concern as behaviour and home–school relations. One problem encountered by schools is the low turn-out of parents for the meeting.

annual report to parents   A report published each year by governing bodies of maintained and special schools in England to provide information to parents. It includes decisions such as governing body membership, **national curriculum** assessment results, public examination results (in secondary schools), changes to the school prospectus and a financial statement. All parents must receive copies at least two weeks before the **annual parents' meeting**. Schools have complained that the required report is too lengthy and takes too long to compile.

appraisal   A system for assessing the work of teachers and headteachers, as well as the teaching staff in universities. Appraisal may be connected with schemes of staff development; it may or may not be connected with promotion and/or pay increases.

apprenticeship   A very traditional method of learning a craft or trade by serving under the supervision of a master craftsman, originally for a seven-year period. After the Second World War, apprenticeship numbers declined, probably because there was full employment and high wages available for school leavers. In recent years, the shortage of skilled labour has brought about a revival of apprenticeship in various modernised forms. (See also **Modern Apprenticeship**)

aptitude   An individual's potential **ability** to acquire skills or knowledge (i.e. not existing achievement or ability). For example, there are tests that are designed to indicate mechanical aptitude or mathematical aptitude. One problem with such tests is, however, that although they are intended to be predictive (i.e. indicating potential rather than actual achievement), they necessarily involve performance now, which may be partly dependent on **skills** or techniques already learned. In practice it is difficult to distinguish between aptitudes and abilities, despite the conceptual differences between them and the desirability for some purposes of establishing potential (i.e. aptitude) rather than present achievement (ability). (See also **attainment test**, **performance test**, **vocational guidance**)

Area Training Organisation (ATO)   The **McNair Report** recommended that ATOs should be established in each area, responsible for the co-ordination and validation of teacher training. From 1947, **Institutes of Education**, based on universities, were officially recognised as ATOs. As a result of the restructuring of teacher training, ATOs ceased to exist from August 1975.

articled teachers (AT)   The articled teachers scheme was introduced by the Department of Education and Science in 1991 partly as a way of encouraging a more school-based version of **initial teacher training** (ITT), and partly to offer an alternative to the two established routes – the **Bachelor of Education** (BEd) and the **Postgraduate Certificate of Education** (PGCE). The scheme was available to suitably qualified applicants – graduates or those with at least two years of higher education in 'teaching subjects'; most of their training would be school-based but some 'theory' would be involved.

In some respects the course resembled a part-time PGCE course spread over two years. At first **local education authorities** were responsible for some of the costs involved, but in 1992 the **Department for Education** (DfE) announced that from April 1993 the AT bursary would be entirely covered by government funding under the Local Education Authority Training Grants Scheme (LEATGS). This scheme has now been superseded by the **Graduate and Registered Teacher Programme**.

AS Level   (See **Advanced Subsidiary (AS) Level**)

assessment   A range of methods for evaluating student performance and attainment.

assessment criteria   Statements that describe performances and place them in context with sufficient precision to allow valid and reliable assessment. (See also **performance criteria**)

assessment for learning   In his speech to the **Qualifications and Curriculum Authority** (QCA) annual conference in June 2001, the Chief Executive, David Hargreaves, stated that the most important development in assessment was 'assessment for learning', which had replaced the older term **formative assessment** to cover the means by which teachers gather and use evidence about teaching and learning to decide where students are in their learning and what changes are needed to help them take the next steps. Assessment for learning concerns: the need for teachers and pupils to have a clear understanding of the desired standard; the recognition of the gap between the student's current performance and the desired standard; and the need for both to be ready to adjust what they do to help the student to close that gap.

assessment grid   A plan prepared by a Chief Examiner at **GCSE** level to indicate how assessment objectives and weightings are to be met in question papers.

assessment objective   One of a set of statements in a syllabus describing the focus of assessment. For **national curriculum** subjects, the assessment objectives at GCSE must reflect the **Programmes of Study** set out in the Subject Order.

assessment of pupils   Headteachers have a statutory duty to secure the implementation of the **national curriculum** in schools, including the assessment and reporting arrangements. All maintained **primary schools** must use a baseline assessment scheme accredited by **Qualifications and Curriculum Authority** (QCA) to assess children in reception class or Year 1.

Teacher assessment is an essential part of the national curriculum assessment and reporting arrangements. The results from teacher assessments must be reported together with the test results.

Assessment of Performance Unit (APU)   Established by the Department of Education and Science in 1974, its terms of reference were 'to promote the development of methods of assessing and monitoring the achievement of children at school and to seek to identify the incidence of under-achievement'. Much of the work of the Unit has been concerned with the first task. It set out to assess children's development in seven areas – aesthetics, mathematics, science, social and personal skills, physical skills, language skills, and modern languages. In 1978, tests were administered covering the performance in mathematics of 11- and 15-year-olds in England and Wales, followed by tests in foreign languages, English and science. It was decided not to proceed with tests of social and personal development or aesthetic development. The Unit was eventually abandoned because its work was replaced by much of the assessment work connected with the **national curriculum**.

assessment of special needs   Section 5 of the 1981 **Education Act** required local education authorities to assess children's needs where there are special needs or learning difficulties. A **statement** of how these needs are to be met may then be drawn up. There were five scales of need, with stages three to five attracting extra resources, with pupils in the fifth stage receiving a statement of extra help which might be needed. The new **code of practice** published in November 2001 streamlined the way children are graded, with the five stages now being reduced to three. (See also **special educational needs**)

assignment   A task given to a pupil or student by a teacher either as part of a learning programme or as a means of **assessment** (or both). Assignments are usually set out as individual exercises, often for **homework**, but co-operative assignments are sometimes set for completion by two or more students. In primary schools 'assignment' tends to be used with much the same meaning as **project**. (See also **coursework**)

assistant head   A post first officially introduced in schools in autumn 2000. The assistant head is a member of the school's **senior management team,** ranking between a **deputy head** and **head of department.** The duties vary from school to school. As yet, few **primary schools** have appointed assistant heads.

Assistant Masters and Mistresses Association (AMMA)   (See **Association of Teachers and Lecturers (ATL)**)

Assisted Places Scheme (APS)   This scheme introduced as part of the **Education Act** (1980), was designed to assist academically able children whose families could not otherwise afford the tuition fees to attend one of the independent secondary schools in the scheme. It was criticised by advocates of **comprehensive schools** and was abolished by the Labour Government in 1997.

Association of Colleges (AoC)   The Association, established in 1996, represents the interests of 485 colleges in England and Wales both at local and at national levels. Membership includes **tertiary**, general, specialist and **sixth form colleges**. The equivalent in Wales is Fforwm, and in Scotland, the Association of Scottish Colleges.

Association of County Councils (ACC)   The Association, founded in 1974, put forward policies for County government after receiving approval from its executive committee, which represented the 47 member counties. It discussed issues with ministers, civil servants and MPs and appeared before select committees. Central to the ACC's work was the problem of finance. It argued its case with the government through the Consultative Council on local government finance and at officer level through technical working groups. It also took part in national negotiations on pay and conditions of service for local authority employees. In 1997, it ceased to exist when it became part of the newly founded **Local Government Association**.

Association of Headmistresses (AHM)   This Association was founded in 1874 by nine secondary school headmistresses for the advancement of girls' secondary education and for the holding of annual conferences. From the beginning, the Association welcomed a wide range of secondary schools and there never existed a division corresponding to that between the Headmasters' Conference (now the **Headmasters' and Headmistresses' Conference**) and the **Headmasters' Association**. From 1976, it became absorbed into the **Secondary Heads' Association** (SHA). (See also **teachers' unions**)

Association of Metropolitan Authorities (AMA)   The AMA, which was formed in 1974, was funded by subscription from the metropolitan authorities. Its task was to keep them informed of what was happening in Government circles and to represent the authorities at governmental and parliamentary levels. Each major area of interest had its own service committee, and specialist staff dealt with planning, housing, social services, and legal matters. In 1997, it ceased to exist when it became part of the newly founded **Local Government Association**.

Association of Principals in Sixth Form Colleges (APVIC)   During the 1970s and 1980s the idea of a **sixth form college** taking students aged between 16 and 18 from several **comprehensive schools** in a district grew in popularity. The heads of such colleges tended to be called **principals**, and formed themselves into a discussion group/pressure group to ensure their specialist requirements were kept under review.

Association of Teachers and Lecturers (ATL)   This Association originated from an amalgamation of the Assistant Masters Association and the Association of Assistant Mistresses in 1978 when it took the name Assistant Masters and Mistresses Association (AMMA). In 1993, to reflect the growing number of members from the further education sector, it changed its name to the Association of Teachers and Lecturers. Membership consists of about 183,000 teachers. It is non-party political and is not affiliated to the Trades Union Congress. The Association lays great stress upon professionalism and equal opportunities for men and women. (See also **teachers' unions**)

Association of University Teachers (AUT)   In 1909 a meeting was called in Liverpool 'to consider a proposal to form an association for bringing the members of the junior staff more in touch with one another and with the life of the University'. From this sprang the AUT, which now represents university teachers and related associated administrative grades in professional and salary matters. Most of the AUT's 43,000 members are in the 'old' universities. (See also **National Association of Teachers in Further and Higher Education, teachers' unions**)

attainment   The present (i.e. achieved) learning of a particular skill or area of knowledge as demonstrated by evidence of some kind, including the evidence of teacher assessment. 'Attainment' should be regarded as different from '**aptitude**'.

Attainment Target (AT)   In the **national curriculum**, subjects were divided into sub-sets (e.g. in English 'speaking and listening', 'reading' and 'writing'). Since 1995 some subjects have had a single attainment target. Attainment targets are sub-divided into levels. (See also **level descriptions**)

attainment test   A test that is designed to measure the degree of **learning** that has already been achieved in a particular subject area or skill, rather than the potential **ability** of an individual, which might be measured by a specific **aptitude test**. (See also **performance test**)

attendance and absence   Children between 5 and 16 must be in regular education, and it is the responsibility of parents to ensure that this is attained.

Heads must report to the **local education authority** (LEA) if a pupil is absent for ten consecutive days or more. From March 2001, parents who commit school attendance offences could be fined up to £250 and /or given up to three months' imprisonment. The **Education Welfare Service** employs officers to liaise between school and parents. Heads are required to maintain an admissions register and an attendance register, the latter of which is taken twice a day. (See also **Education Otherwise**, **exclusion**, **school leaving age**, **truancy**)

audio-visual aids (AVA)   Equipment for using recorded sound and visual images in schools and other educational institutions. A distinction is sometimes made between AVA hardware (equipment such as film projectors, television screens and audio players) and the software (e.g., films, audio tapes, film strips, slides). Posters, wallchart and other display materials are included in AVA, but not books. (See also **educational television**)

audit   A term borrowed from the world of commerce and accounting to indicate a means of publicly checking standards in education, especially universities. The **Academic Audit Unit** (AAU) was established in 1990 but was replaced by the **Quality Assurance Agency for Higher Education** (QAA) in 1997. (See also **Audit Commission**)

Audit Commission   An independent body established by the Government to scrutinise publicly funded services in order to encourage greater effectiveness and accountability.

auditor/auditor-moderator   The school assessment arrangements for 1993 require **local education authorities** to appoint auditors to be responsible for setting and maintaining standards at **Key Stage** 1. It seemed to be felt that in the past local education authority moderators had not been sufficiently authoritative. From 1993 the auditor's role has included developing teachers' assessment skills as well as adjudicating where there is disagreement within a school. In addition to local education authority auditors, there are independent agencies for **independent** and overseas schools. Any independent school participating in Key Stage 1 assessment must have its **Standard Assessment Task** results validated by an agency.

Auld Report   A Report for the **Inner London Education Authority** by Robin Auld QC who presided over a public inquiry in 1975 into the teaching, organisation and management of the **William Tyndale School**.

aural   Aural refers to the ears and to hearing: as in 'aural training', which is designed to teach partially-hearing children to identify speech sounds. Because the two words have the same pronunciation, 'aural' is sometimes confused with 'oral', which refers to speech.

authentic assessment   Some methods of assessment, e.g. multiple-choice tests, have been criticised for being artificial or far removed from the knowledge or skills that need to be tested. Instead examiners have been encouraged to give greater priority to **validity** than **reliability** by seeking the kind of assessment that looks at realistic **project** work or **continuous assessment** of other kinds. Such assessment is regarded as more 'authentic' even if it is more difficult to assess. Other kinds of authentic assessment include, e.g., portfolios of work produced over a period of several months. Critics of 'authentic' assessment have pointed out several problems, including the difficulty of being sure that all the work presented is that of the candidate. (See also **continuous assessment**)

authentication   Confirmation that work has been produced solely by the candidate concerned.

autistic   Autistic children appear to be unable or unwilling to communicate with other individuals, including their own parents. Even if such children are of average or above-average intelligence, they are likely to be educationally **retarded**; in the past they would probably have been considered to be mentally sub-normal or classified as feeble-minded. The causes of autism are not known, but researches in the field of special education have established improved methods of teaching autistic children, some of whom have been able to make considerable progress. Considerable claims have been made for the Hungarian Peto method, and in February 1992 the Spastics Society set up a Peto Centre in London. (See also **special needs**)

autonomy   One of the aims of education in a democratic society is said to be the development of a pupil's ability to make rational decisions for him or herself 'autonomously' rather than to simply carry out instructions. 'Moral autonomy' is the highest level of moral development. (See also **moral development**)

award   A general term for qualifications issued by examining or validating or **awarding** bodies.

awarding   The process in **GCSE** and **A Level** by which candidates' grades in a subject are determined by examiners on the basis of available evidence.

B

Baccalauréat   A school leaving examination in French secondary schools. General *lycées* offer a general *Baccalauréat* and the technical *lycées* offer the *Baccalauréat Technologique*. These general and technological *Baccalauréats* are not of equal prestige. In 1985 a third type, a four-year vocational course followed by the *Baccalauréat Professionnel*, was introduced. (See also **International Baccalaureate**, **Technological Baccalaureate**)

Bachelor of Education (BEd)   It was recommended in the **Robbins Report** (1963) that teaching should become an all-graduate profession. By the end of the 1970s, Teachers' Certificate courses had been replaced by three- or four-year courses leading to the award of a Bachelor of Education **degree**. This degree includes a professional teaching qualification and may be taken at a large number of **colleges of higher education** and **university departments of education**. Courses will include curriculum subject studies, educational and professional studies, school experience and **teaching practice**. Most students preparing for teaching careers in primary schools follow this 'concurrent' pattern of initial teacher education and training. Applicants for BEd courses are expected to have a good general education and will normally be required to have passed **General Certificate of Education** examinations in English and mathematics, at an appropriate level, together with two subjects at **A Level**. Some BEd degrees have been renamed Bachelor of Arts (BA) with professional qualifications. Several institutions of higher education also offer a BEd degree for serving teachers who hold a certificate qualification but wish to achieve graduate status. In-service BEd courses focus largely on the academic study of education. Such courses have also proved to be suitable for teachers from overseas who are seeking to upgrade their professional qualifications. Since the Government introduced salaries for postgraduate teacher trainees in March 2000, many institutions have been restructuring their BEd courses to include shortened primary courses, or are offering a three-year course followed by a **Professional Graduate Certificate of Education**.

backwardness   Educational backwardness is used in reference to a child whose attainment in the basic skills of reading and arithmetic falls below the levels of achievement of those in his or her age group, irrespective of intelligence. Backwardness should, therefore, be distinguished from educational retardation which arises, in the main, from low intelligence. Backwardness can be remediated but teachers have to be alert to a wide range of causative factors, e.g., physical, emotional and environmental. (See also **special educational needs**)

banding   The division of a school-year group into two, three or four bands, mainly on the criterion of ability, such as verbal reasoning or reading tests. Each band is sub-divided into a number of classes, though not necessarily of equal **ability**. Aimed at giving schools a balanced intake, in practice there are often widely different proportions of pupils between the bands. (See also **mixed-ability grouping**, **setting**, **streaming**)

Barlow Report   A Committee on Scientific Manpower was appointed by the Lord President of the Council in 1945 and chaired by Sir Alan Barlow to consider the development of scientific resources in the following decade. It recommended that the output of science graduates should be doubled, from 5,000 to 10,000 a year, and that universities should be enlarged to accommodate this expansion. Priority was to be given to teaching and fundamental research, the needs of the Civil Service (both government and industrial), and defence science. The Committee also endorsed the findings of the **Percy Report** (1945) on higher education in the public sector and requested that urgent consideration be given to the development of two or three Institutes of Technology.

baseline assessment   Maintained primary schools in England use a baseline assessment scheme, accredited by the **Qualifications and Curriculum Authority** (QCA), for all children as they begin school. This includes language, literacy, numeracy, personal and social education. This information helps teachers to assess individual children's needs, and later gives a picture of progress made.

basic English   A phrase that ought to be used as a technical term rather than as a parallel to basic maths, basic science, etc. Basic English was developed between 1926 and 1930 by C. K. Ogden as a possible international language. Its basis was the listing of 850 commonly used keywords that could communicate all ideas and any kind of message. However, it was increasingly used as a means of teaching English to foreigners rather than as a complete language in its own right. It was also used in some studies of **readability** and graded reading.

basic skills   Skills – especially in the three Rs, which provide a kind of competency, such as being able to add up and multiply – that are thought to be necessary for participation in everyday adult life. They are sometimes related to more advanced skills, which became known as **core skills**, later renamed as **key skills**.

Basic Skills Agency (BSA)   Formerly the **Adult Literacy and Basic Skills Unit** (ALBSU), the BSA, founded in 1995, is a limited company and registered charity concerned with developing literacy, numeracy and related basic skills in England and Wales. It produces teaching and learning material for children, young people and adults to improve their skills, carries out research and runs programmes at all levels. The National Basic Skills Resource Centre at the University of London Institute of Education houses a wide range of teaching and learning material which is available for consultation.

beacon schools   Originally an idea from the USA, beacon schools were launched in England in 1998. They are nursery, primary, secondary or special schools that have been identified by their **local education authorities** or by the Government as amongst the best in the country, representing examples of successful practice. By working in partnership with other schools they raise standards and spread good practice. Beacon schools tend to be located in cities, or have a school partner in an area of deprivation, urban or rural. Lower performing schools are encouraged to twin with beacon schools. The Green Paper, *Schools: Building on Success* (2001), proposed an expansion of **secondary schools** to 400. In June 2001, a further extension of the scheme was intended to bring the total number of beacon schools up to 1,000. The Green Paper also promoted the notion of advanced beacon schools. Each school receives an extra grant of £50,000 per year from the **Standards Fund** for an agreed programme of activities.

behavioural objective   A specific statement of intent by a teacher about the changes in behaviour that a student must show as a result of a teaching programme. The emphasis is on pupil or student behaviour rather than on teacher behaviour or teacher intention. An essential feature of a behavioural objective is that the behavioural change must be specified in advance, in terms of student behaviour that can be measured. Opponents of the behavioural objectives approach criticise this view of **curriculum** planning for a number of reasons, including the suggestion that teachers will tend to concentrate on what is easily tested, i.e. the most trivial aspects of a subject. Another criticism is that human learning is a much more complex process than this simplified view would appear to suggest. (See also **objectives**)

behaviourism, behaviouristic   A school of psychology that rests on the assumption that all human activity can be explained in terms of conditioning, i.e. behaviour is rewarded or punished and habits are formed as a result. Some teachers of severely retarded children adopt a simple step-by-step approach that is close to behaviourism. (See also **behavioural objective**)

Beloe Report   The terms of reference of a Committee appointed by the **Secondary School Examinations Council** were 'to review current arrangements for the examination of secondary pupils other than by the **GCE** examination, to consider what developments are desirable, and to advise the Council whether, and if so, what, examinations should be encouraged or introduced, and at what age levels'. The chairman was Mr Robert Beloe, and the Committee's report, issued in 1960, recommended that a new examination, appropriate for pupils at the end of their fifth year of a secondary school course when they would normally be aged 16, should be devised. This was to be for candidates in the next 20 per cent of the ability range below those attempting **GCE O Level** in four or more subjects. At least four subjects were to be taken; a further 20 per cent of the age group could attempt individual subjects. Two important points were emphasised: that the examinations should not simply provide a replica of GCE examinations but should be specially designed to meet the needs and interests of the pupils, and that they should be largely in the hands of the teachers who would use them. The **Ministry of Education** accepted these recommendations and consequently the **Certificate of Secondary Education** (CSE) examination was created.

benchmark   A term used (originally borrowed from surveying) to indicate a certain kind of standard. The original meaning was a mark cut into a rock, or other permanent feature, that could be used as a point of reference for levelling. In education, a benchmark normally means a standard that is easily recognised. A slightly different meaning of benchmark developed in the 1990s when it was defined as the process of measuring **standards** of actual performance against those achieved by others with broadly similar characteristics. The perceived problem was that some schools were more successful than others in helping pupils to achieve their potential. Schools with very different intakes tend to achieve different results; but some schools with similar intakes also achieve widely differing results. The benchmarking process was intended to lead to the identifying of good practice and the opportunity to learn from those schools that perform better in order to raise the standards of achievement in any particular school. In **higher education**, subject benchmarks for first degrees were introduced by the **Quality Assurance Agency for Higher Education** (QAA) in 2000 to operate from 2002. (See also **targets**)

benchmarking academic standards   The **Quality Assurance Agency for Higher Education** (QAA) published, in April 2000, 22 benchmark statements making explicit the general academic characteristics and standards of honours **degrees** in the UK. The 22 standards included one for education studies. The statements represent the work of groups of subject specialists who were charged with the task of stating the minimum subject content and processes for groups of honours degrees.

bilateral school   A school in which any two of three main elements of secondary education, i.e. grammar, technical or modern, were organised in clearly defined 'sides'. Pupils, though on the same site, remained in their allocated courses during their **secondary school** life. Some local authorities after the Second World War retained separate grammar schools, confining bilateral schools to the technical and secondary modern streams. (See also **bipartite system**, **tripartite system**)

bilingualism   A term used for pupils who are fluent in more than one language. 'Bilingual' may also be used as a euphemism for children who begin school knowing little English.

binary system   In a speech given at Woolwich Polytechnic in 1965, Anthony Crosland, then Secretary of State for Education, announced the Labour Government's acceptance of a plan to develop a system of **higher education** within the further education sector, separate from the university sector. In 1966, the Government's White Paper, *A Plan for Polytechnics and Other Colleges: Higher Education in the Further Education System*, added substantial weight to the argument, leading to the establishment of 30 **polytechnics** in the next six years. Margaret Thatcher's White Paper, *Education: A Framework for Expansion*, published in 1972, endorsed the binary policy, recommending that polytechnics should play a leading role in the development of higher education in the 1970s. The Further and Higher Education Act (1992) granted university status to polytechnics. However, **colleges of higher education** seeking university status under the Act have to meet stricter criteria than those required from polytechnics and argue that a new binary divide has been created.

bipartite system   A system consisting of selective and non-selective schools, usually of the **grammar** and **secondary modern** type respectively.

Black Papers   The title adopted for a series of occasional publications that first appeared in 1969 attacking modern teaching methods, the **Plowden** philosophy, the alleged decline in educational standards, and **comprehensive** schools. They advocated the retention of **selection** for secondary education, and the provision of super schools for the gifted. Contributors consisted of academics, teachers, writers, and politicians holding right-wing views, including G. H. Bantock, Rhodes Boyson, C. B. Cox, A. E. Dyson, Kingsley Amis, Cyril Burt and Jacques Barzun. Many of the issues aired in the Black Papers have subsequently been taken up and amplified by such organisations as the National Council for Educational Standards (NCES), the **Centre for Policy Studies** (CPS), the **Institute of Economic Affairs** (IEA) and the **Hillgate Group**.

block release   A period of time granted by employers to their workers in which to pursue study leading to a vocational qualification. These courses are usually held in **colleges of higher education** (CHEs).

Board of Education   Set up in 1900 in order to meet the need for a single central authority in education, one of its main functions was to put into effect the provisions of the 1902 Education Act and to ensure that the new **local education authorities** (LEAs) provided well-maintained and efficient schools. It also administered grants, withholding them from authorities failing to comply with the Board's requirements. The Board was also responsible for establishing schemes for the constitution of education committees and for making orders for voluntary school managers. In 1944, the Board was superseded by the **Ministry of Education**.

boarding school   Predominantly found in the independent sector of education – but with some **local education authorities** maintaining a small number – boarding schools normally require their pupils to be resident during term-time. Most independent boarding schools follow the **national curriculum** and offer the same range of examinations as in maintained schools. Special houses belonging to the school accommodate the pupils under the supervision of a master or mistress. In recent years the strict division between boys' and girls' boarding schools has been weakened: now accommodation is often provided within a school for both sexes. A survey published in April 2001 by the **Independent Schools Council Information Service** (ISCIS) showed a small increase in the number of girl boarders. Weekly boarding is becoming increasingly popular. In the State sector, the majority of such provision is for children with special needs. There is a **Boarding Schools' Association**, which represents 630 associated boarding schools. (See also **day school, house system**)

Boarding Schools' Association (BSA)   This Association represents all schools which are accredited by the **Independent Schools Council.** It provides information on boarding to its members, organises training programmes for staffs and governing bodies and conducts and funds research on aspects of boarding education.

borderline   (1) Those points on a scale of marks near (i.e. on either side of) cut-off points. For example, if the pass/fail cut-off point is a mark of 40, then the range of marks 36 to 44 might be regarded as borderline. Similarly, in the marking of **honours degrees**, there would be a cut-off point or mark for first class–upper second, but the range of marks either side of the cut-off point would be regarded as borderline and normally subject to special scrutiny. (2) Candidates who fall into the category near the cut-off point are sometimes referred to as borderline.

brain drain   A tendency for highly educated professionals to leave the home country in order to work abroad. There are a variety of reasons for such a move, including improved salary or working conditions, or the opportunity for recognition of one's achievements. In recent years, the term has been extended to cover those highly qualified graduates who leave the country because they are unable to find suitable employment within the UK.

brain storming   A technique, originating in the USA, designed to encourage creative solutions to a problem or series of problems. A group of colleagues meet to discuss a problem, but agree to suspend criticism until the concluding session. The theory is that by removing the fear of criticism, ideas flow more readily and much more creative solutions are generated.

British Accreditation Council for Independent Further and Higher Education (BAC)   Established in 1984 to improve standards in **independent**, **further** and **higher education** institutions in the UK by acting as an accreditation body. The Council accredits some 100 colleges which offer courses ranging from **A level** to **postgraduate** level. Teams of experienced inspectors carry out **full inspections** of accredited institutions every five years. (See also **crammers**)

British and Foreign School Society   The first public meeting of 'The Society for Promoting the Royal British or Lancasterian System for the Education of the Poor' was held in 1808. Joseph Lancaster's system, embracing a complete scheme of primary instruction, was unsectarian though Christian, and attracted many influential supporters, including Lord Byron and James Mill. It included provision at Borough Road for training monitors. The Society was reorganised as the British and Foreign Society in 1812. Flourishing societies were established not only in Great Britain but on the continent and throughout the Empire. (See also **British School**)

British Association for the Advancement of Science (BAAS)   Commonly called the British Association, it was established in 1831 by a group of scientists concerned to ensure that science and technology made a contribution to the life of society. In May 1991, the BAAS set up a **National Commission on Education** (NCE).

British Baccalaureate   The idea of a British Baccalaureate was first discussed in January 1990 at an **Institute for Public Policy Research** (IPPR) seminar. The background was the perceived failure of the education of 16–19-year-olds in England and Wales, and in particular the failure to bridge the gap between academic **A Levels** ('narrow, specialised and old-fashioned') and **vocational courses** ('too job-specific, low-level and ill-coordinated'). An IPPR paper, *A British Baccalaureate* (1990), described England and Wales as suffering from 'an early selection–low participation system'. The proposed solution was a new qualification, to some extent based on the French **Baccalauréate** and the **International Baccalaureate**, that would also combine aspects of academic and vocational learning as well as community projects. The British Baccalaureate would be divided into three levels – foundation, advanced and higher, with overlap between the three. The foundation level would progress from **Key Stage** 4 of the **national curriculum**, replacing the **General Certificate of Secondary Education** (GCSE); the advanced stage would replace A Level and equivalent courses at that level. The advanced diploma would have three domains: social and human sciences, natural science and technology, and Arts, languages and literature. Each domain would have core, specialist and work/community-based modules. All students would choose a balanced curriculum including all three domains and all three types of module. When the Labour Party was in opposition they gave some support to the idea of the British Baccalaureate; when in office, after 1997, they preferred less radical reforms for this age group, apparently still regarding A Levels as the gold standard. (See also **Welsh Baccalaureate**)

British Council The Council, an independent, non-political organisation, was established in 1934 to develop closer cultural relations with, and to promote a wider knowledge of Britain in, other countries. The majority of its funding is provided by the Foreign Office and the Commonwealth Office. A large part of its activities is devoted to education, such as the teaching of English, to providing educational assistance in developing countries, and to maintaining and running libraries. The Council is represented in more than a hundred countries.

British Education Index (BEI) A quarterly publication listing and analysing by subject content all articles on education appearing in periodicals published in the British Isles.

British Educational Communications and Technology agency (BECTa) One of the leading agencies for **information and communications technology** in education. Its aim is to raise standards, widen access and improve skills in this area in primary and secondary schools. BECTa works in partnership to develop the **National Grid for Learning**.

British School   A shortened term for nonconformist schools established by the **British and Foreign School Society** from 1814. The majority of them became state schools after the 1870 Education Act.

British Standard BS 5750   The British Standard on 'quality systems' was originally devised for contracts in which two parties were involved either with the manufacture of a product or the delivery of a service. It is now being awarded to **colleges of further education** and training organisations who match up to the criteria. The scheme affords the opportunity for institutions to raise **standards**.

Brougham Reports   Henry Brougham, later Baron Brougham, successfully moved for an inquiry in the House of Commons in 1816 into the state of education among the poor in the Metropolis. A **Select Committee** on the Education of the Poor was appointed the same year with Brougham as chairman. In its report, the Committee demonstrated that educational endowments for the poor were being misapplied and that there was a grave shortage of **elementary schools**. A second committee in 1818 reinforced the findings of the earlier report and recommended that Government schools should be established to fill the gaps. An Education Bill, introduced by Brougham in 1820, proved abortive and no action was taken on these far-sighted proposals.

Bryce Report   A Royal Commission was appointed in 1894 'to consider the best methods of establishing a well-organised system of secondary education in England.' The Commission, chaired by James Bryce, recommended three major reforms in its Report the following year: a central authority for secondary education under a **Minister for Education**; the extension to local authorities of responsibility for secondary as well as elementary education; and the provision of scholarships to provide a **ladder of opportunity** for elementary pupils. It also noted the comparatively meagre supply of secondary school places for girls. Although these recommendations were not adopted, they were influential in subsequent changes made at the beginning of this century. (See also **eleven plus examination, girls' education**)

bulge   A metaphor used to indicate the increase in the number of pupils reaching a stage in the educational process. The term was used in the UK to indicate the growing demand for school places resulting from the increased number of births immediately following the Second World War. The bulge was responsible for the shortage of teachers and overcrowded classrooms in the early 1950s; but when the bulge passed out of the system, the problem of falling rolls produced the reverse effect, namely too many teachers and schools having to be closed. The bulge also caused problems subsequently in the higher education sector. There was a second but less dramatic bulge beginning in 1958.

Bullock Report   The Committee Of Inquiry appointed in 1972 by the Secretary of State for Education and Science chaired by Lord (then Sir Alan) Bullock was given three tasks: to consider, in relation to schools, all aspects of teaching the use of English, including reading, writing and speech; to report on how present practice might be improved; and to suggest ways in which arrangements for monitoring the general level of attainment in these skills could be introduced. In the Committee's Report, issued in 1975 under the title *A Language for Life*, it stated that every teacher should be a teacher of English, but linked this with the need for a systematic policy in schools. Language across the curriculum was advocated, starting with pre-school children and continuing through the secondary stage. Together with a recommended increase in resources for English, especially in secondary schools, greater in-service facilities for teachers were necessary. (See also **English curriculum**, **language deficit**)

bullying   A survey of 4,000 English children carried out between 1984 and 1986 claimed that over one-third of them had been bullied at school. The Elton Report on Discipline (1989) stated that bullying was 'a problem that is widespread and tends to be ignored by teachers'. It recommended that school staff should be more alert to signs of bullying and should take firm appropriate action: systems should also be devised to support the victims. Schools must take into account the **Human Rights Act** (1998) in devising anti-bullying policies. Evidence about bullying is vague and contradictory, but it tends to take place outside the classroom; boys rather than girls are more likely to be the targets; and bullying is less common in schools where there is order and **discipline**. (See also **disruptive units**, **exclusions**)

Burnham Committee   Named after its first Chairman, Lord Burnham, the Committee met in 1919 to draw up national pay scales for elementary school teachers. Soon after, secondary and further education teachers' pay came within the Committee's remit. In 1945, the Burnham Agreement came into force, which established a single salary scale for primary and secondary teachers. There were two committees, one for primary and secondary schools, the other for further education.

Burns Report (Northern Ireland)   Until devolution in 1999, Northern Ireland had been out of step with England on the issue of **selection** for **secondary schools**, and even further apart from Scotland and Wales, where **grammar schools** had ceased to exist. In September 2000, a research report by Professors Gallagher and Smith, *The Effects of the Selective System of Secondary Education in Northern Ireland,* was published. It was critical of the selection process and, at the launch of the report, the new Minister of Education, Martin McGuinness, announced the establishment of a Review Body on Post-Primary Education, to be chaired by Gerry Burns. A report, the Burns Report, was published in October 2001 making three recommendations:

1. the abolition of the Eleven-Plus Transfer Tests at the earliest possible opportunity, and the ending of selection on academic grounds;
2. the development of a progressive 'Pupil Profile' that would inform the individual learning needs of each pupil;
3. the creation of a 'Collegiate System' of schools across Northern Ireland.

bursar   (1) Originally a treasurer of a college, the term now applies to a school or college post that involves financial responsibilities and other duties such as the maintenance of the buildings of an institution. Since the introduction of **local management of schools**, the scope of the post has been widened to include income generation, public relations and the organisation of in-service work and conferences. Now a key member of staff, the bursar – also known as the business manager or the senior administrative officer – is often a full member of a school's **senior management team**. In the 2001 General Election campaign, the Labour Party, in its manifesto, promised to fund up to 1,000 training places at the **National College for School Leadership** for State sector bursars by 2006. Fifty per cent of all schools now have a bursar. There are three times as many female bursars as male bursars. (See also **registrar**.) (2) Holder of a monetary award, a **bursary**, for maintenance on an education course.

bursary   An award, granted by an educational institution such as an independent school or other body, which assists the student in covering expenses for a course of study. (See also **entrance award**)

Business and Technology Education Council (BTEC)   Set up in 1974 as the Business and Technician Education Council, it was the result of a merger of the Business Education Council (BEC) and the Technician Education Council (TEC). In 1995, BTEC as an organisation took over the responsibility for the University of London's School Examination Board's **A Level** examinations and **General Certificate of Secondary Education** (GCSE). BTEC was then renamed Edexcel, and became one of three awarding bodies offering both academic and vocational qualifications, the other two awarding bodies being the Assessment and Qualifications Alliance (AQA), and the Oxford, Cambridge and Royal Society of Arts (OCR). (See also **examination boards**)

business education A number of reports since the Second World War, such as that by **Haslegrave** on technician courses and examinations (1969), led to the establishment of business studies degrees and diplomas. The subject also exists at **GCSE** and **A Level** and awards in business education are made by a number of vocational awarding bodies, in particular by the **Business and Technology Education Council**. (See also **GNVQ**)

Business Education Council (BEC) Set up the year after the **Technician Education Council** (TEC) in 1974 following the **Haslegrave Report**. It planned and administered a national system of courses in business and public administration below degree level in England and Wales. It was later merged with the TEC and became the **Business and Technology Education Council** (BTEC).

Butler Act The name given to the 1944 Education Act, after its architect, R. A. Butler, then President of the Board of Education. The Act was planned during the Second World War and made many important changes to the schooling system. It stipulated that public education should be reorganised into three progressive stages: primary, secondary and further education; and that children were to be educated according to their age, ability and aptitude. A **Ministry of Education** replaced the existing Board, with a Minister possessing greater powers to ensure that the **local education authorities** carried out their duties. The 1944 Act determined the nature of educational administration for the next four decades, but was superseded in many of its aspects by the Education Reform Act (1988), and by the Education Act (1996).

C

Campaign for Real Education (CRE) The CRE was formed in 1987 by a group of parents concerned by 'falling standards'. Although its ideas are right wing, it claims to be affiliated to no political party. The Secretary is Nick Seaton.

Campaign for State Education (CASE) A **pressure group** set up in 1960 to improve the quality of local maintained schools, consisting of parents and others interested in education. Local groups operate within the framework of national CASE policy.

campus   The grounds in which a school, college or university is situated, forming a self-contained entity. The term originated in the USA in the late nineteenth century at Princeton University.

canon   This term is used in educational terminology to indicate lists of novels, poems and plays that are so highly valued as part of cultural heritage that they should be regarded as essential aspects of a curriculum. 'Canon' began to be used in discussions of the **English curriculum** from 1988 onwards. Some wanted to prescribe texts for each **Key Stage**, others wanted to leave all choice to the teachers. A compromise was eventually reached by issuing a list of suggested texts; only Shakespeare was compulsory. The controversy is well described in Brian Cox, *Cox on the Battle for the English Curriculum* (1995).

capitation allowance   An amount given each year by a **local education authority** (LEA) to a school in order to buy such things as books and stationery. The amount a school receives depends on the number of children in the school (capitation, therefore, refers to an amount 'per head'), but the amount usually increases with the age of the children. Normally authorities give more for secondary school pupils than for primary school pupils, and are more generous for **sixth formers** in secondary schools. Since the 1988 **Education Act** local education authorities have been obliged to pass on much higher sums of money (at least 85 per cent of the total education budget) to schools. The major element in this formula is 'capitation' – i.e. the number of pupils enrolled at the school.

Career Entry Profile (CEP)   At the end of successful completion of a student's **initial teacher training** course, he/she will, in conjunction with a tutor, fill out a Career Entry Profile. This consists of a listing of areas of strength and areas for development. When **qualified teacher status** (QTS) has been formally recommended, the initial teacher training provider signs the CEP. During the subsequent **induction** period, the **newly qualified teacher** (NQT) shares the CEP with the school. The objectives set for induction are based on the CEP and the school context, so that by the end of the first year of teaching, the teacher reaches **Induction Standards**.

case study   (1) A method of teaching in which a situation ('case') is presented to students by means of film or sets of documents as a basis for discussion and analysis. (2) A method of 'holistic' research or **evaluation** in education relying less on statistical measurement and more on other kinds of data gained by means of interview or content analysis of documents.

catchment area   A geographical area from which a school or institution draws its pupils or students. One view of the **comprehensive school** is that it should be a **neighbourhood school** drawing pupils from the catchment areas of a small number of **primary schools**. The 1980 **Education Act** changed the picture for, under Section 5, parents could state a preference for schools and also express a preference for schools in other **local education authorities** (LEAs). The 1988 Education Act went further in this direction of **parental choice**, by obliging schools to respect parents' preferences so long as the school was not completely full.

Central Advisory Councils   These Councils, one for England and one for Wales, which replaced the Consultative Committee under Section 4 of the 1944 **Education Act**, differed from the Committee in that they included persons of experience from outside the education field. The Council's functions were to advise the Secretary of State in matters of educational theory and practice referred to them, and to offer advice on their own initiative. Three important reports emanating from the Councils were: the **Crowther Report** (1959) on the education of 15- to 18-year-olds; the **Newsom Report** (1963) on the secondary modern school curriculum; and the **Plowden Report** (1967) on the state of primary education. The Councils have not been reconstituted since the Plowden Report was issued. (See also **Royal Commission**)

central school   Sometimes called 'intermediate' or 'modern' schools, central schools provided an education for brighter children of the **elementary school** population who failed to secure a place at a selective secondary school or chose not to take it up. The first ones opened in London in 1911 and were followed by some in Manchester in 1912. The 1918 **Education Act** encouraged **local education authorities** to make available more schools of this type. Entry was often competitive. A general education was given to the age of 15. Unlike **secondary schools**, which were geared to university entrance, central schools looked to a combination of apprenticeship and technical and commercial colleges.

centre   A school, college or other institution entering candidates for public examinations.

Centre for Educational Research and Innovation (CERI)   Created in 1968, the Centre functions within the **Organisation for Economic Co-operation and Development** (OECD). It is concerned with the promotion and development of educational research, the testing of innovations in education systems, and promoting co-operation between member countries in the field of educational research and innovation. It has published reports such as *Education at a Glance, OECD Indicators* (1992).

Centre for Information on Language Teaching and Research (CILT)   CILT was established in 1966 as an independent charitable trust supported by government grants with the aim of collecting and disseminating information on all aspects of the teaching of modern languages. CILT is based in London, but it operates throughout the UK. It carries out its work under a Board of Governors who are appointed in accordance with a Scheme of Government that deals with its remit, its relationship with sponsoring bodies, and the composition of its Board. The main objects are to promote a greater national capability in languages, and to support the work of all those concerned with language teaching and learning.

Centre for Policy Studies (CPS)   The CPS is one of the most active of the right-wing pressure groups. It was established in 1974 by Sir Keith Joseph and Margaret Thatcher, and has produced many publications critical of the education system.

Centres of Vocational Excellence (CoVEs)   These Centres, described in an official publication, *Colleges for Excellence and Innovation* (2000), are specialist **further education** colleges recognised for their expertise in vocational training. They offer programmes organised by the **Learning and Skills Council**. The Green Paper, *14–19: Extending Opportunities, Raising Standards* (2002), aimed at the improvement of the quality of provision in vocational education and raising the standards achieved. It stated: 'The Centres of Vocational Excellence are the key to our modernisation programme. We intend that 50 per cent of colleges will have CoVEs by 2004. This will enable them to achieve a step-by-step change in the delivery of vocational learning and in their links with local employers.'

There will be 16 colleges in the first phase and an additional 70 in the second.

Certificate of Pre-Vocational Education (CPVE)   In May 1982, the Department of Education and Science published a statement, *17 Plus – A New Qualification*, giving details of this award. It was designed as a one-year course for young people at 16 plus who had had few examination successes. The course, which began to operate from September 1983, was intended to prepare them for work, preferably with a training component, or to follow a particular vocational course at a later stage. The CPVE was administered by a joint board of the **Business and Technology Education Council** (BTEC) and the **City and Guilds of London Institute** (CGLI), together with representatives of the **Royal Society of Arts** (RSA), and the GCE and CSE boards. It was superseded by **National Vocational Qualifications** (NVQ).

Certificate of Secondary Education (CSE)   An examination introduced in 1965 as a school-leaving examination for pupils for whom the **GCE O Level** was considered unsuitable. In 1988 the two examinations were abolished and replaced by a single examination for all (or nearly all) 16-year-olds – the **General Certificate of Secondary Education** (GCSE).

certification   The process of awarding a certificate or diploma that indicates the achievement of certain specified standards of proficiency. One of the purposes of assessment or types of assessment is certification: i.e. **summative assessment** that results in a public award of some kind.

chancellor   In medieval times, the chancellor of a cathedral near where the university was sited granted licences to teach. Later, his authority was delegated to a **vice-chancellor**, who was usually the elected head of the teachers. Chancellors now have only ceremonial duties, particularly in connection with regard to degrees. Members of the Royal Family and distinguished public figures often take on this role. In the old Scottish universities, the chancellor is elected by their **graduates**. (See also **honorary degree**)

change of category   When a governing body decides that it wishes to change the category of a school, a large-scale consultation exercise must follow. DfEE Circular 9/99, *Organisation of School Places*, sets out the procedures: parents of children attending the affected school must be consulted as well as other interested parties. Governors may put forward mandatory proposals to change from **voluntary aided** to **foundation** or **voluntary controlled** status. The second type (i.e. non-mandatory) applies to any other maintained category that allows schools to change from their existing category. **Local education authorities** (LEAs) are more restricted, being limited to changing community or community special schools to foundation or foundation special schools. (See also **school categories**)

change of character   Schools may only increase their enrolment significantly (i.e. by 20 per cent or more), take children of different ages, or begin to select pupils by ability with the approval of the Secretary of State.

charitable status   Bodies calling themselves charities have to be registered with the **Charity Commission** and are governed by rules laid down by the Commission. The advancement of education is accepted as one of the objects of charity. Those who raise funds for schools, such as parent–teacher associations, may wish to register as a charity. One benefit would be that, where parents are encouraged to contribute to a covenant scheme, the tax can be reclaimed for the benefit of the school. The 1992 Charities Act made important changes in charitable status and the investment and care of charity funds. In September 2002, a Government Report concluded that schools enjoying charitable status should be allowed to retain it, but should be required to demonstrate public benefit.

Charity Commission   The Commission, established in 1843, consisted of four Charity Commissioners, at least two of whom were to be barristers, and was charged with the investigation of any charities in England and Wales. Their scope was extended in 1860 and an important aspect of their work was the making of new educational schemes and checking abuse of existing charitable funds.

charity school   Founded by the Society for Promoting Christian Knowledge from 1699, these schools provided education and clothing for poor children. Their aim was to teach reading and writing, the Church catechism, and habits of industry. Local subscriptions and endowments financed the schools, many of which originated in London. In the nineteenth century, the **Charity Commissioners** investigating these schools found that many of the endowments had been misappropriated. (See also **free education**)

chief education officer (CEO)   The principal officer of a **local education authority** (LEA) responsible for advising the local council on a range of educational matters, writing reports for the Education Committee and carrying out its policies. The post dates from the 1902 **Education Act** when local education authorities replaced school boards. In some authorities the chief officer is called the **director** of education. (See also **Society of Education Officers** (SEO))

child-centred education   A version of **progressive education** which places the child rather than the teacher or subject matter at the centre of the educational process. In its milder versions, child-centred education may be regarded as little more than a reaction against the inhumane practices of some nineteenth-century schools, but extreme versions of the doctrine would suggest that the child's interest alone should determine what is taught in class, and therefore any kind of curriculum planning would not be appropriate. (See also **teaching methods**)

child guidance clinic   Child guidance clinics are centres for the **diagnostic** assessment and treatment of children with behavioural problems and other developmental disorders. They are usually administered by **local education authorities** and staffed by psychiatrists, educational psychologists, and psychiatric social workers. Many clinics work on the basis of family therapy. The main referring agents are schools and family doctors but some clinics have an open-door policy. Parents and adolescents may be self-referring. (See also **school psychological service**)

child in need Broadly defined in the **Children Act** (1989) to include children with disabilities and any child unlikely to achieve a reasonable standard of health or development without help. The social services department of a local authority has responsibility for children in need under five, and for all children in need outside school hours and in school holidays. For children in need of school age, the **local education authorities** share responsibility. The Act encourages collaboration between local authority departments.

childhood, history of Recent interest in the concept of childhood has led to the publication of a number of studies, especially in the USA. Aspects such as child rearing, socialisation, the curriculum, and adolescence have been explored. Writers differ in their interpretations of the history of childhood. De Mause, for instance, states that the central force for change in the status of childhood arises from psychogenic changes in personality occurring because of successive generations of parent–child interactions. Laslett notes that written evidence from the past is too slight to support such a theory and favours socio-historical influences. Neither of the authors examines the effects of the process of schooling on the family.

childminding Childminders look after other people's pre-school children in their own homes and receive payment. The requirements to be complied with by persons providing day care for young children were closely prescribed in the **Children Act** (1989). Local authorities were also given a larger supervisory role.

Children Act (1989) The Children Act came into operation in October 1991. One of its purposes was to co-ordinate existing private and public law concerning children: its dominant principle was that the child's welfare should be the major consideration in any decision relating to upbringing; it is assumed that upbringing is normally best within the child's own family. The main responsibility for implementing the Act (which is a complex document of ten parts and 14 schedules) lies with the social services department, but it is recognised that co-operation with other departments – including health and education – is essential. A key concept of the Act was the **child in need**.

chronological age (See **age: chronological and mental**)

circular Issued by the Department for Education and signed by the Secretary of State or the Permanent Secretary for the guidance of **local education authorities** and others on matters concerning government educational policy. Circulars do not have the force of a legal requirement but represent the policy of the central authority and cannot be ignored completely by local education authorities.

citizenship education (CE)   Citizenship was not included in the **national curriculum** (1988), but an attempt to fill the gap was made by the **National Curriculum Council** (NCC), which recommended supplementing the ten subjects of the **national curriculum** by cross-curricular themes, one of which was 'education for citizenship'. This did not prove to be a successful solution. In 1997, the Secretary of State for Education, David Blunkett, set up an advisory group on citizenship education (CE). CE had three strands: social and moral responsibility; community involvement; and **political literacy**. The advisory group was chaired by Professor Bernard Crick. It produced a report in 1999, the contents of which became part of the review of the national curriculum for implementation in September 2002, when CE becomes compulsory at **Key Stages** 3 and 4.

city academy   City academies, first promulgated in April 2000, are independent, all-ability secondary schools, based on the **city technology college** (CTC) model and run by private companies and the voluntary sector. Sponsors provide up to 20 per cent of the initial capital costs, and the **Department for Education and Skills** (DfES) the remainder. They are intended to tackle the problems facing schools in disadvantaged areas, and offer an innovative **curriculum** with study support as part of school life. Pupils may be selected by aptitude. The first six academies, in London, Liverpool and Middlesborough, were announced in December 2000, and specialise in one particular area, for example, science or **information and communications technology**. Teachers are selected by the governors, and salaries are outside the national pay conditions. The White Paper, *Schools: Achieving Success* (2001), set a target of 20 such schools by 2005.

City and Guilds of London Institute (CGLI)   The City and Guilds is Britain's largest awarding and assessment body. It was founded in 1878 as an independent organisation operating under Royal Charter. It offers qualifications in over 500 subjects at all levels from basic skills to high professional standards. In 1995 it had more than 3.5 million component entries per year. (See also **National Vocational Qualification**)

city learning centres (CLC)   These centres are specially designed for an age range from infants to adults, are set in attractive buildings, and offer, e.g. full **information and communications technology** facilities, design technology and other innovative features. They act as hubs for a number of schools in an area. The centres are open for at least 12 hours a day throughout the year to encourage learning. Each centre is administered by a management board made up of representatives from the centre, the **local education authority** and other partners.

city technology college (CTC)   A new category of schools that are independent although partly funded originally by the Department for Education. CTCs were established as part of the 1988 **Education Reform Act** (ERA). The original idea of CTCs, as conceived by Kenneth Baker, then Secretary of State for Education, was that they would be financed by industry and commerce and would provide an alternative to **local education authority** schools, whilst not being selective schools. Education is free and they cater for all abilities. In practice, it has been difficult to attract sufficient money from the private sector and considerable state funds were provided for these schools. Only 15 colleges were set up. Some have responded to the Government's initiative to join the broader family of schools, and some have become **beacon schools**.

civic universities   (See **universities, history of**)

Clarendon Report   Public criticism of the **public schools** resulted in a Royal Commission being appointed in 1861, charged with the tasks of inquiring into the endowments and revenues as well as the curriculum offered, in the nine leading schools: Eton, Winchester, Westminster, Charterhouse, St Paul's, Merchant Taylors', Harrow, Rugby and Shrewsbury. Reporting in 1864, the Commission recommended that the statutes of foundations should be modified whenever they required a closer adaptation to the needs of modern society. Governing bodies were to be reformed and were to undertake a revision of statutes in order to remove local restrictions on masterships and **scholarships** and to reorganise expenditure on prizes and scholarships. Of great general interest was that part of the Report that dealt with the curriculum of schools. The Chairman of the Commission, the Earl of Clarendon, favoured a more liberal approach to the education of the elite, stating 'A young man is not well educated who cannot reason or observe or express himself correctly…if all his information is shut up within one narrow circle.' The Commissioners, whilst denouncing the domination of the classics, agreed that these should continue to hold the principal place. The influence of the German *Gymnasien* is noticeable in their findings. Natural science was to be taught for one or two hours a week; mathematics, divinity, modern languages, drawing and music also formed part of the curriculum. Ancient history and geography were to be taught in connection with classical teaching. Progress in putting some of these recommendations into practice was slow, chiefly because the old universities could not give a lead in teaching methods in non-classical subjects. However, modern studies were encouraged by the Public Schools Act of 1868 which recast the governing bodies and the ancient statutes of these institutions. (See also **Taunton Report**)

class   (1) A group of pupils or students of varying size, but usually between 25 and 35 in number. Members of a class are normally of the same age group, except where **family grouping** is adopted. A class may, however, consist of a range of abilities. The term is interchangeable with **form**. (2) Refers to the division of an **honours degree**, according to performance: normally first, second (upper or lower), and third. (See also **class size**)

class size   The important link between class size and pupil achievement, especially in early years, was acknowledged by the School Standards and Framework Act (1998). From September 2001, **local education authorities** and governing bodies were obliged to limit to 30 the number of pupils between five and seven years taught by a qualified teacher. (See also **class**)

classroom assistant   (See **teaching assistant**)

clearing house   An information-gathering unit to enable, e.g., applicants for university places to make a general application in order of choice rather than having to apply individually to each institution. In the UK the **Universities and Colleges Admissions Service** (UCAS) processes the applications from students in terms of their priorities and the response gained from the universities, passing on 'offers' to successful applicants. Another example in the UK of a clearing house is the **Graduate Teacher Training Registry** (GTTR).

Clegg Report   A Standing Commission on Pay Comparability, chaired by Professor Hugh Clegg, was appointed by the then Prime Minister, James Callaghan, in March 1979, at the request of the **Burnham Committee**, to establish acceptable bases of comparison with terms and conditions of work between teachers and other similar occupations. In the light of the Commission's findings, new salary scales came into effect from 1 April 1979. (See also **Houghton Report**)

cloze   The cloze procedure is a method of testing **readability** of a text by requiring students to show their comprehension of a passage where a proportion of the words have been deleted. It is claimed that this process tests both the reading ability of the student and the difficulty of the passage: this is one of the limitations of the procedure.

coaching   Special tutorial help given to a student, or students, often in preparing for an examination. There has been a substantial increase in private tuition, with pupils being given extra help in preparation for national assessment tests, due to parental worries over the teacher shortage. (See also **crammer**)

Cockcroft Report A Committee of Inquiry into the teaching of mathematics in primary and secondary schools was established in 1978 under the chairmanship of Dr (now Sir) Wilfred Cockcroft. Its report was issued in January 1982 under the title *Mathematics Counts*. The Committee noted that many teachers of the subject were not adequately qualified, a situation that should be changed by offering higher salaries to new recruits and more **in-service training** for serving teachers. On the question of **standards**, the Committee found no evidence that the 'back to basics' approach in mathematics teaching yielded better results than more enlightened methods. It did, however, advocate that more attention should be paid to mental arithmetic and to practical work. A common core of useful mathematics, covering less than is attempted in many schools, was favoured. The existing examination system was heavily criticised on the grounds that it destroyed pupils' confidence. The Committee suggested instead a range of examinations for different abilities ranging from a super 16 plus for the most able to a system of graduated or **graded tests** for the least able. (See also **numeracy**)

Cockerton Judgment In 1900, the Local Government auditor, Cockerton, brought a law case in the High Court against the School Board for London, on the ground that it had exceeded its powers in teaching certain branches of science and art in **higher grade** and evening schools. The Court ruled that **school boards** were not empowered to teach beyond the range of elementary subjects and then only for pupils up to 16 or 17 years of age. This decision was upheld in the Court of Appeal in the following year. The judgment hastened educational reform: the 1902 **Education Act** abolished school boards and the new **local education authorities** were responsible for both elementary and secondary education.

code of practice A set of rules about 'good practice' that are either voluntary (but strongly recommended) or compulsory. For example, the **Qualifications and Curriculum Authority** (QCA), operates as a regulatory body, with codes of practice for both **A Level** and **General Certificate of Secondary Education** (GCSE) examinations, specifying required procedures at every stage of the organisation of the examinations in very precise detail. There are also many other kinds of code of practice drawn up locally: e.g., most universities now have a code of practice to be observed when interviewing candidates for posts.

Codes Until 1860, the regulations of the **Committee of the Privy Council on Education** for schools wishing to receive a parliamentary grant were in the form of Minutes. These dealt with the syllabuses of **elementary schools**, conditions of grants, instructions and advice on the training of pupil-teachers and students in **training colleges**. Robert Lowe, as **Vice-President**, consolidated the Minutes into a Code in 1860, which was thenceforward issued annually. From 1904, the Codes dealt only with matters of minor detail and were finally replaced in 1927 by the *Handbook of Suggestions for Teachers*.

co-education   The education of boys and girls together in the same school and in 'mixed' classes within that school. In England, the term 'co-education' tends not to be used for institutions of further or higher education. Nearly all **primary schools** are co-educational, and there has been a steady trend towards co-education in **secondary schools**, particularly since 1944. It is usually thought that co-educational schools are better for boys, but there is some evidence to support the view that girls achieve better academic results in single-sex schools. (See also **girls' education**)

cognition/cognitive   Cognition is the act of knowing, perceiving or conceiving, as opposed to emotional (affective) experiences. In Bloom's *Taxonomy of Educational Objectives* (1956), cognitive is one of three kinds of objectives, the other two being affective and psychomotor.

cognitive development   The gradual growth of a child's ability to understand concepts, relationships and complex patterns of ideas. Piaget in *The Development of Logical Thinking From Childhood to Adolescence* (1958), Bruner in *The Process of Education* (1960), and others, have theorised about stages of cognitive development: e.g., sensory-motor, preoperational, concrete operations and formal operations (Piaget); and **enactive, iconic and symbolic** (Bruner). (See also **cognitive map**)

cognitive map   The mental picture or diagram that an individual has of a particular environment. A cognitive map will differ from one individual to another in terms of being more or less complete; individuals will also differ from their viewpoint of the same environment.

collective worship   It is a requirement of **maintained schools** that they must hold a daily collective act of worship for all pupils, unless parents have grounds for withdrawal. This is usually carried out in an assembly. It is normally Christian in character and decided by the **headteacher** with the approval of the governing body. Where it is felt that a Christian form of worship is inappropriate, the school can, after the parents have been consulted, apply to the local **Standing Advisory Council on Religious Education** (SACRE) for exemption. In **foundation schools** of a religious character and **voluntary schools**, collective worship should be according to the terms of the trust deed.

college of education   Following the recommendations of the **Robbins Report** (1963), the 155 teacher training colleges were renamed colleges of education. In 1972, a **White Paper**, *Education: A Framework for Expansion*, stated that a substantial reduction in the number of teacher training places was necessary to avoid a surplus of teachers. As part of the reorganisation it proposed that colleges should merge with **polytechnics** or further education colleges; some, however, chose to join universities or to become institutes of higher education. Many subsequently closed. A few colleges remained independent but their degrees were validated by a university. (See also **college of higher education**)

college of higher education (CHE)   Colleges of higher education emerged from the reorganisation of teacher education and advanced further education in the 1970s. Many **colleges of education** were merged with **universities** or **polytechnics** but about 50 became self-standing diversified colleges of higher education. The principals of these colleges of higher education formed the Standing Conferences of Principals (SCOP). When polytechnics became universities in 1992 the future and the status of the CHE was questioned, but it seems likely that those offering specialist courses not available in universities will probably survive.

College of Preceptors   Incorporated by Royal Charter in 1849, it promoted the in-service training of teachers both in the UK and overseas. It is probably best known for its work as an examining body for practising teachers. During the second half of the nineteenth century, the College made a number of unsuccessful attempts to become a registration council for teachers. The College awards an Associateship (ACP) and a Licentiateship (LCP) – both graduate level qualifications – as well as diplomas in Advanced Study in Education. Two more recent classes of membership are Member (M Coll P), to recognise good professional practice, and Ordinary Fellow (F Coll P), reserved for those who have made an outstanding contribution to education. The College changed its name by Supplemental Charter to the College of Teachers in 1998. (See also **General Teaching Council**)

Colleges of Advanced Technology (CAT)   The White Paper, *Technical Education* (1956), envisaged a large increase in advanced courses in **technical colleges.** Most of the work was to take place in Colleges of Advanced Technology (CATs), which were to be formed from technical institutions already providing substantial **advanced level** and **postgraduate** work. The White Paper designated eight CATs, and by 1962 these had been increased to ten. An important feature of the course was the **sandwich** element of a year in industry. After the **Robbins Report** the CATS became fully fledged universities. (See also **Percy Report**, **universities, history of**)

collegiate university   From the middle ages, the colleges of Oxford and Cambridge Universities were established by money given by pious founders. Each college has considerable autonomy. It controls its own property, elects its own **Fellows**, chooses its own head and, subject to university regulations, admits its own **undergraduate** students. The hallmark of such a college is its corporate identity, in contrast to that of a **federal** system. Durham University is also organised on a collegiate basis. (See also **universities, history of**)

Command Paper   A document presented 'by Her Majesty's Command' to either House, the Command Paper is in fact the responsibility of a minister. It may be, e.g., a **White Paper** or a Blue Book and is not in pursuance of an Act of Parliament. All Command Papers bear a number, such as the White Paper, *Higher Education: A New Framework* (1991), Cm 1541.

Committee of the Privy Council on Education   Established in 1839 to superintend grants provided by the Government for the provision of schools and **training colleges**. It consisted of four members, the **Lord President of the Council**, the Lord Privy Seal, the Chancellor of the Exchequer and the Home Secretary. Its first Secretary was Dr James Kay (later Kay-Shuttleworth). Meeting about once a month, the Council published its decisions as Minutes of the Committee of the Council on Education. It evolved a policy that ensured that grants given for specific purposes were properly used. The Council appointed the first two inspectors, **HMIs**, to assist in this task. With the growth in the activities of the Committee, an **Education Department**, headed by a **Vice-President**, was established in 1856 and took over the Council's work.

Committee of Vice-Chancellors and Principals (CVCP)   The Committee was established in 1918 and reconstituted in 1930. It represented heads of university institutions. Its membership was considerably enlarged as a result of the Further and Higher Education Act (1992), which converted **polytechnics** into universities. The CVCP was renamed **Universities UK** in 2000. (See also **principal**, **vice-chancellor**)

common curriculum   (See **curriculum, common**)

Common Entrance Examination   An examination taken by pupils wishing to enter a senior department of an independent school at 11 plus, 12 plus, or 13 plus. Begun in 1904, the examination syllabuses are prepared by the Independent Schools Examinations Board, which is made up of members of the **Headmasters and Headmistresses Conference**, the **Girls' School Association** and the **Incorporated Association of Preparatory Schools**. It is not a public examination and is usually held in the candidates' own junior or preparatory schools. Some 14,000 pupils – 10,000 boys and 4,000 girls – sit the papers each year. There are seven compulsory subjects but, by 2003, it is intended to reduce the number to three – English, mathematics and science – to encourage State school pupils to take the examination. A number of independent schools devise their own examination instead of the common entrance. (See also **preparatory school**)

community college/school   A concept of education that seeks to involve individuals as members of communities in educational activities, regardless of age. This notion, derived from the **village college** and recommended in the **Plowden Report**, has been translated into programmes located in community colleges or schools, with an intake of secondary pupils usually between 14 and 18 years of age. Parents make use of resources during the day as well as the evening, taking part in academic and recreational activities alongside their children. As well as housing a school, the campus may include a **further education** college, a library and a sports complex. The buildings are often in use late at night for leisure and cultural activities, and for meetings of local clubs and societies. Since the School Standards and Framework Act (1998), community schools have become similar to former **county schools**, where the **local education authority** employs the staff and owns the school buildings. (See also **adult education**, **community education**, **neighbourhood school**, **village college**)

community education   Educational planning that involves educational activities outside the school or beyond the **community college** or **village college**. The concept of community education is related to the ideas of **continuing education**, namely, that education does not stop when a person finishes the period of full-time schooling, but continues into adult life. Many schemes of community education would involve teaching staff venturing into the wider community ('**outreach**') as well as bringing adults into the educational institution. Another of its aims is to improve the environment and the quality of life of the community in general.

Community Service Volunteers (CSV)   A registered charity, founded in 1962, with the aim of supporting teachers, youth workers and others interested in developing community involvement projects with young people both inside and outside the formal education system.

comparability   The extent to which the same awards reached through different routes represent equivalent levels of attainment. During the 1990s, there was a major debate about whether the standards of school examinations (**GCSEs** and **A Levels**) were falling: this is sometimes referred to as a question of comparability over time.

compensation   An agreed process by which candidates can make up for low levels of performance in some parts of an examination by higher level performance in others.

compensatory education   The theory behind compensatory education is that of 'social deficit', i.e., that some children come from homes that do not provide early learning experiences or sufficient stimulation to motivate children in the classroom. Working-class children and children from some ethnic minority groups have been singled out for compensatory education programmes such as Head Start in the USA.

competence   **National Vocational Qualifications** are based on the concept of being competent: i.e., performing to professional or occupational standards. A competent plumber is one who can demonstrate all the skills necessary for a range of tasks.

competency-based teaching (CBT)   Aimed at improving teacher performance in the classroom, CBT employs many forms of teaching methods. The essence of CBT is that 'competence' must be defined in such a way as to make it measurable. In England, CBT was connected with the compulsory curriculum for **initial teacher training**, which became a requirement in 1998 as a result of Circular 4/98, monitored by the **Teacher Training Agency** (TTA), and inspected by the **Office for Standards in Education** (OFSTED). The Circular was reviewed in 2000–2 and much of the detailed prescription removed, but the principle of **outcomes** remains.

comprehensive school   The 1944 **Education Act** legislated for secondary education for all, but did not specify any one type of secondary school organisation. Circular 144/1947 set out various forms of organisation and defined a comprehensive school as 'one which is intended to cater for the secondary education of all children in a given area'. After many **local education authority** experiments with **tripartite systems** (grammar, technical and secondary modern schools) in the 1950s and 1960s, the comprehensive alternative rapidly gained in popularity during the 1970s. The 1976 Education Act attempted to make comprehensive schools the only kind of permitted secondary school, but was repealed by the 1979 Act, after the election of the Conservative Government under Margaret Thatcher. Nevertheless, by 1988 comprehensive schools were catering for 86 per cent of pupils in England, 98 per cent in Wales, and 99 per cent in Scotland. Northern Ireland continued with a mainly selective secondary system, but in 2001 the principle of selection was challenged by the **Burns Report**, and it seemed that in time the selection process would be modified if not abolished. In England, in 2002–2, comprehensive schools were encouraged to develop distinctive features, some becoming **specialist schools**. The trend was encouraged by statements by Ministers and others talking about the 'post-comprehensive era'.

compulsory competitive tendering (CCT)   The 1988 Local Government Act requires some services, such as school cleaning and school meals, to be opened up to competition by inviting other organisations, in addition to local government, to tender for the contract. **Local education authorities** are required to ensure that complete fairness is observed. The list of affected services was extended by the 1992 Local Government Act. (See also **Local Government Acts**)

compulsory curriculum   (See **curriculum, compulsory**)

computer-assisted learning (CAL)   Sometimes also referred to as computer-aided instruction (CAI). The use of a computer is not only intended to present instructional material to students, but also to provide a reaction to their response. (See also **information and communications technology**)

conditional offer   Best exemplified by the **Universities and Colleges Admissions Service** (UCAS) procedure for pupils wishing to proceed to university. Such an offer is made by the appropriate university department, conditional upon the pupil obtaining stipulated grades in GCE **A Level** examinations which have yet to be taken at the time of the offer. (See also **entry qualification**)

Confederation for the Advancement of State Education (CASE)   A **pressure group** set up in 1960 to improve the quality of **maintained schools**, consisting of parents and others interested in education. Local groups operated within the framework of national case policy. It espoused numerous causes including support for a fully **comprehensive school** system, and the abolition of **streaming** and **corporal punishment**.

Connexions   An advice and guidance service for 13–19-year-olds which gives career guidance, encourages young people to continue their education or training and make an effective transition from school to work.

Schools are also involved, together with the heads and those key teachers responsible for careers guidance and personal, social and health education. Connexions cover the same geographical areas as the **Learning and Skills Councils** (LSCs). The first 16 areas started in 2001, and the remaining 31 areas in 2002. The local management committees, consisting of representatives from employment, voluntary agencies, health and youth justice, oversee the operation. By February 2002, 70 advice and guidance 'shops' had opened and there were more than 1,600 **Personal Advisors**.

conscience clause   From 1833, attempts had been made to protect Non-conformist consciences from the enforced teaching of the catechism, and attendance at church by those attending school. The matter was not settled until the 1870 Education Act which stated that schools receiving a parliamentary grant placed no religious conditions on the admission of children and that pupils could be withdrawn by their parents from any religious observance or instruction. The nature of that instruction was settled by Section 14 of the Act, called the Cowper-Temple clause after its promoter, that it should be one 'in which no religious catechism or religious formulary which is distinctive of any religious denomination shall be taught'.

constructivism   An aspect of the study of child development and **learning theory** based on developments of the work of Vygotsky and **Piagetian** psychology. A basic principle is that children should not be regarded as passive learners – empty vessels to be filled with knowledge – but as active learners who constantly try to construct a meaningful reality out of what they perceive.

Consultative Committee   Set up by the Board of Education Act (1899) to advise the new Board on any matters referred to it. The first Committee consisted of 18 members, the majority of whom were from universities. After its reconstruction in 1920, and under the chairmanship of distinguished academics, influential reports, such as those of **Hadow** (1926, 1931 and 1933) and **Spens** (1938), covering the whole field of elementary and secondary education, were issued. After the 1944 **Education Act**, the Committee was replaced by two **Central Advisory Councils**, for England and for Wales.

continuing education   A term that overlaps adult education, permanent education and recurrent education, but is not synonymous with any of them. With continuing education the emphasis is on the idea that education in its true form proceeds throughout an individual's life. Thus the emphasis in continuing education is on breaking the barrier between formal and informal education, institutions of education and real life. (See also **University of the Third Age** (U3A))

continuing professional development (CPD)   During the 1990s successive governments paid more attention to improving the quality of teaching. Part of the programme was to focus attention on the kind of professional development that would improve classroom performance. Despite criticisms that this was a narrow view of professional development, the Labour Government, after 1997, increased expenditure on CPD, produced a framework, and put forward the idea of development as a continuing process from **initial teacher training** (ITT), to **induction**, and to continuing professional development through the whole of a teaching career.

continuous assessment   The assessment of a student's work throughout a course instead of (or in addition to) a formal terminal examination. The purpose of continuous assessment is **formative** rather than **summative**, providing useful feedback to the student in order to improve future performance, but the marks awarded may also count towards a summative assessment. (See also **coursework**)

contract school   A new type of **secondary school** for which private or voluntary sponsors may take responsibility for a **failing school** for a fixed term contract of 5–7 years but which may be renewable. Contract schools are based on the model used at King's Manor, Guildford, Surrey, the commercial branch of the **city technology college** at Kingshurst. They are subject to national policies on admissions.

convergent thinking   A way of thinking or problem-solving that concentrates on finding only one solution to a problem. This assumes that there is only one 'best' or 'correct' solution to any given problem. A person habitually inclined to convergent thinking may be referred to as a 'converger'. (See also **creativity** and **divergent thinking**)

core curriculum   (See **curriculum, core**)

core skills   A programme of work on core skills was initiated by the **Department of Education and Science** (DES) in 1989. Various bodies including the **National Council for Vocational Qualifications** (NCVQ) and the **School Examinations and Assessment Council** (SEAC) were asked to explore the feasibility of specifying and assessing core skills which were common to **A Level** qualifications and their vocational equivalents. A list of agreed core skills in communication, application of number, and information technology were drawn up. Responsibility for this area was later taken over by the **Qualifications and Curriculum Authority**, and core skills were renamed **Key Skills**.

core subject   The 1988 **Education Reform Act** national curriculum gave priority to three **foundation subjects** by designating them core subjects. They are English, mathematics and science. In Wales Welsh is a core subject in Welsh-speaking schools.

corporal punishment   Once common in primary and secondary schools (maintained and private), the practice was already diminishing rapidly by

1986 when it was made illegal in State schools as part of the Education (No. 2) Act (1986). This does not preclude the use of force in some circumstances, e.g., to prevent personal injury or damage to property. **Independent schools** still have the right to use corporal punishment, but suspended exercising it after a Government warning that teachers could be blacklisted as a result. (See also **discipline**: **punishment, philosophy and psychology of, Society of Teachers Opposed to Physical Punishment** (STOPP))

correlation (correlation coefficient)   The relationship between two sets of data; e.g., individual candidates' scores in two papers or the scores given by two examiners to the same set of scripts. Correlation coefficients are expressed on the scale +1.0 to −1.0 where +1.0 indicates perfect correlation, and −1.0 indicates a complete inverse relationship. Coefficients between different components in the same subject **examination** tend to fall in the range +0.5 to +0.8. If the correlation coefficient were +0.4 or lower, there would be grounds for a full enquiry.

correspondence course   A course of study, conducted by means of written work, between student and tutor through the post. (See also **distance learning, Open University, self-instruction**)

correspondence theory   A view put forward by some sociologists that suggests that the major purpose of schooling is to service the needs of industrial society. Pupils are taught in schools to be punctual and obedient, and to work hard under supervision, so that they may become docile factory workers and clerks when they leave school.

Council for Curriculum, Examinations and Assessment (CCEA) In Northern Ireland this Council's responsibilities are roughly equivalent to those of the **Qualifications and Curriculum Authority** (QCA) in England. Its role is to keep under review all aspects of curriculum and assessment and to advise the **Department of Education Northern Ireland** (DENI) accordingly. The Council works closely with other partners in the education service, and is also responsible for setting and marking the tests for the transfer procedure from primary to secondary schools.

Council for Education in World Citizenship (CEWC)   Founded in 1939, the Council provides information, projects and practical help on international issues, without political bias. The Council has over the years held national conferences for secondary school students; it has organised teachers' seminars on international understanding; it has provided speakers for schools; and disseminated information through its information service. The Council in England went into suspension in England in April 2001 but its work continues in Wales and Northern Ireland.

Council for Independent Further Education (CIFE) An association of 24 independent **sixth form** and **tutorial colleges**, concerned with maintaining high quality. They are regularly inspected by the **British Accreditation Council for Independent Further and Higher Education** (BAC), the **Independent Schools Council** (ISC) and, where appropriate, the **Department for Education and Skills** (DfES).

Council for National Academic Awards (CNAA) A body set up by the Government in 1964 to validate courses, especially degree courses, offered by colleges and polytechnics. At the time the CNAA was the only non-university body in the UK permitted to award degrees. The Council was abolished in 1991 as part of the reform of higher education.

Council for the Accreditation of Teacher Education (CATE) CATE was established in 1984 'to advise the Secretaries of State for Education and Science on the approval of initial teacher training courses in England and Wales'. Unless courses were 'approved' they did not carry **qualified teacher status** (QTS). CATE was reorganised in 1990 with a smaller council, and new criteria were designed to build on the first five years of experience of CATE as well as to cater for the **national curriculum** in schools. The 1994 Education Act established a **Teacher Training Agency** (TTA) which has replaced CATE.

Council of Europe An organisation established in 1949 with the aim of achieving greater unity between its members, safeguarding and realising their ideals and principles, and facilitating their economic and social progress. Its headquarters are in Strasbourg and committees of ministers from the member countries meet there as well as in the Parliamentary Assembly. A Council for Cultural Co-operation was established in 1962 to promote cultural and educational programmes. Conferences, seminars and symposia on many issues including education are held from time to time and their proceedings are published.

Council of Local Education Authorities (CLEA) In 1975, the **Association of Metropolitan Authorities** (AMA) and the **Association of County Councils** (ACC) formed this new Council so that the education authorities of England could speak with one voice. The Council deals with a large range of matters, from discussing teachers' conditions of service to making representations to the Secretary of State on issues affecting local education authorities. It became part of the **Local Government Association** in 1997.

counselling Counselling has been defined as helping people to understand their own motives and reasons for actions, so that they can come to their own conclusions about what they will do and how they can do it. It means helping them to define their needs and discover what resources are available to them to work out the best ways of making and sustaining satisfactory relationships with others. In a school setting, counselling is focused on personal, educational and **vocational guidance**. The first full-time courses for experienced teachers in Britain were established in 1965 and were much influenced by the ideas and work of Carl Rogers, the American psychotherapist.

county college   The 1943 White Paper on Educational Reconstruction recommended that **local education authorities** should provide compulsory part-time education for 15–18-year-olds. The Education Act of 1944 provided for county colleges to be opened by 1950. But priority was given to the raising of the school leaving age and the scheme was dropped. The **Crowther Report** revived the idea in 1959 but it was not implemented.

county school   (See **maintained school**)

course   The most common usage refers to a 'course of study' meaning a series of lessons, lectures or seminars, of specified duration (often a year). Thus a **Programme of Studies** would consist of several courses. Ambiguity arises, however, when reference is made, e.g., to a 'degree course' when the more appropriate terminology would appear to be 'degree programme'. In recent years, some degree programmes have been organised on a **modular** basis.

coursework   Work carried out by a student during a course of study. Its nature may range from essay-writing to practical tasks. According to the course regulations, such work may be compulsory and be taken into account in forming a final assessment of the student's merit. As regards **GCSEs**, there has been a dispute between teachers (especially teachers of English) who want a higher percentage of assessment to be by coursework, and successive Secretaries of State who have limited coursework to 20 per cent, apart from those subjects that require more to comply with Orders. (See also **Cox Report**)

Cox Report   Professor Brian Cox, editor of the **Black Papers** and member of the **Kingman** Committee, was asked by Kenneth Baker in 1987 to chair the Working Party for National Curriculum English. He produced a report (correctly known as the *Report of the English Working Party, DES, 1988*). This was a moderate document, which was generally acceptable to most teachers of English, but was criticised by the right wing of the Conservative Party for paying insufficient attention to formal grammar, spelling, and other traditional concerns, and for including too much emphasis on **oracy**. John Patten (Secretary of State, 1992–94) yielded to pressure and asked the

National Curriculum Council to revise the Cox version of National Curriculum English. The result was much less acceptable to teachers of English (and to Cox), who provided a detailed account of the events in *The Great Betrayal* (1992) and in *Cox on the Battle for the English Curriculum* (1995). The English curriculum was further modified after the **Dearing Reports** (1993 and 1994).

crammer A name given to an independent tutorial college of further education where students of 16 years of age and over attend to prepare for school examinations and special examinations with a view to entering the professions and universities. There are often short intensive courses for those wishing to improve **A Level** grades. Some guarantee of quality is provided by membership of the **Council for Independent Further Education** (CIFE).

creativity Partly as a reaction against the use of intelligence tests, which were said to measure **convergent thinking**, some psychologists developed tests that would test **divergent** thinking or creativity, e.g. 'write down as many uses as you can think of for a brick'.

credit Formal recognition of achievement, usually counting towards the award of a degree or diploma.

credit accumulation The process by which components of a qualification can be separately counted and stored for a future award.

credit transfer The recognition of credit gained in one course as satisfying some of the requirements of a different qualification.

Crewe Report The last of the **Prime Minister's Reports**, on the position of Classics in the UK, was issued in 1921. The Committee, chaired by the Marquess of Crewe, included Sir Henry Hadow, W. P. Ker, Gilbert Murray and A. N. Whitehead. Its remit – 'to advise as to the means by which the proper study of these subjects may be maintained and improved' – led to a wide-ranging investigation of the teaching of Classics in schools and universities. The report painted a gloomy picture. In **public schools**, Greek and Latin occupied no preponderant position, and in **secondary schools**, whilst the position of Latin was not discouraging, Greek was threatened with extinction. It recommended that while French would normally be the first foreign modern language, liberty of experiment should be encouraged and Latin should be taught first. Some teaching of formal grammar was desirable in **elementary schools**, whilst in secondary schools greater stress was to be laid on the historical and archaeological backgrounds to the texts.

criterion-referenced test A test designed to establish a candidate's performance in terms of a given **level** or **standard** rather than being better (or worse) than other candidates. In England, the driving test is often quoted as the most familiar example of a test that demands performance at a certain level on a number of known criteria. A criterion-referenced test may express the notion of 'pass' either in terms of a 'cut-off point' or test score, or in terms of reaching a standard of competence on a number of related criteria (such as the use of mirror and braking in the driving test). (See also **norm-referenced testing**)

criterion-referencing   Assessment based on a **level** or **standard** rather than on an individual's performance compared with that of other candidates.

critical learning period   One theory in child development suggests that the times in childhood when individuals may acquire particular skills are limited. If an opportunity is missed during the 'critical period' it is then thought to be difficult or perhaps impossible to acquire a skill at a later stage. Critical learning periods are likely to exist in other animals, but some psychologists doubt their existence in human beings. Language acquisition is sometimes suggested as the most important example of a skill acquired during the critical learning period, but this is by no means established.

Cross Report   In 1886, Sir Richard Cross, then Conservative Home Secretary, was appointed chairman of a Royal Commission 'to inquire into the working of the Elementary Acts, England and Wales'. Both the Catholic and the Church of England authorities were concerned at the position of **voluntary schools** under the 1870 Education Act; as a result, religious interests were well represented on the Commission. Because of divisions of opinion within the Commission, two reports were issued in 1888. The majority report supported voluntary schools and a minority report voiced Nonconformist objections to allowing Church schools to have a share of the rates. However, there was agreement on a number of issues. Whilst recommending the eventual abolition of '**payment by results**', it favoured the retention of standards and a core curriculum, consisting of the **three Rs**, needlework for girls, history, geography and elementary science. The teaching of Welsh was officially sanctioned. The Committee also called for a definition of the term 'elementary' by Parliament. (See also **university day training college**)

Crowther Report   Sir Geoffrey Crowther was chairman of the **Central Advisory Council** (England) which issued a Report in 1959 on the education of boys and girls between the ages of 15 and 18. One of its chief recommendations was that the **school-leaving age** should be raised to 16 between 1966 and 1968 to encourage pupils to continue at school until 18, with compulsory part-time day education to this age to be provided in **county colleges** for those who had left school. The second volume of the report provided valuable statistical and sociological evidence of the importance of home background on educational achievement. (See also **numeracy**)

CSE   (See **Certificate of Secondary Education**)

culture   Culture refers to knowledge, beliefs and attitudes, passed on from one generation to the next, and by definition any society possesses a culture or way of life that members of that society share. In a complex industrial society this transmission process is much more complicated than in a technologically and economically simple society. In a complicated society not all values and beliefs are held in common – there are sub-cultures within the major society – but there are always some cultural features held in common, i.e., a common culture, as well as sub-cultures.

culture of the school   Studies of **school effectiveness** and **school improvement** indicate that a key characteristic of **effective schools** is that they possess a certain kind of positive ethos or culture. Lists of characteristics have been drawn up, but it is said to be important that they are not treated in isolation but together as part of the culture of the school.

curriculum   A narrow definition would limit curriculum to a 'programme for instruction'; wider definitions would include all the learning that takes place in a school or other institution, planned and unplanned. In recent years curriculum has been defined as a selection from the culture of a society; and the curriculum is planned by a process of cultural analysis. (See also **syllabus**, **national curriculum**)

curriculum, common   A curriculum planned to cater for all pupils in a school. It is 'common' in the sense that all pupils study certain subjects or have certain educational experiences 'in common' by the end of the period of compulsory schooling. 'Common curriculum' can also be used nationally to indicate the desirability of all children in the country having certain planned experiences 'in common'. Both uses depend to some extent on the idea of a common **culture**.

curriculum, compulsory   The idea that a properly planned curriculum would either be wholly compulsory or that there would be compulsory elements distinguished from the optional. The **national curriculum** was an example of a compulsory curriculum for schools, and a compulsory curriculum for **initial teacher training** was established by the **Council for the Accreditation of Teacher Education** (CATE) and continued by the **Teacher Training Agency** (TTA).

curriculum, core   Often confused with common curriculum, but is usually used as a weaker term to indicate that there are some subjects that are more important than others, and therefore should be compulsory, or given priority in some way.

curriculum, entitlement   The 'entitlement curriculum' was a term used by **HMI** to indicate a curriculum for all pupils based on what was regarded as worthwhile knowledge and experience. The idea was discussed in DES a document *Curriculum 11–16: Towards a Statement of Entitlement* (1988).

curriculum, hidden   An ambiguous term. One meaning implies that there are certain kinds of learning that are not included in the timetable, but which will be transmitted by institutional arrangements, such as a prefect system or the cadet corps (CCF). A related meaning refers to the possibility of pupils acquiring attitudes and behaviour patterns not intended by school authorities. (See also **timetabling**)

curriculum, spiral   Learning planned in such a way that a pupil encounters important concepts at a number of stages – concrete before abstract, simple before complex, easy before difficult. The intention of the originator, Jerome Bruner, was to indicate that important concepts should not be regarded as something to be learned on a single occasion and then taken for granted; concepts need to be encountered in a variety of contexts, over a period of time, and gradually assimilated.

curriculum control   Part of the study of the politics of the curriculum. In any society there are decision-makers who control or influence the content of what is taught in schools.

Curriculum and Assessment Authority for Wales (ACAC)   The body in Wales that had responsibilities similar to those of the English **School Examinations and Assessment Council**, which was, in 1992, superseded by the **School Curriculum and Assessment Authority** (SCAA).

Curriculum Council for Wales (CCW)   The Council in Wales had responsibilities similar to the English **National Curriculum Council**. It was replaced by the **Curriculum and Assessment Authority for Wales** which was, in 1999, renamed the **Qualifications Curriculum and Assessment Authority for Wales**, which is directly responsible to the **National Assembly for Wales**.

curriculum development project   A study of a particular subject or area of the **curriculum** often with a view to improving that part of the curriculum by supplying teachers with attractive teaching materials, sometimes in the form of 'packages'. In recent years there has been less emphasis on 'materials' but greater effort to encourage teachers to rethink aims and methods for themselves. (See also **dissemination**, **Man – A Course of Study** (MACOS))

Curriculum Online   Introduced in September 2002, Curriculum Online is a partnership between the **Department for Education and Skills**, the educational software industry and the British Broadcasting Corporation, formed to provide and enhance online education for schools and individual pupils. It provides a web site, linking with the **National Grid for Learning**, for online curriculum resources; schools will have access to 'e-learning credits' to buy resources. Curriculum Online aims to provide materials that will motivate pupils and raise standards through individualised learning.

curriculum planning   The process of designing and organising the whole curriculum either at national level or within a single school.

Curriculum 2000   One of **Dearing** Committee's Report (1996) recommendations was that the **sixth form** curriculum for 16–19-year-olds should be broadened. This was much in line with previous reports such as **Higginson** (1988). The main suggestion for Curriculum 2000 was that **Advanced Subsidiary (AS) Level** qualifications should be redeveloped at a level between **General Certificate of Secondary Education** and **A Level**. Students in the first year after GCSE should be encouraged to take four or five AS Levels, preferably spanning arts and science subjects, and then concentrate on two or three A Level subjects in their final year at school. During the year 2000–1 there were some complaints by students and teachers, mainly on grounds of over-assessment. Following a review by David Hargreaves, the Chief Executive of the **Qualifications and Curriculum Authority** in 2001, the **Department for Education and Skills** accepted the need for simplified assessment procedures in following years.

cut-off point   A point on a mark list or rank order that is used to separate 'passes' from 'failures' or first class from second class, etc. For example, a group of examiners, after looking at a number of examination papers, might decide that a mark of 40 per cent would be the lowest level of pass and all candidates with 39 per cent would fail. Forty per cent would thus be the cut-off point, but all candidates with marks of, say, 37 to 43 per cent would probably be regarded as **borderline**, and submitted to special scrutiny. In such a case, the examiners would have certain criteria or **standards** in mind which would justify passing some and failing others: the mark of 40 per cent would be arbitrary, but the standard it represented would not.

D

Dainton Report   A Committee chaired by Sir (then Dr) Frederick Dainton, set up in 1965 to inquire into the flow of candidates in science and technology into higher education. Its report issued three years later warned of the harm both to individuals and society of the relative decline in the study of science and technology, especially in the **sixth forms**. This 'swing from science' it suggested, could be dealt with by introducing a broad span of studies in sixth forms and delaying premature specialisation. Schools and **local education authorities** should also ensure that the majority of secondary school pupils should come into early contact with good science teaching and should study mathematics until they leave school. (See also **Swann Report**)

Dalton Plan   A system of teaching and learning devised by Helen Parkhurst and first introduced at Dalton High School, Massachusetts, in 1920. It was based on two major principles: first, that the pupil must be free to continue without interruption upon any subject that may arise in the course of her/his study; and, second, that the Plan would transform the learning process into a co-operative adventure. The basis of the Plan was that the curriculum was divided up into jobs and the pupil accepted the task appointed for his class as a contract. The contract job comprised a whole month's work, designed to accord with the pupil's ability. The Plan postulated the establishment of laboratories, one for each subject in the curriculum, with a specialist in that subject attached to each laboratory. Helen Parkhurst's scheme was rapidly taken up in England, notably by Rosa Bassett at Streatham School for Girls, London.

Dame schools   Traceable as far back as the seventeenth century, these schools were for young children, usually in rural areas, and staffed by unqualified women. The standard of instruction given was normally very low.

day continuation schools   A Consultative Committee on Attendance at Continuation Schools, reporting in 1909, favoured the 'systematic encouragement of suitable and practical kinds of continued education beyond the now too early close of the elementary school day course'. The **Lewis Report** (1917) examined post-war educational needs.

day nursery   Unlike other types of nursery education, day nurseries are normally organised by local authority social services departments. They are for children in need under five and have qualified staff. They are open often throughout the year from 8.00 a.m. to 6.00 p.m. Another type of day nursery is that provided by either private enterprise or an employers' organisation for children of parents going to work. They are often heavily subsidised and are registered with a local authority. (See also **Children Act** (1989))

day release   A method of organising courses in **further** or **higher education** whereby students on courses are in employment and are released for perhaps one or two days a week during the term for training, general education or to pursue a formal qualification. (See also **Youth Training**)

day school   A term generally applied to most maintained schools as well as to an increasing number of **independent schools**. The main characteristic is that pupils attend during school hours and do not normally board at the school.

dean   (1) The person responsible for a faculty or department in a university or higher education institution. (2) A **fellow** or senior member of a university who supervises the conduct and discipline of students.

Dearing Reports/Reviews   In 1993, teachers decided to boycott the **national curriculum** testing arrangements. Sir Ron Dearing, Chairman of the **School Curriculum and Assessment Authority** (SCAA), was asked by the Secretary of State for Education to review the national curriculum and to make his individual recommendations on slimming down the curriculum, and improving its administration. Dearing made an Interim Report in 1993 and a Final Report in 1994 after a period of consultation. It was recommended that the slimmed down national curriculum should not be altered for five years and that national tests should be simplified without sacrificing validity or reliability. The revised curriculum was implemented from August 1995.

In April 1995, Sir Ron Dearing had been asked to review the framework of qualifications for 16–19-year-olds. He produced an Interim Report, *The Issues for Consideration*, in July 1995, with a Final Report, *Review of Qualifications for 16–19-Year-Olds* in 1996.

In 1997, Dearing was asked to look into **higher education** (HE) in the UK. His Report, *Higher Education in the Learning Society*, included more than 90 recommendations. They included: changes in funding and participation; changes in the curriculum; and changes in qualifications (a proposal for a new **framework for higher education qualifications** throughout the UK). The implementation of the framework was to be monitored by the **Quality Assurance Agency for Higher Education** (QAA).

deficit model   A theory put forward to account for the 'under-achievement' of certain minority groups and working-class children. The theory suggests that failure is connected with certain cultural 'deficits' which handicap them in the learning process at school. The theory was implicit or explicit in many of the well-known reports on education such as those by **Crowther**, **Newsom**

and **Plowden**. Some sociologists have reacted to this model by suggesting that schools often fail to provide adequate teaching for certain groups of children, or that society itself is at fault in various other ways. Whereas the deficit model 'blames' the family of an under-achieving child, later theories tend to blame teachers or society in general. (See also **compensatory education**, **disadvantaged**, **enrichment programme**)

degree benchmarks   The **Dearing** national committee of enquiry into higher education (1997) recommended that the **Quality Assurance Agency** (QAA) should develop benchmark information standards for degree courses. In May 2000, 22 benchmark statements were published setting out the knowledge, understanding and skills that a student was expected to gain from the relevant degree programme. The benchmark statements were intended to be introduced into **higher education** institutions from 2002. The degree benchmarks were intended to be used by employers as well as students. (See also **benchmarking academic standards**)

degree class   The system of dividing degree performance into classes such as first, upper second, lower second, third and pass has been criticised for many years for being both crude and often inaccurate. One proposal for reform was that a detailed **transcript** should be prepared for each graduate, on completion of the degree, showing what had been covered as well as the standard achieved in each topic. An experiment began in 2000, which was supported by the **Committee of Vice-Chancellors and Principals** (CVCP) (later **Universities UK**), and monitored by the **Quality Assurance Agency** (QAA). It was expected that most universities would be participating by 2002–3. The transcript system is sometimes also known as **Progress Files**.

degrees   Awarded by universities and other institutions of higher education as the result of successful completion of a course of study: the candidate may be tested by examination, continuous assessment, a viva, a thesis, or a combination of any of these. There are three levels of degrees:

(1) *Bachelor*, usually a first degree, except for degrees such as Bachelor of Philosophy (BPhil) and Bachelor of Literature (BLitt), and for degrees awarded by some Scottish universities. The course is normally of three years' duration. Examples are the Bachelor of Arts degree (BA) and the Bachelor of Science (BSc).

(2) *Masters*, are usually higher degrees obtained after one or two years of study and may include an element of research. In Scotland, the Master of Arts (MA) is normally a first degree. At Oxford and Cambridge, it is awarded seven years from the time of matriculation upon payment of a fee.

(3) *Doctor*, usually awarded as a result of research, presented in the form of a thesis. The initials PhD or DPhil (Doctor of Philosophy) indicate such an award. There are also higher doctorates, such as Doctor of Law (LLD) and Doctor of Literature (DLitt), which are awarded on the basis of the submission of publications. Medical practitioners are, as a matter of convention, entitled to be called doctors on becoming qualified, even without obtaining a doctorate qualification in medicine (MD). Degrees are normally awarded by a faculty and may be indicated by abbreviations following the title. For instance, the Bachelor degree by the faculty of economics at the University of London is written as BSc (Econ).

The majority of degree courses are for internal students, but some universities, notably London, offer **external degrees** for both home and overseas candidates. The **Open University** offers degree courses with the assistance of distance learning material. (See also **diploma**, **graduate**, **honorary degree**, **honours degree**, **postgraduate**, **undergraduate**)

delegacy   A group of individuals in a university who are given responsibility for a particular task or organisation. For example, in some universities **extramural** studies are organised by a delegacy; in others, school examinations are the responsibility of a delegacy. Although these responsibilities are delegated, they are normally reported back to another university committee, perhaps **Senate**.

delegated budget   That part of the budget given to governors of a school or institution to control and manage.

delegated management of schools   See **local management of schools**

Demos   A left-of-centre think tank founded in 1992 by Geoff Mulgan and Martin Jacques (a lapsed Marxist). Demos is particularly concerned with **citizenship** and community.

Department for Education (DfE)   In 1992, when the DES became the Department for Education, the science component of its work was hived off to form the Office of Science and Technology under the Chancellor of the Duchy of Lancaster. From 1992 to 1994, when the DfE was expanded to incorporate many aspects of training and became the **Department for Education and Employment** (DfEE), the responsibilities of the Department for the Welsh Office remained unchanged.

Department for Education and Employment (DfEE)   Created in July 1994, it replaced the former **Department for Education** (DfE). It was seen as an opportunity to span both education and employment. The respective roles of the DfE and the Employment Department had become blurred with the establishment of the **Manpower Services Commission**, the **Youth Opportunities Programme** and the **Youth Training Scheme**. Therefore, under the Department for Education and Employment, the two Departments merged. This larger Department enabled a more co-ordinated approach to schooling and continuing education. The DfEE was replaced by the **Department for Education and Skills** (DfES) in July 2001.

Department for Education and Skills (DfES)   After the General Election in 2001, some of the Employment responsibilities were removed from the **Department for Education and Employment** (DfEE) and the department was renamed the **Department for Education and Skills.** The Department retained responsibility for training as well as all aspects of education.

Department of Education and Science (DES)   In 1964, the **Ministry of Education** became the Department of Education and Science. In addition to absorbing the Ministry of Science, the DES took over from the Treasury responsibilities relating to the **University Grants Committee**. There was a Secretary of State, a Minister of State (Arts) and three Parliamentary Under-Secretaries. There was a separate Secretary of State for Wales. It also formulated policies for non-university education in England and for universities in England, Wales and Scotland and determined priorities in the allocation of resources to the education service. The DES worked in partnership with **local education authorities**, but had powers under the 1944 Education Act to intervene where authorities or schools failed to discharge their duties. Subsequent legislation further strengthened the powers of the DES at the expense of local authorities whilst the Education Reform Act of 1988 led to an even greater centralising of the education system.

Department of Education Northern Ireland (DENI)   Education in Northern Ireland has tended to be similar in structure to the English system but with some significant differences. The need for some local autonomy was reflected by the Education and Libraries (Northern Ireland) Order (1972) which created five education and library boards (somewhat similar to local education authorities in England). The 1978 Education (Northern Ireland) Act established the idea of controlled integrated schools in an attempt to break down barriers between Catholics and Protestants. This move received further support from the Education Reform (Northern Ireland) Order (1990). Until devolution, education in Northern Ireland was the responsibility of DENI but since devolution, responsibility for education in Northern Ireland is shared between two departments, each with its own Minister: the Department for Education, mainly concerned with schools, and the Department for Employment and Learning, concerned with further and higher education.

departmental committees Similar to **Royal Commissions**, except that they deal with subjects of lesser importance and do not enjoy the same prestige. A departmental committee is appointed by a minister to investigate a topic drawing on a range of specialist advice. Its report may be either a **Command Paper** or a non-parliamentary publication and is usually referred to by the name of its chairman. (See also **Parliamentary Papers**)

deputy head A post in the hierarchy of a school between the head and second master/mistress. There is no one standard job definition, but the holder of the post traditionally acts as a liaison between the head and the rest of the staff and frequently exercises powers delegated by the head. Large schools often have two or more deputy heads. Primary schools normally have one deputy head. With the advent of **local management of schools**, there have been changes in senior management teams in order to carry out the many new functions given to schools. One example is the introduction of the school manager or **bursar**. As a result, the post of deputy head has sometimes either disappeared or diminished in importance.

deschooling A term invented by Ivan Illich in *Deschooling Society* (1971) to encourage the idea of developing true education without schools. Schools, according to Illich, are too bureaucratic and expensive, as well as being a very inefficient means of educating the young. Developing countries in particular, in his view, would be better off without schools. Some of his followers have concentrated instead on changing schools by weakening the links between schools and the job market. (See also **alternative schooling**, **compulsory education**, **free schools**)

descriptors (See **level descriptions**)

designated courses Local education authorities have a duty to provide grants, called **mandatory awards**, to all students who are following a course which the **Department for Education and Skills** has listed under this heading. (See also **discretionary award**)

detention A form of **discipline** that involves keeping a pupil in at playtime, lunchtime or after school. Pupils in detention are usually set written work to complete during this time. Although heads have the authority to detain pupils after school, parents must be given 24 hours' written notice and the reasons for the punishment. The school has to ensure that it takes into account the implications of the **Human Rights Act** (1998).

development plan Most educational institutions draw up plans that review their positions, set targets and state how these are to be achieved and monitored. The plans may be on a short-term basis, i.e. annually or for longer periods of time.

developmental testing   A kind of **formative evaluation** particularly used by the **Open University**. Teaching materials are tried out on students on a trial basis before the final version is put into production. The trial group of students are asked to comment on particular difficulties or confusing passages, which are then analysed by educational psychologists and others skilled in textual presentation.

Devonshire Report   The Devonshire Commission took its name from its chairman, the seventh Duke of Devonshire, who was interested in the application of science to industry. The Royal Commission on Scientific Instruction and the Advancement of Science issued a series of reports between 1872 and 1875 on many aspects of scientific education, including the universities. Many of its recommendations were forward-looking. The **Revised Code** had prevented the development of science in **elementary schools**. Advances were to be made by the recruiting of scientifically qualified men for the Inspectorate and professorships were to be established in order to produce a supply of well-qualified science masters. It also deplored the lack of science teaching in endowed schools and recommended that laboratories should be build for practical instruction in physics and chemistry. (See also **Samuelson Report**)

diagnosis   The analysis of pupils' abilities and learning difficulties. This may be by using specially designed attainment tests, and diagnostic tests in the basic subjects. Pupils can be referred to **child guidance clinics** staffed by educational psychologists, for an investigation of physical, psychological or emotional dispositions that may affect school performance. Schools are also being urged to establish programmes to meet the individual needs of these children. (See also **school psychological service**)

diagnostic test   A test designed to discover an individual pupil's strengths and weaknesses in a particular subject area, often arithmetic or reading. Such a test is not designed to find out a pupil's competence or where he stands in relation to the rest of an age group. It is designed as an aid to learning. (See also **attainment, diagnosis, child guidance clinic**)

differentiated examinations   A method of testing different levels of **attainment** by the use of different examination papers. This may be operated in three ways: candidates may take one or more compulsory papers with either easier or more difficult components; they may take the easier components and some harder components; or they may take two or more components which overlap in difficulty. In the **General Certificate of Secondary**

Education (GCSE) there are **differentiated papers** for weaker and more able students.

differentiated papers   Examination papers within a scheme of assessment which are targeted at different levels of attainment. Differentiated papers may be tiered (overlapping) or stepped (non-overlapping).

differentiation/by task/by outcome   The provision of opportunities within a scheme of assessment for candidates across the whole attainment range to show what they know, understand, and can perform. Differentiation can be achieved by outcome (different candidates respond at different levels to the same task) and by task (different candidates succeed on tasks pitched at different levels).

difficulty index   Measure of the difficulty of an item in a test. It might be measured by the percentage of candidates answering correctly according to some models of test construction. An item with either a very low or a very high difficulty index would be omitted from the final version of the test. (See also **facility index**)

dilution   A fear that if unskilled or untrained helpers are employed in schools to do some of the less professional work previously done by teachers, then the whole of the profession becomes 'diluted'. For this reason many professional teachers' organisations are officially opposed to the employment of **teachers' aides** or classroom helpers of any kind. The opposing argument is that if more non-professionals were employed in schools this would release teachers for their more skilled professional duties. (See also **ancilliary staff**)

diploma   (1) A qualification granted by an institution at the end of a course of study. Diplomas may be of sub-degree standard or may be confined to graduates, for example **Postgraduate Certificate of Education** (PGCE). Many professional associations grant their own diplomas. (2) A document describing a candidate's performance following a course of study. (See also **degree**)

Diploma of Higher Education (Dip HE)   Introduced in 1974, the Diploma was a two-year course of study at first degree standard. There was a wide range of subjects to choose from in education: the arts, humanities, and the social and physical sciences. Most students went on to study for a degree, very often choosing between a **Bachelor of Education** (BEd.) or a **Bachelor of Arts** (BA); some institutions had specially designed courses to which successful Diploma students could transfer. The entry qualification was two **GCE A Levels**, or by access courses or by special entry arrangements for mature students. With the development of credit transfer, the Dip

HE has tended to be replaced by other flexible, usually modular, structures. (See also **credit accumulation** and **credit transfer**)

Diploma of Vocational Education (DVE)   Formerly the **Certificate of Pre-Vocational Education** (CPVE) available post-16, the DVE was intended to cover the 14–19-year age range. It was piloted in 1991–92, but was generally superseded by the development of **GNVQ**.

direct grant school   A type of secondary school, usually a selective grammar school, first established in 1926, which received a grant direct from the central authority for education. The arrangement included a guarantee that a proportion of places would be reserved for children from primary schools to be paid by **local education authorities** or the schools' governors in accordance with the direct grant regulations 1959. From September 1976, this arrangement ceased to operate: direct grant schools either joined the **maintained** system or became **independent** schools.

direct method   This method of teaching modern languages stemmed from work done in Germany towards the end of the nineteenth century. It avoided the analysis of grammar, but stressed that the teacher employed oral techniques, especially conversation and question and answering, which allowed the pupil to become immersed in the language itself. The direct method was very popular in English schools between 1900 and 1914: by the 1920s it was under attack, to be finally laid low by a staff inspector at the Board of Education, F. H. Collins, between the years 1929 and 1932. (See also **language laboratory**)

director   (1) Director of education: an alternative title to **chief education officer**, the leading officer of a local authority education department. (2) Director of studies: a person in a school or college responsible for a course or advising groups of students in academic matters. (3) A title for the head of an educational establishment, particularly in institutions of higher education.

director of studies   A member of the school's **senior management team,** with responsibilities for all aspects of teaching and learning. The duties may include curriculum development and training and support of teaching. The post may be combined with that of **head of department**.

disadvantaged   Those whose life chances are diminished by various social, physical, economic or family handicaps, or a combination of them all. The 'cycle of deprivation' hypothesis is often linked to the 'culture of poverty' argument, both laying stress on family process. Another view is that society and its structure is most to blame. The chances of avoiding disadvantage depend much on the individual's external avenues of escape. (See also **compensatory education**, **deficit model**, **enrichment programme**, **positive discrimination**)

disapplication   The **national curriculum** is a statutory requirement: schools are legally required to follow the provisions for all pupils unless they make a request to the **Department for Education and Skills** (DfES) for disapplication of one or two of the **foundation subjects** for individual pupils in order to provide for work-related learning, or to consolidate learning, or to emphasise a particular curriculum area. A **Qualifications and Curriculum Authority** (QCA) survey monitoring disapplication showed that about one third of schools were using disapplication arrangements for about 5 per cent of pupils. The most common subject for disapplication was modern foreign languages, followed by design and technology.

discipline   In schools, usually a term used to indicate 'classroom control' or 'keeping order'. The formulation of school rules is the responsibility of the headteacher. (See also **disruptive units**, **detention**, **exclusion**)

disciplines, academic   An area of human knowledge, e.g. history, geography, physics or geology, which has been developed, often in universities, as a separate subject area for purposes of teaching and research. A discipline would be associated with **learned journals**, professional associations and perhaps written or unwritten codes of practice. Some philosophers, e.g. Paul Hirst, have tried to avoid the ambiguity of 'disciplines' preferring to subdivide knowledge into 'forms' and 'fields'. (See also **disciplines of education**, **interdisciplinary studies**)

disciplines of education   The subject areas that, according to one view of professional teaching, all teachers should be introduced to as part of their initial training. The disciplines were traditionally considered to be philosophy, psychology and history of education; but from the late-1950s and early-1960s, sociology tended to be included, sometimes at the expense of history. (See also **academic disciplines**)

discretionary award   In contrast to a **mandatory** award, **local education authorities** give discretionary awards according to their own determined policies, and cases are considered individually. These are for a variety of courses, usually below first degree level. (See also **entrance award**, **maintenance grant**)

discrimination   The identification of different levels of attainment in relation to a task, an examination component or an overall scheme of assessment.

discrimination index   A measure of the success with which an item in a test can discriminate between 'good' and 'poor' candidates on the test as a whole. The easiest way of measuring the discrimination is to see to what extent success on a particular item correlates with success on the test as a whole. In some test models, items that do not discriminate are omitted from final versions of the test.

disruptive behaviour   The disruption of lessons by pupils, which is either deliberate or due to emotional or behavioural difficulties. This can take the form of violence against other children and the verbal abuse of staff. Schools often exclude such pupils for short or longer periods. Parents have a legal right to demand a place for their child in another school, but in practice this presents difficulties. (See also **discipline**, **exclusion**)

disruptive units   Children who cause undue disruption in ordinary schools may be placed in a disruptive unit, on either a part- or full-time basis. Units may be part of the campus of a school or an off-site provision. There is a high staff–pupil ratio and the aim is to combine therapy with an appropriate curriculum. Although such units are regarded, in the main, as temporary measures, many pupils do not return to their classrooms.

dissemination   Part of the process of **curriculum** development. A well-planned scheme of curriculum development would not only consist of planning the desired change, preparing materials and methods to implement change, but also the means of getting these new ideas across to a large number of teachers. In the early days of curriculum development, it was thought that this process of spreading ideas would occur naturally by a process of diffusion, but this proved to be an unwarranted assumption and plans for dissemination in an active way were built into later curriculum development projects. (See also **research and development**)

dissenting academy   The passing of the 1662 Act of Uniformity deprived some **Oxbridge** tutors of their fellowships and clergymen of their livings. A number therefore set up their own academies and brought with them a liberal and broadly based curriculum, which often included both history and science. The academies became very popular throughout England, offering up to five years' study. One of the most famous was Warrington Academy, which included on its staff Joseph Priestley, the discoverer of oxygen. By the beginning of the nineteenth century the movement was in decline, partly through lack of endowments and partly through sectarian differences.

dissertation   A treatise based on research submitted in connection with an award or qualification. Although the term dissertation and **thesis** are often interchangeable, the latter might often be more demanding. In some universities, a dissertation is shorter than a thesis. (See also **degrees**, **viva**)

distance learning   The most obvious kind of distance learning is the **correspondence course**, but the term now includes other media besides the written and the printed word, such as television, video tapes, World Wide Web, and radio programmes. Distance learning is normally based on a pre-produced course that is self-instructional but where organised two-way communication takes place between the student and a supporting institution. Distance learning is now seen as a useful adjunct to face-to-face learning. The **Open University** is a good example of this form of learning and it has long been common in Australia. Cable and/or satellite television may prove to be very important in distance learning in the future. (See also **e-university**, **study skills**, **University for Industry** (UfI))

distractor   In a **multiple choice test** each question will be followed by one correct answer but several incorrect answers or distractors. The candidate has to choose the correct answer from the incorrect, and at least some of the incorrect answers should be sufficiently plausible to distract the candidate. If all the incorrect answers were too obviously wrong, the candidate would be able to 'guess' at the correct answer without really knowing the right one.

divergent thinking   A thinking process which tends to look for a variety of solutions rather than a single correct answer. Liam Hudson in his book, *Contrary Imaginations* (1972), contrasted the **convergent** thinking of boys who tended to become scientists and those who, as a result of his tests, were classified as divergers who tended to be better at art subjects. (See also **creativity**)

don   Originating from the Spanish word 'don', to denote a nobleman, it was later applied to **Oxbridge Fellows**, but has now been extended to include university teachers in general.

Donnison Report   Whilst the Public Schools Commission under the chairmanship of Sir John Newsom was deliberating, its terms of reference were extended to include **direct grant** and **independent day schools**. (See **Newsom Report on Public Schools**). Members of the Commission, in their second report published in 1970, were divided in their opinions on the funding and status of direct grant schools. The return to office of a Conservative government shortly after this report was published ended further consideration of the proposals, though after the Labour victory in 1974 the direct grant arrangements were terminated. (See also **Assisted Places Scheme**, **Endowed Schools Commission**, **Fleming Report**)

Down's syndrome   A condition, also known as mongolism, named after the nineteenth-century physician Langdon Down who wrote up cases studies of the condition. The condition is now believed to be caused by chromosome abnormalities resulting in flattened facial features, stubby fingers and mental retardation. Children of this kind used to be taught in **special schools**, but recent attempts have been made to integrate them (especially children with the milder forms of Down's syndrome) into normal classes. (See also **special educational needs**)

dual system   The existence of Church and State schools alongside each other dates from the time of the 1870 Education Act. Under this Act, Church schools were given building grants for new buildings. By the 1902 Act, rate-aid was extended to Church schools in return for concessions such as the nomination of school managers by the local education authorities and their supervision of non-religious aspects of the curriculum. The 1944 Act modified the system by dividing **voluntary schools** into three categories – aided, controlled and special agreement – according to the type of financial arrangement desired in return for concessions made with the local authority. It should be noted that the Act introduced compulsory religious worship and instruction in all county and voluntary schools. Legislation in 1959 and 1967 allowed for building grants for Church schools for the first time in a century.

Duke of Edinburgh Award   A scheme began in 1956 to 'help the young generation, first to discover their talents and then how to use them, particularly in the service of others'. The scheme is available to organisations and individuals between the ages of 14 and 25. For each award, young people have to meet the requirements in one activity from each of the following four different sections: service, expeditions, skills, and physical recreation. Awards – bronze, silver and gold – are given for a range of interests which include, e.g., life-saving, youth leadership, drama, sailing and expeditions on land or sea. Between 1956 and 1991, over two million young people took part in the scheme.

Dunning Report   Published in 1977, this Report complemented the work of the **Munn** Committee. The remit of the Committee, under its chairman, Mr J. Dunning, was to identify the aims and purposes of assessment and certification in the fourth year of Scottish secondary education, the higher grade Scottish Certificate of Education and the Certificate of Sixth Year Studies. The Committee's recommendations were quite radical. The **O Level** grade examination should be replaced by a three-level certificate – foundation, general, and credit – according to achievement. Assessment of the examination was to be based on a combination of internal and external marks. Teachers would be assisted in ensuring standards by the recommendation that national guides in each subject were to be prepared. (See also **Munn Report, Scottish Education Department**)

dyslexia Defined by the World Federation of Neurology in 1968 as 'a disorder in children who, despite conventional classroom experience, fail to attain the language skills in reading, writing and spelling, commensurate and with their intellectual abilities'. In the UK, some doubt has been expressed on whether a clearly defined syndrome exists. The **Bullock Report** rejected the term and the **Warnock Report** preferred the use of a more general term, 'children with special learning difficulties.' However, it is believed that one in ten children in British schools suffers from some kind of dyslexia. A recent American study suggests that children between eight and ten with serious dyslexia could successfully achieve higher grades in reading if individual teaching programmes and lessons, on a one-to-one basis, were available for two months.

E

Early Excellence Centres (EEC) A programme to support integration of early education with day care. Twenty-nine pilot centres give high quality early education, child care and family support services and link up with other programmes such as **Sure Start**. They are community based and involve **local education authority** participation. Fourteen new Centres were announced by the Government in October 2001. (See also **early years education**)

Early Years Development and Child Care Partnerships (EYDCP) These partnerships, beginning in 1997, were extended to include child care the following year. Their purpose is to provide a forum in the 150 **local education authorities** where schools, employers, parents and colleges can supervise the provision of early education and child care and draw up plans for action. These include the year of entry to **reception classes**, early identification of **special educational needs** and the provision of child care after school. The deliberations of the Partnerships are available for the public from local education authorities.

Early Years Directorate (OFTOT) The Early Years Directorate, more popularly known as OFTOT, was established in September 2001 under the Care Standards Act (2000). It took over the responsibilities of the Children Act (1989) for the registration and inspection of nurseries, crèches, playgroups, after-school clubs and **childminders**. It is also responsible for the safety and quality of the education of early years children. The setting up of the Directorate involved the mass transfer of 1,200 early years inspectors employed by local education authorities. Wales has its own Early Years Directorate, called ESYN, and has a Care Standards Inspectorate for Wales. (See also **Foundation Stage and Early Learning Goals**)

early years education   This takes place in a wide range of settings such as **day nurseries, playgroups, nursery schools, reception classes** in **primary schools**, and by **childminders**. Several governmental initiatives have been launched to improve the quality of education and standards of supervision at this stage. Free early education for four-year-old children is funded by the Nursery Education Grant paid by the Department for Education and Skills to local authorities early years development partnerships. From September 2000, the **Foundation Stage and Early Learning Goals** were introduced for ages 3 to 6. These set out what should have been achieved by the end of this period and prepare children for learning in **Key Stage** 1. Free places for four-year-olds have been available since September 1998 and the entitlement will be expanded to three-year-olds from September 2004. (See also **rising fives**).

Economic and Social Research Council (ESRC)   Established in 1983 to replace the **Social Science Research Council** (SSRC) because the then Secretary of State for Education, Sir Keith Joseph, objected to the term 'social science' (he did not consider such studies to be 'scientific'). No funds would have been provided unless the title of the Research Council were changed. The ESRC responsibilities include providing funding for university research in education.

educability   A measure or estimate of the extent to which an individual pupil or a group might be capable of responding to or benefiting from a given educational programme. Some educationists concerned with children with **special educational needs** (SEN) have shown their dislike of this concept by declaring that 'no child is ineducable'.

education action zones (EAZ)   Education action zones are local partnerships between groups of schools, local education authorities, business, parents and the local community intended to raise standards in deprived areas. Each zone operates through an action forum, consisting of the main partners, who draw up an action plan to fix targets for each school in the zone, and the zone as a whole. Funding comes from the **Department for Education and Skills** (£750,000 per annum) and private sponsorship (£250,000 per annum). Since September 1998, 73 EAZs have been set up nation-wide, initially for three years but with a possible further two-year extension. One disappointing feature of the enterprise has been the lack of commercial sponsorship, with few zones achieving their targets. The Government has turned increasingly to the **Excellence in Cities** programme which incorporates a number of the small EAZs. None of the zones will be renewed when they reach the end of their five-year funding.

Education Acts Since the nineteenth century, a series of Education Acts passed by Parliament, have signalled reform and reorganisation of all aspects of education. The earliest ones, 1870, 1876 and 1880, were mainly attempts to establish adequate school accommodation and to enforce attendance. The 1902 Act laid the foundations for a coherent education system, bringing hitherto disparate elements under a central body, the **Board of Education**, as well as creating **local education authorities**. Welfare aspects were dealt with by the 1906 Act (school meals) and 1907 (medical treatment), whilst the school leaving age was raised by those of 1918, 1936 and 1944, which also organised education in three stages: primary, secondary and further. Since 1979 there has been a succession of Acts, some of greater significance than others:

1979 Education Act Repealed 1976 Act compelling local education authorities to have comprehensive plans.

1980 Education Act Introduced **Assisted Places Scheme**; stated that all independent schools should be registered; gave parents the right to express a preference for a school; gave parents the right to be represented on the governing body; stated that local education authorities and **governors** were now required to provide information on examination results, criteria for admission etc.; imposed greater control over the advanced further education pool (capping); restricted local education authority rights to refuse places to outsiders.

1981 Education Act Following the **Warnock Report** (1978) local education authorities were given responsibilities for special education; and parents were given the right to be consulted and to appeal against the local education authority.

1984 Education (Grants and Awards) Act Allowed Government to allocate money to local education authorities for specific purposes (e.g. reducing local authority control over grants).

1986 Education Act Introduced local education authority training grants schemes (LEATGS) and grant-related in-service training (GRIST) – an extension of the 1984 Act, earmarking funds for specific training.

1986 Education (No. 2) Act Required every maintained school to have a governing body; set a formula for numbers of representatives on governing body (parents' representation strengthened); required governors to present annual report to parents and arrange meeting to discuss it; abolished corporal punishment in State schools; made governors responsible for policy on sex education and for preventing political indoctrination; and made governors responsible for policy document on curriculum which could modify local education authority policy.

1987 Teachers' Pay and Conditions Act   Abolished Burnham negotiating machinery.

1988 Local Government Act   Clause 28 forbade local authorities to 'promote teaching in any maintained schools on the acceptability of homosexuality as a pretended family relationship'.

1988 Education Reform Act (ERA)   Introduced a **national curriculum**; publication of information on schools; open enrolment; and **grant maintained schools** (GMS).

1992 Education (Schools) Act   Required schools and local education authorities to publish examination performance **league tables** and provides for the inspection of all schools every four years by the **Office for Standards in Education** (OFSTED).

1992 Further and Higher Education Act   Introduced quality assurance and new funding arrangements, abolished the binary line in higher education.

1993 Education Act   The Act was based on the White Paper *Choice and Diversity* (1992), the main purpose of which was to encourage the development of grant maintained schools. The Act also abolished the **National Curriculum Council** (NCC) and the **School Examinations and Assessment Council** (SEAC), replacing them with the **School Curriculum and Assessment Authority** (SCAA); likewise the **Curriculum Council for Wales** (CCW) was replaced by the **Curriculum and Assessment Authority for Wales** (CAAW).

1994 Education Act   Dealt with two issues: teacher training in England and Wales, and students' unions in Scotland, England Wales.

1996 Education Act   A large consolidating Act repealing the last surviving parts of the **Butler Act** (1944).

1996 Nursery Education and Grant Maintained Schools Act   Introduced the voucher scheme for nursery education and gave governing bodies of **grant maintained schools** power to borrow money.

1996 Schools Inspection Act   Consolidated existing legislation on school inspection.

1997 Education Act   Established the **Qualifications and Curriculum Authority** (QCA) to replace the School Curriculum and Assessment Authority and the **National Council for Vocational Qualifications** (NCVQ).

1997 Education (Schools) Act   Abolished the **Assisted Places Scheme**.

1998 School Standards and Framework Act   Gave **local education authorities** and the Secretary of State authority to intervene where schools were deemed to be failing. **Education action zones** were established, categories of secondary schools changed, with community, and foundation replacing county and **grant maintained schools**. The **Funding Agency for Schools** was abolished.

1998 Teaching and Higher Education Act   Established a **General Teaching Council** for England, laid down compulsory qualifications for head teachers, and clarified the role of the **Office for Standards in Education** in inspecting **initial teacher training**.

2002 Education Act   The Act puts into legislation much of the content of the White Paper, *Schools: Achieving Success* (2001). Concerned mainly with **secondary education**, the Act was intended to raise standards and modernise structures in schools. Some categories of schools are encouraged to achieve greater diversity and flexibility in terms of curriculum, organisation and financial management. Some of the provisions, especially those favouring **faith schools** and **specialist schools**, were controversial and much criticised by those committed to comprehensive education.

Education and Learning Wales (ELWa)   ELWa was established in 2000–1 by bringing together as a unified organisation the work of the National Council for Education and Training for Wales and the **Higher Education Funding Council** for Wales (HEFCW).

Education Association (EA)   The 1993 Education Act proposed that inspection reports would identify schools that were 'at risk' of failing to give their pupils an acceptable education. The governing body was charged with preparing an action plan, and the local education authority would supply a supporting commentary. The Secretary of State has the power to appoint an Education Association to take over the management of an 'at risk' school or group of schools from their governing bodies and local authority. The Association had the same powers and funding as a **grant maintained school** governing body. The Education Association was intended to manage the schools until the Secretary of State was satisfied that they had achieved a satisfactory level of performance; the schools could then be considered for grant maintained status. The School Standards and Framework Act (1998) abolished Education Associations, replacing them with the **Fresh Start** scheme. (See also **failing schools**)

education committee   (See **local education authority**)

Education Department   The **Committee of the Privy Council on Education** was set up in 1839 to administer grants to **voluntary schools**. With the growth of its responsibilities, particularly the amount of money to be allocated, the Council was replaced by an Education Department in 1856. It was represented in the Commons by a **Vice-President of the Council** who was virtually the **Minister of Education**, and by a **Lord President** in the Lords. The Department continued to flourish until the Board of Education Act (1899) established a Board, headed by a President, responsible for elementary, secondary and technological education.

education maintenance allowance (EMA)   In July 1998 the Chancellor of the Exchequer, as part of his discussion of his Public Expenditure White Paper, announced a pilot scheme to encourage young people from low-income families to stay on in education after 16. The pilot scheme was designed as a three-year project from 1999, with the possibility of becoming a permanent arrangement after 2002.

Education Otherwise (EO)   Formed in 1977 by a small group of parents, EO now has a membership of well over 1,000 families. Education Otherwise takes its name from Section 36 of the 1944 Education Act which states: 'It shall be the duty of the parent of every child of compulsory school age to cause him [*sic*] to receive efficient full-time education suitable to his age, ability and aptitude, either by regular attendance at school *or otherwise*.' Families who join EO are sent a guide to the meaning of 'or otherwise' and a booklet, *Suggestions About Learning at Home*. (See also **school phobia**)

education vouchers   A scheme whereby vouchers are given to parents to enable them to purchase education at schools of their choice. A two-year study of vouchers carried out in the Ashford area of Kent in 1977 showed that, apart from the expense of the scheme, it would be difficult to administer. A voucher plan was operated in the Alum Rock school district of San Jose, California, from 1972 to 1976, but was not regarded as a success.

Education Welfare Service (EWS)   The Service is required, on the one hand, to exercise enforcement powers of school attendance through court proceedings; and, on the other hand, to provide material benefits, such as necessitous clothing allowances and maintenance grants. Other duties of education welfare officers (EWO) include child employment certification, transport of children and assessment for free meals. Their job descriptions include counselling and guidance with pregnant school girls, monitoring child employment, groupwork with persistent non-attenders or disruptive pupils, and liaising with social service agencies. Section 36 of the **Children Act** (1989) stipulates the conditions under which a **local education authority** may apply to a court for an education supervision order for a child of compulsory school age who is not being properly educated. Pilot schemes in 16 local education authorities were mounted in September 2000 in an attempt to discover if **attendance** and **truancy** levels increased or decreased if education welfare officers are managed by schools rather than by local education authorities.

Educational Institute of Scotland (EIS)   The Institute was founded by Royal Charter in 1847 and is the oldest teachers' union in the world. Apart from its original aim – 'the promotion of sound learning' – it also represents 85 per cent of teachers in Scotland, ranging from nursery schools to higher education institutions. In 2002 there were over 52,000 members. The EIS deals with teachers' salaries and conditions of service. In recent years it has campaigned to protect the distinctive nature and quality of Scottish education. (See also **teachers' unions**)

educational psychologist   Most **local education authorities** employ or contract psychologists who have been trained as specialists in diagnosing the problems of children, whether they are of an emotional or behavioural kind (e.g. children who do not respond to normal teaching methods), or whether they have some other kind of **special educational need** such as **dyslexia**. (See also s**chool psychological service**)

educational television (ETV)   A term with two different but overlapping meanings. The first refers to any television programme that is intended to be educational, e.g. documentary films or discussions about politics. The second meaning refers to television films that are made specifically for educational purposes in schools and other educational institutions. The latter may often be referred to as 'school television'. The **Open University** has made some major advances in etv for adult learners.

educationally subnormal (ESN)   Children described as educationally subnormal will be intellectually impaired in either a moderate (M) or severe (S) form. Many ESN children will have associated disorders in areas of physical and emotional development. Approximately one-third of mildly mentally retarded children have significant problems in the area of behavioural disorders and may have problems of physical co-ordination. The severely mentally retarded are usually multi-handicapped and some need nursing and social care rather than educational management. (See also **special educational needs**, **special schools**)

effective schools   For some years after the US Coleman Report (1966) the conventional wisdom was that schools made little or no difference to the levels of **attainment** of their pupils – social background was the dominant factor. However, a number of studies in the USA, UK and elsewhere, in the 1970s and 1980s, showed that the performance of children from similar backgrounds was different according to the **culture of the schools**. An effective school has a number of positive features – e.g. collaborate planning, co-operative commitment to **goals**, staff stability, maximum use of learning time, etc. But it must always be stressed that these cannot be regarded as separate factors to be treated in isolation – they are features of the culture of an effective school. Changing the culture of a school is very difficult. (See also **Rutter Report**, **school improvement**)

EFL   (See **English as a foreign language**)

Eldon Judgment   In an attempt to widen the school's curriculum, the governors of Leeds Grammar School put forward a scheme to Chancery in 1797 which would have allowed mathematics and modern languages to be taught. Eight years later Lord Eldon, the Lord Chancellor, ruled that Greek and Latin only could be taught. In 1840, a Grammar School Act allowed for the introduction of a broader curriculum.

e-Learning Foundation   A registered charity established in 2001 and funded by the Government and the private sector with the aim of ensuring that all UK pupils have access to a computer within 5–7 years. The Foundation operates through a network of 35 local e-Learning Foundations which raise funds for schools to buy **information and communications technology** hardware.

element   NVQ: the smallest specification of **competence** within a statement of competence; **GNVQ**: a statement of **achievement** within a **unit** of achievement.

elementary school   A type of school that existed until 1944 offering an education for children from 5 to 14 years of age. The **1944 Education Act** made provision for primary education for all up to the age of 11 and secondary education thereafter.

eleven plus examination   Term commonly used for tests administered by local education authorities for entrance into selective **secondary schools**.

emeritus   A title conferred on a **professor** on his or her retirement. In some universities it is also conferred on **readers**.

emotional intelligence   During the 1990s, the idea of intelligence as 'general mental ability' was increasingly criticised. Daniel Goleman, in *Emotional Intelligence* (1996), claimed that emotional intelligence was more important than the qualities measured by conventional intelligence tests. (See also **intelligence quotient** (IQ))

enactive, iconic and symbolic   The American psychologist, Jerome Bruner, put forward a theory of children's intellectual development in which he distinguished three sequential modes of representing experience. First, the *enactive* mode during which a child experienced the world by means of purely motor responses; second, the *iconic*, which involved pictorial images or models; and, third, the *symbolic*, which involved language or abstract formulae. An example that is often given to illustrate these three modes is that of 'balance'. At a very early stage of intellectual development, a child might experience balance in terms of a see-saw – the *enactive* mode. Later he/she might understand some of the principles of balance by looking at various pictures and diagrams – the *iconic* mode. Finally, he/she might be able to make calculations about various kinds of balance by purely mathematical formulae – the *symbolic* mode. Bruner's modes clearly have much in common with Piaget's stages of development, but some teachers have found them to be more useful in classroom planning. (See also **Piagetian**, **stages of development**)

encyclopaedism   A view of schooling that suggests that up to the compulsory school leaving age all education should be general and should be planned to cover the major kinds of **knowledge** and experiences. Thus a good education would be a balanced selection from the major forms of human knowledge and experience. (See also **essentialism**)

end-of-Key Stage Statements   For those **foundation subjects** that do not have specified **Attainment Targets** with **level descriptions**, (i.e. art, music and PE), Orders define the knowledge, skills and understanding that pupils are expected to achieve at the end of each Key Stage.

end-of-module test   A test taken by a **GCSE** or **A Level** candidate on completion of a module within a modular syllabus. The test is normally set and marked externally.

Endowed Schools Commission   The **Taunton Commission** reported in 1868 on the need to reform the endowed schools. Following the passing of the Endowed Schools Act in 1869 a Commission, consisting of three full-time members, was set up to frame a number of model schemes as a basis for making sweeping reforms in matters of charitable endowments. There was much opposition from the larger foundations and the work of the Commission soon became a political issue. With the return of a Conservative government in 1874, the Commission was dismantled and its duties were transferred to the **Charity Commission**.

English as a foreign language (EFL)   EFL is a commonly used abbreviation describing the teaching of English either to foreign students in the UK or in overseas countries. In the USA English as a second language (ESL) is often preferred, but the two are by no means identical. In recent years an attempt has been made to cover both fields by the term ESOL (English for speakers of other languages), since it is not always possible to make sensible distinctions between those for whom English is a foreign language, and those for whom English is a second language but not a foreign language. The problem is particularly acute in countries such as the UK and USA where large immigrant communities exist using their first, native language, but for whom English is not a 'foreign' language. (See also **language schools**)

English curriculum   Of the ten subjects in the **national curriculum**, English has become the most controversial. The major debate has been about differences between traditionalists and those who advocate more progressive methods. These differences include attitudes to the teaching of grammar and **spelling**. The controversy has sharpened since 1997 with the introduction of the **National Literary Strategy** and the **literacy hour**. (See also **Cox Report**)

enrichment programme   A programme of school activities designed either to compensate children from a deprived background, e.g. the American **Head Start** programme, or to provide additional stimulating experiences for the able.

entrance award   At Oxford and Cambridge, financial awards may be made to certain applicants who are successful in the colleges' entrance examinations. These awards are either **scholarships** or **exhibitions**, the former being of greater vale. There are both open and closed awards. Open awards are given solely on the basis of merit, whilst closed awards are restricted to certain categories, either of subject or of students from a particular school. (See also **bursary, discretionary award, entry qualification, mandatory award**)

entry level   The lowest level of the national qualifications framework. It is intended for those who wish to demonstrate achievement at a level below that of the **General Certificate of Secondary Education** (GCSE). Entry levels are available from **examinations boards** in a variety of fields, but are often concerned with 'life skills and working life', including languages, geography, English, hairdressing, textiles, information technology and science (double award or single). They have some credibility with employers and can be used as a first step towards vocational qualifications. (See also **national qualifications framework**)

entry qualification   Most courses in higher education have prerequisites of some kind in the form of entry qualifications or entry requirements. For example, most masters degrees would require at least a second class honours degree at bachelor's level: most first degrees would require students to have passed at least two **A Levels**.

equal opportunities   The Sex Discrimination Act (1975) (Sections 53–61 and Schedule 3) provided that a commission should be appointed by the Home Secretary to work towards the elimination of discrimination on the grounds of sex or marital status, to promote equality of opportunity between men and women and to keep under review the working of the Sex Discrimination Act (1975) and the Equal Pay Act (1970). The Sex Discrimination Act was amended in 1986 but the main provisions of the first Act are largely unchanged; the amendments being designed to extend its scope though not in relation to education (to cover small businesses or retirement ages). The **Race Relations Act** outlawed racial discrimination on the grounds of colour, race or ethnic origins as well as religious or political beliefs. The Disability Discrimination Act (1995) gave persons suffering from physical or mental disability the right of access to goods or services. These legislative measures have important implications for schools. Staffing levels should conform to the provision of these Acts. Governing bodies must formulate an equal opportunities policy for their schools and monitor the policy and procedures for effectiveness.

ERIC   An Educational Resources Information Centre – this is an American-based system that issues a monthly abstracting journal, *Resources in Education*, on various aspects of educational research. Many libraries are also linked into the system. (See also **information retrieval**, **resource centre**)

essentialism   (1) The belief that there is an 'essential' body of knowledge that all students should acquire. The term is sometimes employed in comparative education to refer to continental school systems such as the Soviet or the French. The term is also sometimes referred to as **encyclopaedism**, which suggests that where there is a compulsory system of education, then this should be general education up to the compulsory school leaving age. (2) In philosophy, the term is used to describe Plato's theory that words only have meaning by reference to the resemblance of a particular object or quality to an ideal form. This kind of essentialism rests on the assumption that ideal forms exist in some meaningful sense. The curricular implications of this theory are that art and poetry are inferior to mathematics: whereas mathematics focuses upon the abstract form, art and poetry are concerned with imitation and, therefore, stray further and further away from ideal forms or 'the truth'.

ethnic minority pupils   For many years it was assumed that children whose parents were either born outside the UK or belonged to a minority group whose native language was not English, would be likely to be **under-achievers** at schools. This assumption does not entirely coincide with the statistical information that has been collected. Some ethnic minority pupils, e.g. Jewish children, tend to over-achieve, that is, they perform better than average. Chinese children and some other Asian minorities also tend to over-achieve. On the other hand, native white working-class pupils tend to under-achieve. It would appear that achievement at school is a complex phenomenon. One relevant factor is **culture**: some kinds of social background appear to favour the development of knowledge and skills that are valued by schools, but others do not. The White Paper, *Schools: Achieving Success* (2001), set out an agenda for raising standards generally but highlighted the fact that children from some ethnic minority backgrounds may be in need of special attention. Such children now form 11 per cent of the pupil population, more than half a million do not have English as a first language, and many start school without an adequate grasp of it. It was recommended that schools should make an effort to raise expectations; have a positive culture and ethos throughout the school; develop strong links with the community and parents; and have a commitment to ethnic monitoring to keep track of pupils' progress. In 2001 the Ethnic Minority and Traveller Achievement programme provided £162.5 million funding to **local education authorities** (LEAs) to support their activities. (See also **achievement**)

ethnography, ethnomethodology   Ethnographic studies refer to small-scale, micro studies of the school or classroom. Ethnomethodology is a branch of sociology invented by the American Harold Garfinkel in the 1960s, which concentrates on the sociology of everyday social life. The stress in these studies would be on the way in which participants interpret the situation. There is, therefore, sometimes a link between ethnomethodology and phenomenology. Both concepts have been used in educational research.

e-university   In October 2000 the **Higher Education Funding Council** (HEFC) published plans for the UK's first national e-university, using

distance learning techniques by means of the internet, to be operational by 2002. At first such electronic courses would be limited to **postgraduate** studies and professional development, but **undergraduate** degrees would follow eventually. At the time of writing, the establishment of the e-university has not been completed but plans are well advanced. The main proposal was that the electronic university would sponsor high quality courses via the internet. The university would be established as a holding company which would license an operating company to produce courses. The e-university would, therefore, be a joint venture between UK universities and the private sector. All **higher education** institutions in receipt of funding from the four UK funding bodies, the Higher Education Funding Councils, would be entitled to apply to become members of the holding company. The e-university will have a Committee for Academic Quality to monitor standards and the **Quality Assurance Agency** (QAA) will be invited to nominate an assessor. Before the e-university had been launched discussions were taking place about how less expensive models might be more appropriate.

European Economic Community (EEC)/European Community (EC)   (See **European Union** (EU))

European Union (EU)   The European Economic Community (EEC) – later European Community (EC) – was established in 1957 with the aim of promoting the development of economic activities, enhancing the standard of living, and encouraging closer relations between the member States by creating a common market. The EU has a permanent Commission in Brussels; member States are represented by Council of Ministers as well as a European Parliament.

evaluation   A term that may either refer to the general process of judging the worth of an educational programme, including judgements about the quality of its content, or more specifically to measurements of the effectiveness of learning experiences – what is often described in the UK as **assessment** of student **attainment**. In recent years, evaluation has been divided into two kinds – the more quantitative approach (sometimes referred to as the agricultural or botanical model); and those who declare that the measurement of educational experiences are much more complex and demand interviews and whole studies of the context of the experience.

evening class   A class for those of post-school age which provides further education, cultural or leisure facilities. Such classes may be held in **local education authority** evening institutes, further education colleges, or community colleges (See also **continuing education**, **recurrent education**)

examination boards   Bodies responsible for the conduct of public examinations. Before 1995 there were eight **General Certificate of Education** (GCE) boards for **A Levels** and four **General Certificate of Secondary Education** (GCSE) groups of boards in England, plus the **Welsh Joint Education Committee**. In 1995 one of the GCE/GCSE boards, the University of London Examination and Assessment Council (ULEAC), and the **Business and Technology Education Council** (BTEC), agreed to explore possibilities of co-operation in order to deliver a framework for qualifications for 14–19-year-olds which would bridge the academic and vocational divide. A full merger took place in January 1996 and this new body was renamed Edexcel. This was very much in accord with the **Dearing** *Interim Report on the Review of 16–19 Qualifications* (1995). Following strong pressure from the **Department for Education and Employment** (DfEE) encouraging co-operation between academic and vocational boards, other mergers took place: the Oxford and Cambridge boards agreed to co-operate with the **Royal Society of Arts** (RSA) under the title Oxford, Cambridge and RSA (OCR); and the Northern board plus the Associated Examining Board (AEB) agreed to merge and co-operate with **City and Guilds of London Institute** under the title of AQA (Assessment and Qualifications Alliance). This process of rationalisation left only three boards responsible for both academic and vocational awards for 16–19-year-olds but still hundreds of minor awarding bodies dealing with specific vocational qualifications. (See also **Curriculum 2000, vocational awarding bodies**)

examination component   A discrete part of a scheme of assessment which makes a significant contribution to reported outcomes, e.g. an oral test in a modern foreign language examination.

examinations, mode of   The traditional mode of public examinations in England and Wales is that a **syllabus** is agreed and examination papers set and marked by **examination boards** rather than by teachers themselves in their own schools. However, with the development of the **Certificate of Secondary Education** (CSE) in the 1960s, teachers were encouraged to be more involved at all levels of the examination process. In particular, teachers were allowed to propose their own syllabuses, to set papers for their own pupils and to mark them. This became known as Mode III examining (in contrast to the traditional Mode I). Mode II was a compromise whereby teachers worked out their own syllabus, but papers were set and marked by the board. When CSE examinations were superseded by the **General Certificate of Secondary Education** (GCSE) in 1988, there was a tendency to revert to Mode I as the normal requirement. (See also **graded assessment**)

examiner, external   (1) At school level, a person responsible for marking the **examination** scripts or **coursework** where the examination has been externally set. For example, **General Certificate of Education** (GCE) and **General Certificate of Secondary Education** (GCSE) boards recruit experienced teachers for this work. (2) At post-school level, particularly in **higher education**, examiners are appointed from other similar institutions to ensure that the standards of students' work are being maintained.

examiner, internal   (1) A member of a school or college staff responsible for marking candidates' scripts or other forms of presentation of an internally set examination. (2) At post-school level, particularly in higher education, a member of staff who undertakes the marking of her/his students examinations. They are then **moderated** by an **external examiner**.

Excellence in Cities (EiC)   Excellence in Cities was originally launched in March 1999 to raise standards in schools in large cities. Extra resources were provided for **gifted** and talented pupils, **learning mentors**, **Learning Support Units**, **beacon** and **specialist schools**, and the establishment of **education action zones** for small clusters of schools. Allocation of resources is based on need rather than by making bids. By September 2001, 48 **local education authorities** and 1,000 **secondary schools** were members of the scheme. From that date also, the programme was extended outside large cities through new Excellence Clusters.

exceptional children   These can be regarded in one of two ways. The first is that they are markedly different from other children, in that they are, e.g. mentally retarded, gifted or physically handicapped. The second regards children as differing in degree rather than in kind from each other, with the differences traceable to the result of the normal process of learning which are made different in their effects by physical, genetic or environmental factors. (See also **enrichment programme**, **giftedness**, **high flier**, **special educational needs**)

exclusion   The problem of exclusion, the banning of a child from attending school, is being tackled in a number of positive ways. Since the 1993 Education Act, pupils who are excluded must be excluded either permanently or for a fixed period not exceeding 15 days in any one term. The Government hope that pupils excluded for more than 15 days should remain in education. In a consultative document, *Revised Guidance on Exclusion from Schools*, issued in February 2002, the **Department for Education and Skills** stated that bullying and the carrying of weapons should lead to exclusion after one offence, with little likelihood of subsequent reinstatement. Other offences recommended to carry equal penalties are: serious actual or threatened violence, sexual misconduct, supplying an illegal drug, and persistent and defiant behaviour. **Pupil referral units**, offering a broad and balanced curriculum but not necessarily the full national curriculum, and situated off-site, have increased in numbers. In September 2001, two thirds of **local education authorities** were providing full-time education for excluded secondary pupils.

exhibition (See **entrance award**)

experiential learning Learning through experience rather than through books or formal instruction. It was strongly advocated in some **Technical and Vocational Education Initiative** (TEVI) programmes.

expressive Expressive attitudes are contrasted with instrumental attitudes; expressive attitudes satisfying emotional needs rather than gaining some extrinsic or instrumental rewards. In the book *Instructional Objectives* edited by W. J. Popham (1969), Elliot Eisner made a similar distinction between expressive objectives and instructional objectives. With expressive objectives, there is no behavioural outcome but there may be change in pupil attitude which is important but not measurable.

external degree A degree for which the candidate does not follow a formal course of study within a university, but sits the requisite **examinations** to gain a qualification. The University of London external degree system has been widely used throughout the world. (See also **degree**)

external examiner (See **examiner, external**)

extramural department A department of a university which provides courses for the general public, mostly in the field of liberal **adult education**. The names of the departments vary, for example, **continuing education**, **adult education**.

extrinsic (See **intrinsic/extrinsic**)

F

facility index A calculation of the ease with which any particular item in a test might be answered. It might be expressed in terms of the percentage of candidates answering that item correctly. (See also **difficulty index**)

factory school The 1802 Factory Act, the first of its kind, required compulsory instruction of apprentices in cotton and woollen mills in the

three Rs. Many factory owners ignored this requirement, though Robert Owen opened a school at New Lanark in 1816 that was divided into infant, junior and upper departments. The Factory Act of 1833 made school attendance a condition of employment. (See also **half-time system**, **industrial school**, **school of industry**)

faculty   (1) A large division in a **higher education** institution that includes all the teaching staff, e.g. faculty of medicine. Colleges themselves are sometimes organised into faculties which may cover a range of allied subjects, e.g. faculty of humanities. Many secondary schools organise their work on a faculty basis. (2) A term once used in psychology to describe mental attributes.

failing school   These are secondary schools where fewer than 15 per cent of pupils obtained five **General Certificate of Secondary Education** grade Cs. In 2000, there were 101 schools in this category. The School Standards and Framework Act (1998) abolished the former **Education Association** option. These schools were given two years to reach minimum targets or faced either being closed down or reopened under the **Fresh Start** scheme. The minimum targets were raised to 20 per cent by 2004 and 35 per cent in 2006.

Fair Funding   The method by which **local education authorities** delegate money to individual school budgets over a period of two years. It was introduced in April 1999 and was followed by the Financing of Maintained Schools Regulations in 2000. School budgets are supervised either by the head on behalf of the governing body or, in a large school, by a **bursar.** A budget plan must be drawn up by the school and is then discussed by the finance committee and finally approved by the governing body. It is then submitted to the local education authority. From April 1999, many financial areas have been delegated to schools, such as repairs and maintenance, staff costs and inspections services and, since April 2000, school meals. The School Standards Grant (SSG) is also paid to all schools to improve literacy and numeracy, based on the number of pupils on roll.

faith schools   Term used to embrace schools under the auspices of different religious denominations. The main providers are the Church of England and the Catholic Church, but some Muslim, Sikh and Greek Orthodox schools are now funded on the same basis, and the number of Jewish schools is increasing. There are in total some 6,340 primary and 582 secondary faith schools. Pupil numbers have remained fairly constant at 7,000 since 1997, the majority being in **primary schools**. In the White Paper, *Schools: Achieving Success* (2001), faiths were required, in contemplating establishing new schools, to 'take into account the interests of all sections of the community'.

All new faith schools have to demonstrate that they are working in partnership with other religious and secular schools in the area.

falling rolls   Since 1977, there has been a continuous decline in the total number of schools and pupils in England. This has led to lower intakes into all types of schools, a drop in demand for teacher recruitment and the closure or amalgamation of smaller schools. In 1981, the Department of Education and Science issued Circular 2/81 urgently requesting **local education authoritie**s to undertake a review of over-provision, and the White Paper on Public Expenditure (March 1982) set the Government's target of removing almost half a million school places by the following year.

In 1992, the **Audit Commission** reaffirmed the need for continuing reduction in school places. However, the 1988 Education Reform Act complicated the picture with its policy of open enrolment. The White Paper, *Choice and Diversity* (1992), stated the Government's determination to eliminate surplus places in schools and release the resources for redeployment.

family grouping   An alternative, found especially in lower primary schools, to grouping by age in different classes. Where family grouping operates, a child remains in the same **class**, with the same teacher, for the whole of his or her time in that part of the school or for a period of several years. An alternative name for this system of organisation is **vertical age grouping**. (See also **setting**, **streaming**)

Fast Track   Probably inspired by the Civil Service Fast Stream, the Fast Track system aims to produce a number of excellent teachers and future school leaders from highly motivated graduates whose talents would be rewarded by an accelerated five-year route through the pay threshold. The scheme, announced in the Green Paper, *Teachers: Meeting the Challenge of Change* (1998), and launched in September 1999, was initially to be operated in ten selected institutions. Candidates, ranging from final year students at university expecting to be awarded a 2:1 degree or equivalent, to existing teachers, would be interviewed, and undergo tests at an assessment centre. For those not currently holding **qualified teacher status**, this would be followed by a one-year **Professional Graduate Certificate of Education** course, supplemented by extra experience in work on initiatives designed to enhance pupils' achievements. Such teachers would be guided through a series of challenging teaching posts. New entrants to teaching are awarded an additional point in their first year after qualifying. The scheme produced its first classroom teachers in September 2002.

feasibility study   A preliminary study that is often undertaken before launching a major research project. Such a study provides the team with preliminary data, and may suggest alternative strategies that can be adopted. It will also test the viability of the larger project before financial resources are committed. (See also **pilot study**)

feedback   A term borrowed from the field of cybernetics where it has a more precise technical meaning. In education feedback normally refers to the process of giving information about results to the students and their teachers with a view to improving performance.

federal university   As distinguished from a **collegiate** university such as Oxford or Cambridge. In a federal organisation, there is central control over the whole university whilst constituent colleges look after their internal affairs. (See also **universities, history of**)

fellow   (1) A senior member of an Oxford or Cambridge college who has a voice in the running of the college. Fellows teach and give tutorials to undergraduates. Before the University Test Act of 1871, Fellows had to be unmarried. (2) A member of a learned or professional society, such as Fellow of the Royal College of Physicians or Fellow of the Royal Historical Society. (3) A member of a college or university engaged in funded research with the title of **Research Fellow**.

field study   A form of work undertaken in an environment outside school or college. For example, geographical and biological studies may involve students in carrying out practical activities in either a rural or an urban setting. (See also **field trip**)

field trip   A journey or excursion to a particular place by students as part of a **field study**.

Finneston Report   A Committee of Inquiry, chaired by Sir Monty Finneston, was asked by the Government in July 1977 to investigate the requirements of British industry for professional and technical engineers, and how far they were being met, and the role of the engineering institutions in the education and qualification of engineers. Arrangements in other industrial countries, particularly in the **European Union**, were to be examined. The Committee's report, issued in 1980, stated that training schemes provided by industry were inadequate and that the talents of graduates were often wasted. It recommended close links between industry and **higher education** institutions.

first degree   An initial **degree**, usually a Bachelor's, obtained by following a course of study at a **higher education** institution or by private study. (See also **external degree, undergraduate**)

first school   The **Plowden Report** (1967) recommended that primary education should be restructured and that the age of transfer to secondary education should be changed. **Nursery education** should be available for children between three and five years to be followed by attendance at a first school from five to eight years. From there the pupils would attend a **middle school** from 8 to 12 years. Children should enter the first school in the September following their fifth birthday. Where middle school reorganisation has not occurred, the traditional **infant school** still exists, spanning the age group of five to seven. (See also **junior school**)

flashcard   Cards bearing words or letters used in schools in connection with the teaching of reading, especially word recognition. (See also **Gestalt**)

Fleming Report   A Committee was appointed by Lord (then Mr) R. A. Butler, President of the **Board of Education**, in July 1942, to consider ways in which the association between **public schools** and the general educational system of the country could be developed. It was also asked to include within its brief girls' as well as boys' public schools. The Committee was chaired by Lord Fleming and reported in 1944. Its recommendations were not generally welcomed by the schools and by parents and the links between the two sectors were never forged. (See also **Assisted Places Scheme**, **Donnison Report**, **Newsom Report on Public Schools**)

flexible grouping   Organising the teaching of a large number of pupils (e.g. a whole year group) in such a way that they could sometimes be taught in very large numbers, sometimes broken down into conventional classes of 25 or 30, sometimes working in much smaller groups, and sometimes as individuals. (See also **timetabling** and **team teaching**)

foreign language assistant (FLA)   Foreign language assistants, who are drawn from a number of different countries, help pupils in their communication skills in modern foreign languages. They help, particularly in oral work, to improve standards in their subject. More than 22,000 FLAs are employed in schools each year. The scheme in the UK is the responsibility of the Education and Training Group (ETG) – formerly the Central Bureau for International Education and Training, at the British Council – and receives funding from the **Department for Education and Skills**.

form   An alternative word for a **class** of pupils in a school. The term is invariably used for the highest class, the sixth form, which caters for those aged 16 and over.

formative assessment   The distinction between formative and **summative assessment** was first made by Michael Scriven in 1967; both terms have now become part of the language of education. Formative assessment is part of the 'formation' or development of a student; it is essentially concerned with providing **feedback** with a view to improving performance. Thus formative assessment has to take place during a course or programme whereas **summative assessment** occurs at the end.

formative evaluation/summative evaluation   The process of making judgments about the value of a new curriculum project or new teaching materials with the intention of improving the project or the materials for the future. Unlike summative evaluation the intention is not to make a judgment about the final value of a project, but is intended to provide useful feedback to those preparing materials or working on the project so that improvements can be made before a summative evaluation takes place. (See also **developmental testing, evaluation**)

formula funding   Most maintained schools are funded through a **local education authority**. There are two possible methods of funding: treating each school as unique, or applying some kind of general formula. In most cases some kind of formula was developed. Normally, a formula for schools would use the number of pupils (usually differentiated by age) as the major factors, but the formula was complicated by such other factors as the age (and running costs) of buildings, and the difficulty of the catchment area. In practice, such a formula was rarely applied mechanically and variations to the formula might be permitted from year to year. In some cases the normal method of allocating funds was to work from an 'historic' base, simply adding on a percentage each year for inflation. This was not always seen to be fair, and in the 1980s there were increasing demands for openness or transparency about funding decisions. The solution was often to publish details of a formula. The 1988 **Education Reform Act** compelled local education authorities to provide for the **local management of schools** by giving schools more spending autonomy, at first giving them 85 per cent of the total amount calculated; that percentage has been increased so that local education authorities have less financial control, leaving schools with greater autonomy – and, of course, greater responsibilities.

foundation course   A basic, introductory course usually designed to prepare students for more advanced courses. The foundation course may be a prerequisite for more advanced courses in the same area. An **Open University** foundation course may be required, for example, in arts/humanities before students proceed to more advanced work in English literature. (See also **general education**)

foundation degree   Unveiled by David Blunkett, the Education Secretary, in a speech at Greenwich in February 2000, the foundation degree is a two-year, vocationally-oriented qualification, largely delivered by **further education colleges**. As its main objective is to fill the skills gap, the degree involves employers, national training organisations and professional bodies. Candidates can specialise in the arts (FDA), sciences (FDSc) and engineering (FDEng). It is intended to attract the large number – over 30 per cent of under 30s – who are at present receiving no form of **higher education**. Bids are received from consortia of universities and colleges to provide courses. Students progress at their own rate and, by using credit accumulation, can go on to take a three-year honours degree. The first pilot schemes began in September 2001: by March 2002, more than 4,000 students had started on courses. Some doubts have been expressed as to its market currency and critics point to the **Diploma of Higher Education**, with which it shares some characteristics.

foundation school   This type of school, several of which were former **grant maintained schools**, is empowered to employ its own staff and decide on admission policy for pupils. It also owns its land and buildings. The first school to change to foundation status opened in September 2001, with many more likely to follow.

Foundation Stage and Early Learning Goals   The Foundation Stage, introduced by the **Department for Education and Skills** (DfES) in September 2000, and covering the ages 3–5 and 6, prepares children for learning in **Key Stage** 1. It is accompanied by a set of Early Learning Goals, which set out what a child should have achieved by the end of their **reception class** year. These consist of six key areas of learning: personal, social and emotional development, communication, language and literacy, mathematical development, knowledge and understanding of the world and creative development. (See also **Early Years Directorate**)

foundation subjects   The 1988 **national curriculum** specified ten foundation subjects: English, mathematics and science for **Key Stages** 1–4 (which were prioritised as **core subjects**); technology and physical education, Key Stages 1–4; a modern foreign language, Key Stages 3–4; history, geography, art and music (which since 1995 are only compulsory for Key Stages 1–3). In Wales, Welsh is a foundation subject.

franchising   A partnership between **further** and **higher education** institutions in the matter of course provision. This may take the form, for instance, of part or whole of the first year of a **degree** course being taken in a further education college.

free education   Moves to provide national **elementary education** that would be secular and free began with the foundation of the Lancashire Public Schools Association in 1846. From 1855 free education became a political issue in election campaigns, and in 1891 the **Education Act** gave parents the right to demand free education for their children.

free period   Can refer either to the time allocated to teaching staff for preparation or marking of lessons, or to pupils who undertake private un-supervised study.

Free Place system   The Regulations for Secondary Schools introduced by a Liberal government in May 1907 stated that **grammar schools** receiving State grants should offer 25 per cent of their places to pupils from public **elementary schools**. No definite age of entry was laid down, but applicants were required to pass an entrance test of **attainment** and proficiency, and **intelligence tests** were later used in many **local education authorities**. The system was replaced by the **Special Place** examination in 1931.

free-response question   (See **open-ended question**)

free school   A type of school which emerged in the early 1970s for parents interested in **alternative education**. It also catered for some children who had made little progress in State schools, having a freer curriculum. A number existed in London, such as the White Lion Street Free School in Islington (opened in 1972) and in other large cities and were largely financed by local enterprise. (See also **deschooling**)

Fresh Start school   The School Standards and Framework Act (1998) gave powers to **local education authorities** to intervene, where schools had been judged by the **Office for Standards in Education** (OFSTED) to be failing. From September 1998, such schools had to be turned around within two years, closed, or be given a Fresh Start. The latter involves reopening the school with a new headmaster and a new name. The scheme has had only limited success. Several of the initial 15 Fresh Start school heads have resigned, largely because of unreal expectations.

Froebel schools   Friedrich Froebel (1782–1852) was an influential German educationist who believed in the natural goodness of children, and believed that there was a need for educators to allow self-development in young children. Rote learning and a rigid age-related curriculum were frowned upon and were replaced by an emphasis on the development of individual pupils, progressing at their own pace. Froebel was the originator of the **kindergarten** and the movement spread rapidly. The first English Froebel school in Tavistock Place, Bloomsbury, was opened in 1851, a Froebel

Society was formed in 1874, and the National Froebel Union (NFU) followed in 1887. The Froebel Education Institute was established in London in 1892 to train teachers and has now been absorbed into the Roehampton Institute. Many of Froebel's ideas have long been a part of the mainstream philosophy of nursery and infant education.

full inspection   A term used to describe the visit of a team of **inspectors** representing a range of subject or phase interests, to an educational institution. The findings of the team are normally enshrined in a report which, from January 1983, became publicly available. (See also **advisers, Her Majesty's Inspectorate, OFSTED**)

full-time equivalent (fte)   In those institutions of **higher education** or **further education** where full-time and part-time students are recruited, it is important from the point of view of staffing requirements and other resources to calculate the whole student body in terms of full-time equivalents. Frequently part-time students would count for half a full-time student. In further education it is often possible to convert part-time students into fte in terms of the 'contact hours'. In universities this is rarely calculated since most part-time students can be converted into fte in terms of the length of the course rather than the amount of instruction which they receive.

functional literacy   The level of skill in reading and writing that any individual needs in order to cope with adult life. It is clearly very difficult to arrive at a satisfactory definition of functional literacy, but in the USA there have been prosecutions brought by parents against a school or school system for failing to equip a child at school leaving age with functional literacy. The idea behind this view of schooling is that functional literacy would be a right of all normal pupils and that it would be the duty of the school to provide it. (See also **literacy**)

Funding Agency for Schools (FAS)   An agency created by the 1993 Education Act, based on the principles of the **Further Education Funding Council** (FEFC) and the **Higher Education Funding Council** (HEFC), to take over some of the responsibilities held by local authorities. It was empowered to fund and monitor **grant maintained schools**, and was concerned with the admission of children to these schools. It was stipulated that as the percentage of grant maintained schools in a local authority increased, the Agency would take increasing responsibility for their governance. After the Labour Government came into office in 1997, the Agency was abolished by the School Standards and Framework Act (1998), and the FAS ceased to exist from the following year.

fund-raising Formerly a fringe activity in schools, fund-raising is widely carried out, often to supply basic educational materials such as books, furniture and teaching equipment such as computers. Primary schools, which receive a lower level of funding than secondary schools, are much involved in this activity. It has been argued that fund-raising highlights the differences between those schools in affluent, middle-class areas, which may raise large amounts, as against those schools in deprived areas where the tradition has not been established.

Further and Higher Education Act (1992) This important piece of legislation approved by Parliament in March 1992 changed the pattern of post-16 education: **sixth form colleges**, and **tertiary** and **further education** colleges were removed from local authority control. The financial aspects would be dealt with by the **Further Education Funding Councils** (FEFC); one for England and one for Wales. It also abolished the **binary** divide and allowed polytechnics to be called universities, those in England sharing a funding agency, the **Higher Education Funding Council** (HEFC), with separate funding councils for Wales and Scotland. During the passage of the Bill, there was much discussion in Parliament on the need for safeguards for academic freedom, which seemed to be under threat by some of the Bill's provisions.

further education (FE) A term covering all types of post-school education apart from that given in universities. Much of it is vocationally orientated though not exclusively so. Much of the teaching is carried out in the 450 further education colleges that, before March 1992, were administered by **local education authorities**. It has been argued that, with their newly gained independence, the colleges should be more responsive to local needs, especially as regards training.

Further Education Development Agency (FEDA) FEDA was established in 1994 by amalgamating the Further Education Staff College with the **Further Education Unit** (FEU). It is now the **Learning and Skills Development Agency**.

Further Education Funding Council (FEFC) The Further and Higher Education Act (1992) established this Council to take control from local education authorities that were previously responsible for the financing of further education colleges. The money for the colleges was channelled through the FEFC, and bids for courses were submitted to it by institutions. Responsibility for financing adult education was divided between the Council and the local education authorities. The FEFC ceased to exist when the **Learning and Skills Council** (LSC) took over its functions in April 2001.

Further Education National Training Organisation (FENTO)
Formerly the FE Staff Development Forum, FENTO is one of 71 **National Training Organisations** (NTOs). Funded by the **Department for Education and Skills**, its aim is to promote the effectiveness of the FE sector by raising training standards. The Standards for Teaching and Supporting Learning were published in 1999. All further education teacher training qualifications in England have been supervised by FENTO since September 2001. Many universities and colleges are involved in the endorsement process. FENTO is governed by a Council of 30 members, representing colleges, trades unions, industry and government. In common with other NTOs, FENTO was given three years' funding, starting in the year 2000, from the **Department for Education and Employment** in order to establish itself; after that time it would be expected to become self-financing. Scotland, Wales and Northern Ireland are represented on the Council. In Wales, there is a separate Cymru FENTO.

Further Education Unit (FEU)   The Unit was established in 1977 to serve as a focal point for further education curriculum matters. Although the Unit was financed by and housed in the Department of Education and Science (DES), it was free to operate independently from the Department's policies. From January 1983 the Unit became an agency independent of the DES. In April 1992, it merged with the Unit for the Development of Adult and Continuing Education. In 1994 it became the **Further Education Development Agency**. (See also **profiles**)

G

games and simulations   Certain kinds of 'games' are designed to be used in teaching to present occurrences in a given order so that pupils can gain insights into some kinds of human interaction. Simulations involve students taking on roles and may be more open-ended than games such as *Monopoly*. A simulation ought, e.g., to involve examining the advantages and disadvantages of siting a new airport: roles might be allocated to students who would proceed to make plans, argue their case and so on.

Gaussian curve   The shape of a graph showing a normal distribution. Sometimes also referred to as **normal** curve. It is a bell-shaped curve that occurs in a graph, e.g., showing how many people obtain each possible score on a measured variable such as height. Psychologists also assume that intelligence falls into a normal distribution, and therefore express **intelligence quotient** (IQ) scores in terms of the Gaussian curve showing very few people as extremely intelligent and very few as extremely dull, with the curve rising to a hump around the average score (in terms of IQ, the score of 100). Opponents of IQ testing frequently complain that it is simply an assumption, not an established fact, to suppose that intelligence falls into the same kind of curve as height. (See also **intelligence test, parametric statistics**)

GCE   (See **General Certificate of Education** (GCE))

GCSE   (See **General Certificate of Secondary Education** (GCSE))

'Geddes Axe'   A Committee on National Expenditure was appointed by the Prime Minister, Lloyd George, in August 1921 to advise on Government economies in the coming year. By the end of the year, the Committee, chaired by Sir Eric Geddes, a former Minister of Transport, had drawn up a report. The most controversial proposals, for education savings, the lowering of teachers' salaries and the exclusion of children under six from **elementary schools**, were rejected by the Cabinet. Part of the £6.5 million reduction in education estimates was achieved by teachers contributing five per cent of their salary towards superannuation and by increasing the size of elementary school classes to 50.

gender and educational performance   From the pre-school and infant stage, boys tend to choose more physical activities while girls choose more creative and social activities. The **national curriculum** has had the effect of narrowing the differences in subjects entered for **General Certificate of Secondary Education** (GCSE) examinations; nevertheless, such subjects as information technology, science and physical education are seen as predominantly boys' subjects and English and foreign languages as girls' subjects at **A Level**. A similar pattern is discernible in higher education, where women tend to study social studies, languages, and business studies. Mathematics and the sciences tend to attract men, except for biology, where over half the undergraduates are female. (See also **girls' education**)

General Certificate of Education (GCE)   The GCE **O** (ordinary) and **A** (advanced) **level** examinations were introduced in 1951, replacing the **School Certificate** and **Higher School Certificate** examinations. GCE **O Level** remained as a school leaving examination for 16-year-old pupils until it was replaced by the **General Certificate of Secondary Education** (GCSE) in 1988. GCE **A Level**, although much criticised, is still the main leaving examination for academic 18-year-old school leavers, and is the normal entrance requirement for higher education.

General Certificate of Secondary Education (GCSE) An examination for 16-year-olds formed from a combination of **General Certificate of Education O Level** and **Certificate of Secondary Education** (CSE). First awards were made in 1988. Part of the original **national curriculum/TGAT** plan for **Key Stage** 4 was that GCSE assessment (Grades A–G) would be brought into line with the TGAT ten levels (i.e. Grades A–G would disappear). Sir Ron **Dearing**, however, recommended that the TGAT levels (1–8) should apply only to Key Stages 1–3 and that GCSE grades would remain for Key Stage 4. It was still necessary for GCSE syllabuses to be harmonised with subject **programmes of study** and **level descriptions**. It was planned to implement the revised Key Stage 4/GCSE from September 1996. In 1994 the **School Curriculum and Assessment Authority** (SCAA) developed new GCSE Regulations (for all subjects) as well as criteria for specific subjects in line with new Subjects Orders. The GCSE Regulations and subject criteria also set out rules for **assessment** – including **tiering** – and the balance of terminal **examinations** and **coursework**. At the same time arrangements were made for two new kinds of award: (a) the GCSE short course covering 50 per cent of the content of a full GCSE; (b) **vocational awarding bodies** were invited to offer **GNVQ** Part I courses in a limited number of vocational areas.

general education Perhaps best described as the opposite of 'specialised' or 'specialist' education. Many educationists believe that before embarking upon a specialist course of study it is important to have covered a wide range of subjects and subject matter. This would apply particularly to **primary schools** and the first three or four years in **secondary schools** in the UK. In some **universities** a general **foundation** course is provided in the first year rather than specialist courses. (See also **liberal education**)

General Education Diploma (GED) The **National Commission on Education** (NCE) in its Final Report (1995) recommended the establishment of a General Education Diploma with the following characteristics: a high-quality national award; two levels – Ordinary (aged 16) and Advanced (aged 18) – but with no fixed age limit; replacing the three-track system at 18 (**A Level**, **General National Vocational Qualifications** (GNVQ), **National Vocational Qualifications** (NVQ)); a group award at both levels. including **core skills** and **citizenship**. This was not accepted by the Conservative Government in 1995, but the Labour Government after 1997 showed interest in the ideas, some of which were incorporated into **Curriculum 2000**.

General National Vocational Qualification (GNVQ) GNVQs were introduced by the **National Council for Vocational Qualifications** (NCVQ) in 1992. The GNVQ was designed to provide vocationally oriented skills and knowledge for progression to employment or university. It is available at three levels: *Foundation*, roughly equivalent in weight to four or five **GCSE** passes at grades D–G; *Intermediate*, roughly equivalent to four or five **GCSE** passes grades A–C; *Advanced*, roughly equivalent to two **A Level** passes. In 1999–2000, GNVQs were renamed Vocational Certificate of Education (VCE or **Vocational A Levels** and became closer to **A Levels** in assessment requirements. (See also **Dearing Reports/Reviews**)

General Teaching Council (GTC)   Since 1860 attempts have been made to found a General Teaching Council for England and Wales, analogous to the General Medical Council (GMC), to govern the profession. A General Teaching Council for England came into being in 1999 following the Teaching and Higher Education Act (1998). The Council, which was established in 2000, deals with matters such as the training, the supply and qualifications of teachers, the establishment of a code of conduct and the raising of professional standards, and has a disciplinary committee. It consists of 64 members with a chairman. There are 25 elected members, 9 teachers appointed by the main teaching unions, 16 appointed by other representative bodies who have an interest in education, 13 Secretary of State nominees and a member appointed by the Disability Rights Commission. Approximately two-thirds of the members have teaching experience.

A GTC for Wales (GTCW) was established in September 1999. Based in Cardiff, it has a chairman, 25 members, 12 elected by teachers, 9 appointed by the National Assembly for Wales with nominations from teaching unions and other educational bodies, and 4 members by direct appointment by the Assembly itself. A Scottish GTC (GTCS) was set up by the Teaching Council (Scotland) Act in 1965. It has more powers than its English equivalent, e.g., it approves new **initial teacher training** courses. A GTC for Northern Ireland was established in 2002.

Gestalt   Gestalt is the German word for 'configuration'. At the beginning of the twentieth century a school of psychology, developed in Germany, was later referred to as 'Gestalt psychology'. Its main assumption was that the human brain has a tendency to organise experience into patterned configurations or wholes. The word 'Gestalt' was used to refer to the whole of a perception or thought process rather than to the individual items within it. In education, Gestalt psychologists have been influential in encouraging teachers to concentrate pupils' attention on the whole (the Gestalt) rather than on parts. In **reading**, this has tended to support 'look and say' or looking at the whole sentence rather than phonic methods of reading. (See also **flashcard**, **learning theory**, **reading age**, **reductionism**)

giftedness   An ambiguous term, sometimes referring to children of supposed high **intelligence quotient** (IQ), for whom schools should make special provision; and sometimes used to identify children with specific talents in fields such as music or dancing. The 'gifted' are also sometimes included in the generic term 'exceptional children' or 'children with special needs'. The Government has recently recognised the need to make special provision for the gifted. As part of the **Excellence in Cities** scheme, a Gifted and Talented Programme (GTP) was introduced in April 2000 into 495 secondary schools in 24 inner city local education authorities. Similarly, some 400 primary schools, mainly in Years 5 and 6, benefited from this scheme. Distance teaching and learning programmes are mounted for 5–10 per cent of pupils in each year group. Two-thirds of the cohort consists of pupils with talents in the statutory curriculum other than in art, music and physical education, and up to one-third with skills in these subjects or any creative art. There is a lead co-ordinator for a cluster of 3–8 schools, and a co-ordinator for each school. National **summer schools** intended for gifted and talented pupils completing Years 6–9 are mounted. The White Paper, *Schools: Achieving Success* (2001), announced the establishment of a new National Academy for Gifted and Talented Youth for 11–16-year-olds. It is based at Warwick University, and follows the model of Johns Hopkins University Center for Talented Youth, Baltimore, USA. (See also **National Association for Gifted Children**)

Girls' Day School Trust (GDST)   This Trust was established in 1872 to promote a scheme for a public day school for girls at Chelsea. The Taunton Report of 1868 had disclosed the grave shortage of suitable educational institutions for girls of middle-class families. The trust now has 25 schools in England and Wales.

girls' education   Views differ on the benefits of single-sex or mixed schools for girls' education. A 1992 survey by **Her Majesty's Inspectorate** entitled *The Preparation of Girls for Adult and Working Life* claims that girls are more likely to develop high aspirations in the best single-sex schools. Self-confidence is created in all-girls schools, partly because 'teachers in mixed schools paid insufficient attention to the ways in which boys sometimes dominate work in classrooms and other key areas of school life'. It is for this reason that in mixed schools classroom management, curriculum policy and pupil counselling all need careful monitoring. (See also **Equal Opportunities Commission**, **gender and educational performance**, **Girls' Public Day School Trust**, **Girls' School Association**)

Girls' Schools Association (GSA)   The Association consists of the heads of 207 leading **independent secondary schools** for girls in the UK.

Member schools include day and boarding types. All schools in the **Girls' Day School Trust** are members.

Gittins Report   In August 1963, the Central Advisory Council for Education (Wales) was asked by Sir Edward Boyle, the then Minister for Education, to examine the state of **primary education** and the transition to **secondary education** in Wales. Its terms of reference were identical to those of the **Plowden** Committee. In its Report, *Primary Education in Wales* (1967), the Committee agreed with its English counterpart and commended the notion of **first** and **middle** schools. It also endorsed the principle of fully bilingual education. The teaching of Welsh as a first or second language was to be encouraged in all Welsh schools.

GNVQ   (See **General National Vocational Qualification**)

Governing Bodies Association (GBA)   This Association, founded in 1944, consists of governing bodies of **independent schools** for boys and co-educational schools, whose heads belong to the **Headmasters' and Headmistresses' Conference, Society of Headmasters and Headmistresses of Independent Schools, Independent Schools Association, or Incorporated Association of Preparatory Schools**. It represents the interests of the 319 membership schools and provides a forum for the discussions of matters concerning schools.

Governing Bodies of Girls' Schools Association   Founded in 1942, the Association represents the governance of girls' independent schools in the UK. In all, 220 schools are members. The heads must belong to the **Headmasters' and Headmistresses' Conference**, the **Society of Headmasters and Headmistresses of Independent Schools**, the **Independent Schools Association**, or the **Incorporated Association of Preparatory Schools**.

Government of Wales Act (1998)   This Act defined the organisation, functions and powers of the **National Assembly for Wales**. Powers delegated from the UK to the National Assembly were listed in the Wales (Transfer of Functions) Orders: these included considerable responsibilities for education.

governors   All maintained schools are required by law to have a board of governors. In recent years the powers and responsibilities of governors have steadily increased. The 1944 Education Act required the duties of governors to be set out in an **instrument of government** and the functions of governors in relation to headteachers and local education authorities to be set out in articles of government.

The 1980 Education Act extended the responsibilities of governors (following the recommendation of the **Taylor Report** (1977)), and stipulated that elected representation of teachers and parents should be included on the board of governors.

The 1988 Education Reform Act added to governors' responsibilities (see **local management of schools**). And in the case of those schools that 'opted out' of local authority control (see **grant maintained schools**) the powers of governors appeared to be very great indeed and gave rise to celebrated disputes. In 2001, there were some 340,000 school governors in England and Wales and approximately 24,500 governing bodies. A recent Education Select Committee Report into the Role of School Governors led the **Department for Education and Skills** to announce a National Strategy for Training and Support for Governors. The Strategy aims to achieve a high quality in governor information and training, working with the **National Governors' Council** and the **National Association of Governors and Managers**, and many other associations. Among the priorities are: developing a national induction training package for new governors, and voluntary accreditation for governors. With the increasing range of responsibilities given to governors by successive legislation, it has been suggested that they should be paid. (See also **manager**)

grade   A mark given to students to denote their achievement *either* in a specific test for a specific assignment, *or* to indicate the level of achievement at the end of a year or course. Grades or **levels** of achievement may be in literal (i.e. alphabetical) or numerical form.

grade criteria   In **criterion-referenced** assessment each level of achievement or grade should be indentifiable by strictly defined criteria. (See also **standards**)

grade descriptions   It is often found difficult to make public examinations **criterion-referenced** in a strict sense; a move in the direction of specifying precisely what is expected of candidates is sometimes achieved by writing grade descriptions – i.e., providing guidance for examiners as to what to expect from a grade A candidate as compared with a grade B and so on. Grade descriptions are used in **GCSE**.

grade review   A consideration of the work of particular **GCSE** and **A Level** candidates by senior examiners and moderators. Candidates are normally included in a grade review if they are 1 per cent or less below the C/D borderline and their provisional subject grade differs by two or more grades from the centre estimate.

graded assessment (GA)   Schemes of graded assessment have been developed as an alternative to **GCE O Level, CSE** and – more recently – **GCSE**

examinations. One purpose is to avoid leaving most assessment until the end of the course; another is to allow pupils to progress at their own individual pace and to be assessed whenever it is most appropriate. It is claimed that graded assessment dramatically enhances student motivation and performance. (See also **examinations**)

graded reader   A reader in this context refers to a book rather than a person. A graded reader is a book that is graded in terms of reading difficulty. Such books are usually produced as a **series** so that a pupil systematically progresses from one level of difficulty to the next. The pupil is gradually stretched, but does not encounter too many difficulties in the same page or chapter of the book. Some teachers and reading specialists, however, dislike this kind of mechanical approach and prefer to use **real books**. (See also **reading**)

graded test   Graded tests are to be distinguished from **graded assessment**. Graded tests have been designed to indicate **levels** of achievement in subjects where progress in specific skills can be measured in a standard way – especially in modern languages and numeracy skills.

graduate   (1) In Great Britain, the term graduate is normally used for a person who has successfully completed an **undergraduate** or **degree** course at a university or higher education institution and has been awarded a degree. (2) An honorary graduate is a person awarded a degree (usually a masters degree or doctorate) without taking a course, as a means of publicly recognising distinction of some kind. (3) In the USA (and some other systems) to graduate means to complete any course – hence the term 'high school graduate'.

Graduate and Registered Teacher Programmes (GRTP)   An inclusive term for the **Graduate Teacher Programme** and the **Registered Teacher Programme**.

Graduate Teacher Programme (GTP)   Introduced in 1998, the Programme is an employment-based training scheme for graduates from other occupations over the age of 24 in shortage subjects – mathematics, English, science, modern languages and technology. The length of training can vary according to the needs of the trainee, but it is usually between one term and a year. The **Teacher Training Agency** (TTA) is responsible for funding the growing number of teachers who enter by this route. Whilst training, the student normally receives £13,000 and a grant is provided to cover the cost of the training. The GTP accounts at present for about 10 per cent of new entrants to the profession, but the scheme was extended in scope from January 2002. All GTPs are overseen by an institution of higher education which is responsible for working with the school to plan the training programme and to assess the candidate against the standards for **qualified teacher status**. (See also **Registered Teacher Programme**)

Graduate Teacher Training Registry (GTTR)   The Registry is a clearing house for courses of initial teacher education. Graduates, or under-graduates in the final year of their degree courses, wishing to take a **Professional Graduate Certificate of Education** (PGCE) register with the GTTR, listing the higher education institutions in order of priority, thus avoiding the need to make separate applications to a number of institutions. The GTTR has recently become part of the **Universities and Colleges Admissions Service** (UCAS) but operates separately from applications to undergraduate courses.

grammar school   The term grammar school was first used in the fourteenth century for a type of school founded to provide free or subsidised education for children, usually boys, in a particular locality. Latin was always an important part of the **curriculum**. By the nineteenth century many grammar schools had deteriorated, and were reformed by the Grammar School Act (1840). The 1902 Education Act gave the newly created **local education authorities** power to provide secondary schools on grammar school lines. The 1944 Education Act stipulated that secondary education should be free and compulsory. Some local education authorities interpreted the Act to mean that three different types of secondary school should be available for three supposed kinds of ability: secondary grammar schools, secondary technical, and secondary modern. By 1990 only about 7 per cent of local authorities had retained any grammar schools. No new grammar schools have been created and the total is now 166. Selection for grammar schools was traditionally based on the **eleven plus examination**. The School Standards and Framework Act (1998) enabled parents to make decisions on future selection admissions, where a grammar school exists, by petitions and ballots. Governing bodies of grammar schools may also publish proposals to end selection. In December 2001, the Labour Government considerably softened its stance on grammar schools by allocating £500,000 to link grammar and **comprehensive schools** in 25 areas of England in order to encourage good practice in the State sector.

grant maintained school   Established by the Education Reform Act (1988) these schools could choose to 'opt out' of local education authority control and received finance direct from the Department. Under the School Standards and Framework Act (1998), these schools were replaced by **foundation schools** from 2000.

graphicacy   A term invented as a parallel to **literacy**, **numeracy** and **oracy**. Graphicacy covers the ability to think visually and spatially as well as the mastery of certain **basic skills**.

'Great Debate'   On 18 October 1976, the Labour Party Prime Minister, James Callaghan, made a speech at **Ruskin College**, Oxford, calling for a public debate on education. The Ruskin speech was followed by eight one-day regional conferences in February and March 1977. As a result, in July 1977, a **Green Paper**, *Education in Schools: A Consultative Document*, was issued. (See also **Yellow Book**)

Greats   The name given to an undergraduate course at the University of Oxford devoted to classical languages, history and philosophy. Its correct title is *Literae Humaniores*.

Green Paper   A government may choose to set out proposals for future policy in the form of a consultative or discussion document. This is known as a Green Paper. (See also **Parliamentary Papers**)

Grubb Institute   Named after its founding president, the late Sir Kenneth Grubb, the Grubb Institute is a group of consultants who work with clients to develop or improve their own management systems. The Grubb Institute has worked successfully with local education authorities (especially the **Inner London Education Authority** before its abolition in 1988) as well as with individual schools or groups of schools. The Grubb 'style' is to try to enable schools (as well as other kinds of organisations) to develop their own management system rather than to impose a package or a formula.

H

Hadow Reports   During the inter-war period, when Sir William Hadow, Vice-Chancellor of Sheffield University, was chairman of the Consultative Committee of the Board of Education, three important reports were issued. The first, *The Education of the Adolescent*, was published in 1926, the second, *Primary Education*, in 1931, and the third, *Infant and Nursery Schools*, in 1933. The return of the first Labour Government in 1924, committed to a policy of secondary education for all, led to a study of the organisation, objectives and curriculum of children up to the age of 15. (The leaving age at this time was 14.) As secondary schools were outside the Committee's remit, the study was only a partial one. Psychological evidence was prominent in the Report. Its introduction includes the statement, 'There is a tide which begins to rise in the veins of youth at the age of 11 or 12. It is called by the name of adolescence.' The Committee recommended a separation of **primary** and **secondary** education at the age of 11. Some type of secondary education should be available to all, either **grammar** or **modern**: pupils would be allocated as the result of an examination. The **curriculum** would differ between the schools, the modern being more 'realistic'. A leaving age of 15 was recommended by the Report, but this was postponed and did not come into force until 1947. The findings were accepted by the Board, and from the 1930s schools were reorganised on Hadow lines. With the break in school life at 11 now official policy, the Consultative Committee's 1931 report on the primary school turned its attention to the consequences flowing from this move. It advocated close co-operation between the primary and secondary stages and the transfer of children at seven from the **infant** department. The curriculum was to be thought of in terms of 'activity and experience rather than of knowledge to be acquired and facts to be stored'. Differences in intellectual capacity between pupils, it believed, should be dealt with by dividing an age group into streams by the age of ten. The third Hadow Report examined infant and **nursery schools**. It encouraged enlightened approaches, giving approval to Froebelian and Montessorian methods, and stressed the need for separate infant schools. Perhaps the most far-sighted recommendation was that a national system of nursery schools should be provided, a recommendation that still awaits implementation. (See also **all-age school**, **Froebel schools**, **Montessori schools**)

half-term   A short holiday given by schools in the middle of each **term**. (See also **academic year**, **semester**, **vacation**)

half-time system   An attempt in the nineteenth century to limit the amount of time spent by children in employment. The 1833 Factory Act stated that two hours' schooling on six days a week should be given for those aged between 9 and 11. Eleven years later, another Factory Act extended the time to three hours' education on five days a week. This was the real beginning of the half-time system. From the time of the 1870 Education Act, public demand for more compulsory attendance and raising of the minimum age of employment resulted in legislation in the following ten years which went far to meet these wishes. However, the half-time system for older pupils continued in some areas until its abolition by the Fisher Education Act of 1918. (See also **factory school**)

hall, university   (1) A building, either on or away from the **campus**, for students' resident. (2) At Oxford and Cambridge, formerly a place, not a college, where students lived under the supervision of a Master of Arts. The title still exists in the name of some of the present colleges, such as Trinity Hall and St Edmund Hall at Cambridge.

halo effect   The psychologist, R. L. Thorndike, observed that in the process of various kinds of **assessment** the judgments of an assessor tend to be biased by a previous assessment (even if the assessment was of a totally unconnected ability). The halo effect can thus be either negative or positive.

Handbook of Suggestions for Teachers   The ending of 'payment by results' at the end of the nineteenth century, left the elementary school teacher free to pursue her/his work without central regulation. The first *Handbook of Suggestions for Teachers* was issued by the Board of Education in 1905 to inform teachers of good practice. All aspects of the elementary curriculum were dealt with, whole chapters being devoted to individual subjects. The *Handbook* was frequently revised, the last one appearing in 1937.

handwriting   The importance of handwriting in schools is becoming increasingly recognised. Studies have shown that pupils with bad handwriting will often disrupt lessons rather than have their lack of skill exposed, and it also tends to lower self-esteem. Many schools, particularly first and middle, have promoted common practices with handwriting development programmes and liaise with parents of pre-school age. Since 1988, it has been part of the English **national curriculum**. A survey by the **National Foundation for Educational Research** (NFER) in 1992 showed that more seven-year-olds needed a 'writing rescue' programme than special help with reading.

Hansard   Verbatim reports on the debates in both Houses of Parliament which are published by Her Majesty's Stationery Office (HMSO). Since 1943, the parliamentary debates, and official reports, have had the name *Hansard* on their covers. This is a reference to the printer, Luke Hansard, who printed the journals of the House of Commons from 1774. *Hansard* is a very useful reference source for researchers on many aspects of education. (See also **Hansard Society**)

Hansard Society   The Hansard Society for parliamentary government is a non-party organisation, founded by an Independent MP, Commander (later Lord) King-Hall in 1944. The Society's original aim was to encourage people to read the daily *Hansard* reports of parliamentary debates. It now has wider aims, and provides information on the workings of British democracy and assessing how well the system continues to serve today's needs. The Society played a part in promoting political education in schools, and it has a Curriculum Review Unit to monitor trends in teaching politics. (See also **Hansard**)

Haslegrave Report   In 1967 the **National Advisory Council on Education for Industry and Commerce** (NACEIC) appointed a Committee on Technician Courses and Examinations 'to review the provision for courses suitable for technicians at all levels … and to consider what changes are desirable in the present structure of courses and examinations'. Its report, issued in 1969, stated that the existing pattern of technician courses and examinations was unsuitable for meeting not only existing needs, but also the changing needs and new needs which were likely to arise in the future. The main recommendation was that there should be a unified body for each of the main two sectors, technical and business, responsible for planning and co-ordinating courses. The Secretary of State for Education and Science was advised to set up as soon as possible a **Technician Education Council** (TEC) and a **Business Education Council** (BEC). (See also **business education**)

Hawthorne effect   In the early days of industrial psychology it was observed in a study by Elton Mayo, of the Hawthorne works near Chicago, that when individuals are being observed, they tend to perform better. This is important in educational studies because if a new teaching method or a new curriculum project is introduced into a classroom, and the pupils improve their performance, this may be caused not by the value of the new approach but simply because the pupils are receiving extra attention. The Hawthorne effect is sometimes extended to mean simply 'the effect of the novelty of a new set of materials which eventually wears off'.

head boy/girl   A pupil, elected or appointed as leader of **prefects** in a school. His or her duties are often concerned with maintaining discipline and the orderly running of the school.

head of department or faculty   Heads of departments or faculties in schools and colleges are persons who are in charge of their subject or a range of subjects at all levels and co-ordinate the work of the department's staff. They are responsible for helping to formulate academic policy in relation to the overall school policy, and in encouraging curriculum development, and often assist the head or principal in deciding on matters affecting the whole institution. A head of department normally holds departmental staff meetings to discuss matters of common concern to teachers working in the department. A **National Foundation for Educational Research** (NFER) survey published in 1989 showed that headteachers all expected their middle managers to be pro-active rather than re-active. The provision of middle management training by schools and authorities varies considerably over the country.

head of house   (See **pastoral system**)

head of year   The holder of this post is responsible for leading a team of **tutors** in schools, to manage the pastoral welfare of students in a particular year; to monitor the students' academic progress; to co-ordinate a programme of personal development; and liaise with parents and outside agencies. (See also **pastoral system**)

Head Start   A nationally funded programme started in the USA in 1964 which provided **disadvantaged** pre-school children with educational and social services. In its early years, notably through a study undertaken by Ohio University and the Westinghouse Learning Corporation, it was believed that **compensatory education** programmes had little effect. However, follow-up studies since 1975 have revealed the long-term benefits of Head Start in achievement in primary and secondary schools as well as in out-of-school behaviour. (See also **enrichment programme**)

Headmasters' and Headmistresses' Conference (HMC)   Originally set up in 1869 to oppose the investigations of the Endowed Schools Commission into grammar and endowed schools, the Conference consists of headteachers of 242 boys' and co-educational **independent schools**. The main mover of the Conference was Edward Thring of Uppingham, and the first gathering took place in his school. Annual meetings are still held. Membership of the Conference has been the hallmark of a **public school**. (See also **Headmasters' Association**, **headteacher**)

Headmasters' Association (HMA)   Established in 1890, the Association had close links with the Headmasters' Conference; all members of the Conference were members of the HMA, but the reverse did not hold true. The HMA, through its membership from secondary schools, from 1976 became part of the **Secondary Heads' Association** (SHA). (See also **headteacher**)

Headship Leadership and Management Programme (HEADLAMP) (See **headship training**)

headship training   There are three national training programmes for headship:

1. *National Professional Qualification for Headship (NPQH)*.   First introduced in September 1997 by the **Department for Education and Employment** (DfEE), it is intended to be a necessary qualification for all first-time heads. Early in 2000, a new model under the supervision of the **National College for School Leadership** was unveiled. This included greater use of information and communications technology and more school-based elements.

The duration of the course is between three months and two years, according to the experience of the candidate, though a new one-year qualification from April 2001 proved very popular. From 2002, all college principals were required to obtain the NPQH before taking up their posts. It will be mandatory for all new heads from 2004.

2. *Headteacher Leadership and Management Programme (HEADLAMP).* This professional programme, initiated in 1998, is intended for new head-teachers appointed to their first post. The two-year funding for training enables heads to follow individually provided courses to meet their particular needs. About 8,000 completed the course between 1998 and 2001.

3. *Leadership Programme for Serving Headteachers (LPSH).* Building on the previous two courses, the LPSH provides existing heads in England with more advanced knowledge on raising standards in schools and analysing their own leadership roles. Heads are able to share their experience and skills with others in a neutral setting and the Programme encourages exploration of practice and research into headteacher effectiveness.

From April 2001, the administration of these three training programmes was transferred from the **Department for Education and Skills** to the National College for School Leadership.

headteacher   The term headteacher covers both sexes, in primary as well as in secondary schools. The head is expected to provide effective leadership. In recent years, systematic training for headship has become increasingly common and, for new heads, the **National Professional Qualification for Headship** will be compulsory from 2004. Since the Education Reform Act (1988) when the majority of schools were given control of their budgets, heads have had greater responsibilities for promoting the school and ensuring financial viability. (See also **headship training**)

Health Education Authority (HEA)   Formerly the Health Education Council, the HEA is a special health authority within the National Health Service. Its task is to provide information and advice about health directly to the public, to support other organisations who provide health education and to advise the Secretary of State on this subject. Health education for young people between the ages of 5 and 19 is an important aspect of the Authority's work. They provide information and encourage skills to enable children to make healthy choices about their lives. Recent work includes the launch of the 'Promoting Health in Primary Schools' project: the training of teachers to use material in connection with the 'Mr Body' project; the expansion of the 'Happy Heart' project, which develops health education through physical activity in primary schools; and the development of the 'Health in Clubs' project by the training of youth workers in respect of health education.

Her Majesty's Inspectorate (HMI)   HMI dates back to 1839, when inspectors were appointed to supervise the spending of public money for the education of the poor. Over the years HMI responsibilities were widened, with all schools and colleges maintained from public funds being open to inspection. By the 1990s the inspectorate had only about 500 members, but their work included providing **in-service training** for teachers, carrying out inspections, preparing reports and discussion documents for publication, liaising with **local education authorities** and serving as observers on many bodies. A scrutiny of the work of HMI by Lord Rayner in 1983 supported the policy of concentrating on general surveys rather than individual inspections. However, the Education (Schools) Act (1992) introduced a new system of privatised inspection. An independent office of Her Majesty's Chief Inspector of Schools – the **Office for Standards in Education** (OFSTED) – was established in September 1992. HMI numbers were reduced and their functions limited mainly to the training and monitoring of newly **registered inspectors** and independent inspectors. HMI provides advice to, and are the permanent inspection staff of, OFSTED.

In 2001, there were approximately 200 inspectors who were assigned to teams, called divisions (ten in number). The divisions are not permanent and change according to the task in hand. Teacher training and school improvement are the largest divisions. Others include: local education authority inspections; phase work for primary and secondary schools and special educational needs; LEA-funded further education; and post-16 education and training. Meetings of inspectors are held within divisions during term time. New HMI are initially given a three-year contract but these can subsequently be made permanent. The problem of Her Majesty's Inspectorate retaining a distinctive identity still remains.

hidden curriculum   (See **curriculum, hidden**)

Higginson Report (1988)   Criticisms of the **Advanced Level** examination began soon after its introduction in 1951: the concentration on two or three subjects was regarded as narrow and over-specialised at such an early age as 16. Several attempts were made to broaden the curriculum for the 16–19 age group (see **Q and F Levels** and **N and F Levels**). In the 1980s a committee was set up under the chairmanship of Dr Gordon Higginson, Vice-Chancellor of the University of Southampton. A Report was published in 1988, recommending a five-subject curriculum, a mixture of **Advanced**

Supplementary (AS) and A Levels. The Report had wide support, but was vetoed by Margaret Thatcher, then Prime Minister.

high flier   Term used for a very able pupil with high attainments. (See also **giftedness**, **exceptional children**)

high school   A term formerly used widely by **grammar** and **independent schools**. It now more commonly describes junior secondary schools, catering for 11- to 14-year-olds.

higher degree   A **postgraduate** degree obtained, either by research or by following a taught course, at the masters' or doctoral levels. (See also **dissertation**, **graduate**, **university department of education**, **viva**)

higher education (HE)   This term is usually used to distinguish courses of study that result in the award of a degree, diploma or similar advanced qualification, from various kinds of **further education** (FE) institutions. So far such work has been conducted in universities, which awarded their own degrees, and polytechnics, which offered them in the name of the **Council for National Academic Awards** (CNAA). **The Further and Higher Education Act** (1992) removed this distinction and replaced it with a single higher education system embodying both institutions.

Higher Education Funding Council (HEFC)   This Council deals with the funding of all the higher education sector that resulted from the **Further and Higher Education Act** (1992). Amongst its tasks is the determination of funding methodology for research and teaching. Since 1993, there have been separate higher education funding councils for Wales, Scotland and England.

Higher Education Quality Council (HEQC)   The Council was established in May 1992 as a company limited by guarantee, owned by the **Committee of Vice-Chancellors and Principals**, the Conference of Scottish Centrally Funded Colleges, and the Standing Conference of Principals. In 1997, most of the functions of HEQC were taken over by the **Quality Assurance Agency for Higher Education** (QAA).

higher elementary school   A type of school bridging the elementary–secondary sectors in its curriculum, legalised in 1900. The Code of 1905 suggested the development of higher elementary schools which would provide education between the ages of 12 and 15 for brighter children who had previously attended an ordinary public elementary school. The Consultative Committee's Report on Higher Elementary Schools (1906) suggested that the courses offered should consist of three strands: humanistic, scientific and manual; and, in the case of girls, domestic. Previously, these schools were required to offer predominantly scientific instruction.

higher grade school   In 1882, a seventh Standard was added to the **Code** to enable older pupils to extend their stay at elementary schools. As an increasing number continued on after passing the seventh Standard, ex-Standard classes were formed. In many cases, **school boards** gathered such pupils into one school called 'higher grade' and offering an education until at least 15. In 1894, there were 60 of these schools in England. (See also **standards**)

Higher National Diploma (HND)   Post-school vocational award more advanced than the **National Diploma**. It is usually regarded as roughly equal to a university pass degree and requires the equivalent of two years' full-time study. (See also **Business and Technology Education Council** (BTEC))

Higher School Certificate   Introduced by the **Secondary School Examinations Council** in 1919, the Higher School Certificate was awarded to pupils who had previously taken the **School Certificate** examination and had normally completed a two-year course of study. The course was of a more specialised nature than that of the School Certificate and candidates sat examinations in two, three or four subjects at main or subsidiary levels. It was replaced by the **GCE A Level** examination in 1951.

Hillgate Group   A right-wing pressure group that has published a number of pamphlets on education.

HMI   (See **Her Majesty's Inspectorate**)

HND   (See **Higher National Diploma**)

Holmes Circular   In May 1910, Edmund Holmes, the Chief Inspector of Elementary Schools of the Board of Education, wrote a confidential memorandum for all the Board's Inspectors on the status and duties of **local education authority** inspectors. Holmes claimed that this body was on the whole inefficient and lacked the type of school and university education that characterised **Her Majesty's Inspectors**. Extracts from the Circular appeared in the Press shortly afterwards and the matter was taken up in the Commons. Holmes had by this time retired but Robert Morant, the Permanent Secretary to the Board who had signed the Circular and who had made enemies of elementary school teachers, was transferred to the newly formed National Insurance Commission. Walter Runciman, the Liberal President of the Board, who handled the affair badly, was removed to the Board of Agriculture. The contents of the Circular were not fully revealed until nearly 70 years later.

Home and School Council   A partnership of four pressure groups, the **Advisory Centre for Education** (ACE), the **National Confederation of**

Parent–Teacher Associations (NCPTA), the **Campaign for State Education** (CASE), and the **National Association for Primary Education** (NAPE). The Council, formed in 1967, produces a number of practical guides for parents, teachers, governors, and those involved in home-school matters.

home education   Section 36 of the 1944 Education Act stated that 'it shall be the duty of the parent of every child of compulsory school age to cause him to receive efficient, full-time education suitable to his age, ability and aptitude, either by regular attendance at school or otherwise'. The final two words give parents the opportunity to educate their children at home in accordance with their own principles. Parents have no general duty to inform **local education authorities** of their decision to educate their children at home. The 1996 Education Act states that pupils could be educated in accordance with the wishes of parents, provided there is evidence of efficient full-time instructions. Home-educated children do not have to follow the **national curriculum** or take tests. An organisation for like-minded parents was formed in 1977 with the title of **Education Otherwise** and has a thriving membership. However, it has been argued that if a child is over-involved with her/his parents, this may lead to difficulties later when the child endeavours to establish an independent life. (See also **compulsory education**, **home tuition**)

home-school   Since September 1999 schools in England and Wales have been required to adopt a home-school agreement, under the Schools Standards and Framework Act (1998). The agreement is produced by school governors, in consultation with the head and parents; it sets out the school's aims and values, standards of education and the responsibilities of parents in respect of attendance, behaviour and **homework**. All parents of children between the ages of 5 and 16 are requested to sign the declaration, though this is not compulsory. A large-scale survey of schools in England and Wales in October 2000 showed that teachers, governors, parents and children displayed a considerable degree of scepticism about the agreements. Whilst they provide parents with a better understanding of the school's aims, it is doubtful if less supportive parents and their children will become more co-operative as a result.

home tuition   Often used by parents whose children need extra coaching in a subject or subjects in order to pass an examination. Home tutors – who may or may not be qualified teachers – often advertise locally and visit homes after the school day is ended. Problems may arise with the **General Certificate of Secondary Education** (GCSE), where there is a proportion of course assessment, when the tutor may unduly and unfairly aid the pupil. (See also **home education**, **Education Otherwise**)

home tutor   A teacher employed by a **local education authority** to give lessons to children who are unable for various reasons to attend school. The work may be done in either the tutor's or the child's home. (See also **home tuition**)

homework   Originally called 'home lessons', the practice of setting extra work out of school began in the early nineteenth century. After the system of '**payment by results**' had been instituted in 1862, the volume of home-work increased in elementary schools: the establishment of the Oxford and Cambridge 'Local' examinations from 1857 had a similar effect on secondary schools. By the 1880s, medical reasons were being advanced against the imposition of homework, but with little effect. In the twentieth century, several government reports dealing with aspects of education commented on the effects of homework on children's out-of-school life, but no action followed. Homework guidelines were issued by the Department in 1996. All schools are expected to have an effective homework policy, which has three aims: to develop home-school partnerships, to consolidate and reinforce skills and understanding; and to extend school learning. New homework guidelines were published by the Department in November 1998, setting out for parents what is reasonable to expect from a child at different ages. For 5–11-year-olds, the emphasis is on literacy and numeracy, and the homework time recommended ranges from 10 to 30 minutes a day. The secondary school guideline spanning the curriculum recommended 90 minutes per day for 11–13-year-olds, rising to between 90 minutes and 2.5 hours a day for 14–16-year-olds. (See also **homework clubs**)

homework clubs   Intended as homework and study support centres for more than 6,000 schools which enable pupils from seven years of age to do homework where there are difficulties in studying at home. First established in 2000 and linked with leading football clubs, the new centres provide quiet places for homework, art activities, sports, and access to computers. They are financed jointly by the **Standards Fund** and the **New Opportunities Fund**.

honorary degree   A **degree** awarded by a higher education institution to persons distinguished in their own field. The degree is conferred at a public ceremony, usually by the **chancellor** or head of the institution.

honours degree   An examination of a higher standard than a pass degree and one that may have a different syllabus. Honours degrees are usually divided into different **classes**, the first being the highest, second (often sub-divided into upper and lower) and third. (See also **class**)

Houghton Report   A Committee of Inquiry, appointed in June 1974, and chaired by Lord Houghton of Sowerby, to examine the pay of non-university teachers in Great Britain. The Report was completed within six months and its findings were swiftly implemented. It was the first independent committee on teachers' salaries for 30 years. At a time when counter-inflation legislation was in force, the Committee regarded teachers as a 'special case' after comparing their salaries with rewards in similar fields of employment. It recommended periodic reviews on teachers' pay to be made independently of the established negotiating bodies, and a common grading structure for **further education** establishments and **colleges of education**. (See also **Burnham Report**, **Clegg Report**, **Pelham Report**)

house system   Originally an essentially **public school** phenomenon, where pupils are allocated to boarding houses under the supervision of a housemaster/mistress. The house system is now found in the great majority of **comprehensive** schools. These schools may be divided into a number of houses, either located in individual buildings or not, for social and academic activities. All members of staff are attached to houses and most of them look after a **tutor** group of up to 30 children for the rest of their school lives. Tutor groups may consist of pupils of the same age group or of a large age range. (See also **boarding school**)

humanities   A term usually employed to group a number of disciplines or subjects together, all of which are concerned with some aspect of human life. History, human geography, literature and philosophy, and sometimes the social sciences are included in the term humanities. In schools, under a humanities umbrella, a number of subjects are drawn upon to provide pupils with a coherent approach to understanding major human and social issues.

Human Rights Act (1998)   This Act, which came into force in October 2000, had several implications for education. Article 2 (on the right to education) raises questions on compulsory school uniform, and the right of excluded students to an alternative education. Article 6 (the right to fair trial) allows legal challenges to **exclusion** if pupils are accused of violence, drug-taking or sexual offences. Article 8 (the right to privacy and family life) restricts the scope of teachers' enquiries into pupils' activities.

hurdle   Refers to a given level of performance that candidates must reach on an examination component in order to succeed. There are a number of factors which govern the level of the hurdle, the most important of which is a consideration of all the candidates' performances.

I

iconic   (See **enactive**)

ideology   Some writers have spoken of different ideologies within the teacher profession; others have concentrated on the influence of ideology on education. An ideology is generally taken to mean a more or less coherent set of values. Since education is inevitably connected with values, it has become increasingly difficult for those who claim that education is, or should be, ideology-free.

ILEA   (See **Inner London Education Authority**)

impression marking   In the marking of essays there are broadly two approaches. The first is to mark the essay as a whole and to give an overall (or impression) mark for style, content and presentation. The alternative is a more analytical approach that sets down beforehand what kind of points a candidate should make; marks are then awarded for each of those points made, possibly with marks being added or deducted for style, spelling and other 'automatic errors'. The fairest or most accurate method is said to be a combination of both ways of marking, namely by a group of examiners some of whom use the analytic style and some the impression marking; the marks for each candidate are then averaged out. This is, however, a very expensive way of treating scripts and is rarely used.

inaugural lecture   A lecture given by a new **professor** on aspects of his or her **discipline**.

incentive allowances   (See **teachers' salaries**)

incline of difficulty   An ordering of a series of tasks so that they become progressively more demanding throughout the examination component.

Incorporated Association of Preparatory Schools (IAPS)   This Association, founded in 1892, consists of over 500 headteachers of **preparatory schools** and, since January 1981, represents girls' as well as boys' schools. It keeps heads informed of developments in education. All schools in the Association need accreditation, which is gained after satisfactory inspection. (See also **Independent Schools Inspectorate**)

independent further education colleges   These differ from maintained **further education colleges** in that they offer specialised courses, such as drama, architecture and languages, and English for foreign students. They are validated by independent professional bodies or by the **British Accreditation Council**

for Independent, Further and Higher Education (BAC). Many of these colleges, on the other hand, are **crammers**, offering intensive courses of study.

independent learning   (See **individual learning**)

independent schools   **Public schools** and other kinds of **private schools** increasingly prefer to be known as independent schools. These consist of both secondary schools and **preparatory schools**. Many private schools are now members of the **Independent Schools Council** (ISC). (See also **registration of independent schools**)

Independent Schools Association (ISA)   Founded in 1879, the ISA represents all types of independent schools ranging from the nursery to secondary stage. Its original title was the Association of Principals of Private Schools, becoming the Private Schools Association in 1895. It assumed its present title in 1927. Membership is vested in the head teacher of each establishment. The Association provides training opportunities to its members.

Independent Schools' Bursars Association (ISBA)   Represents some 800 **bursars** in independent schools. A survey carried out in 2002 showed that 42 per cent were formerly in the Armed Forces.

Independent Schools Council (ISC)   Established as the Independent Schools' Council in 1974, it was reconstituted as the ISC in 1998. There are eight constituent associations: the **Headmasters' and Headmistresses' Conference**; the **Society of Headmasters and Headmistresses of Independent Schools**; the **Independent Schools Association, Incorporated Association of Preparatory Schools**; the **Governing Bodies' Association**; the **Girls' Schools Association**; the **Governing Bodies of Girls' Schools Association**; and the **Independent Schools' Bursars Association.** The ISC acts as a unifying organisation and speaks and acts on behalf of these bodies. Over 80 per cent of children in independent schools attend its 1,275 member schools, which in 2001 had a total of 492,000 pupils. The Council also acts as a lobbying organisation, making representations to government, political organisations and civil servants. The public relations aspects are carried out by the **Independent Schools Council Information Service** (ISCIS)

Independent Schools Council Information Service (ISCIS)   This organisation, the media and public relations branch of the **Independent Schools Council** (ISC) was founded in 1965. It became a national body in 1972, with the title of the Independent Schools Information Service (ISIS); it amended its title to the present one in August 2001. It provides an information service for parents and others interested in independent education, and publicises the schools' academic achievements.

Independent Schools Inspectorate (ISI)   The Inspectorate is a successor to the Accreditation Review and Consultancy Service of the **Independent Schools Council** (ISC). It assumed this title in September 1998. It amalgamated with the **Headmasters' and Headmistresses' Conference** inspection service in April 2000. The ISI is officially recognised by the DfES and carries out inspections in ISC schools. The Inspectorate undertakes initial accreditation of schools, monitors standards and mounts review inspections. Inspection teams usually consist of former heads, **Her Majesty's Inspectors**, and/or **Office for Standards in Education** (OFSTED) inspectors.

Independent State School Partnership Programme (ISSPP)   In 1997 one of the first actions of the new Labour Government was to abolish the **Assisted Places Scheme** (APS). Anxious to avoid this being seen as ideological hostility towards the independent sector, in 1998 the **Department for Education and Employment** (DfEE) set up an advisory group to monitor partnership ideas between **independent** and **State schools**. This developed into the ISSPP. The general idea was to encourage co-operation between independent and **maintained schools**, and in October 1998 a short report on *Building Bridges* was published.

individual education plan (IEP)   Designed for children with learning difficulties and to meet identified needs. At **Key Stages** 2 and 3, pupils have an IEP which sets performance targets, provides individual work programmes, and gives parents sources of help and advice.

individual learning   There are at least two somewhat different meanings to this term. (1) The first focuses on pupils working on their own, perhaps by means of worksheets, perhaps by programmed materials of some kind. (2) The second meaning refers to the need to allow children not only to learn at an individual pace, but also to make use of different approaches, styles of learning, and their personality differences. The latter is much less common than the former. The first of the two meanings is sometimes also referred to as independent learning. (See also **mastery learning**, **programmed learning**)

individual learning plan   The Green Paper, *14–19: Extending Opportunities, Raising Standards* (2002), proposed that the 14–19 phase of learning should begin with a review of achievement, towards the end of **Key Stage** 3. The outcome of the review might be recorded as the beginning of an individual learning plan that would form the basis for monitoring progress from 14–19. (See also **Progress File**)

induction   In the past, some **local education authorities** held short induction courses for **newly qualified teachers** (and newly appointed **head-**

teachers or **deputy heads**). The **James Report** (1972) recommended that all newly qualified teachers should, in the first year at school, be given a light timetable that would enable them to spend one-fifth of the teaching week in some kind of further training. The James Report also recommended that teachers undergoing this induction year should be supported by specially appointed **professional tutors** in the school, possibly one of the deputy head-teachers. This aspect of the James Report was never completely implemented, but a few pilot schemes of induction were tried out with varying degrees of success. Many schemes suffered from the financial problems faced by local education authorities in the late 1970s and early 1980s. In the late 1990s, induction became an issue once again as part of the general concern for improving the quality of teaching and teacher training. The emphasis on school-based **initial teacher training** has also increased the importance of induction in the first year of a teacher's career as well as **continuing professional development**. Since 7 May 1999, all newly qualified teachers (NQTs) must successfully undergo an induction period of three school terms. The NQT must not have more than a 90 per cent teaching timetable and should be provided with support from an **induction mentor** throughout the period. The local education authority, on the basis of the judgment of the induction tutor and/or the school's head, decides if the NQT meets the **Induction Standards**. The induction period replaces the former probationary year.

induction mentor   All **newly qualified teachers** (NQT) should have a named tutor who works closely with them and offers support during their **induction** period. Good practice has been developed by schools, local education authorities and initial teacher training providers.

Induction Standards   These standards are laid down by the **Teacher Training Agency** (TTA) and specify the professional skills and knowledge that teachers have to acquire in order to become fully qualified teachers. The majority of teachers meet these Standards by the end of their **induction** year.

industrial school   Successors to **schools of industry**, these were often established by philanthropic individuals and were residential in character. The Industrial Schools Act (1857) empowered magistrates to send to these schools children who were truants, or beggars, or who had committed a misdemeanour. The 1876 Education Act introduced day schools, for boys and girls, that had a largely vocationally based curriculum.

industrial training   The training of employees in industry either at their place of work or in vocationally oriented courses in **further education**. There have been many unsuccessful attempts to increase the amount of industrial training in the UK. For example, the Industrial Training Act (1964) was intended to increase both the amount and the quality of industrial training. Industrial Training Boards (ITBs) were set up to organise training and to share the cost of training more fairly. The Act was modified by the Employment and Training Act (1973), but in 1982 the Government decided to wind up the majority of the boards, replacing them with 'voluntary arrangements'. When the **Department for Education and Employment** (DfEE) was set up, a network of **Training and Enterprise Councils** (TECs) was established in 1991, the boards of which were responsible to the DfEE. In 2001, the Education Act, *Learning and Skills*, replaced both the **Further Education Funding Council** (FEFC), and the Training Enterprise Boards run by the **Learning and Skills Council** (LSC), with a network of local Learning and Skills Councils.

industry, links with schools   Throughout the twentieth century, and particularly since the 1944 Education Act, schools have frequently made a distinction between education, which was the concern of schools, and training, which was the concern of industry itself. Any kind of vocational training within schools was particularly offensive to many teachers and their professional organisations. One of the themes of James Callaghan's **Ruskin College** speech of 1976 was the insufficient regard paid by schools to the adult world, particularly the world of work. From this time onwards, Department of Education and Science documents emphasised the need for schools to be concerned with the world of work. At the same time, the **Manpower Services Commission** (MSC) and its various training programmes seemed to be preserving the barrier between school and training for work. This continued until 1982 when a proposal was made, financed by the MSC, to introduce technical education into schools as well as colleges of **further education** starting with 14-year-old pupils in some selected schools. This was known as the **Technical and Vocational Education Initiative** (TVEI). Links between schools and industry were further encouraged by various aspects of the **Education Reform Act** (1988). (See also **'Great Debate'**, **industrial training**)

Industry Lead Body (ILB)   A lead body is an institution or group recognised as having responsibility for setting standards within a given area of competence in **NVQ**.

infant school   A school catering for children between the ages of five and seven. Most now form part of a **primary school** with a **junior** department and perhaps a **nursery**.

information and communications technology (ICT)   Information and communications technology draws heavily on three complex technologies that have converged: computing, micro-electronics and telecommunications. Many schools make considerable use of this technology, e.g. personal computers (PCs), the Internet and CD-ROMs. In many ways, ICT has helped to transform teaching and learning in schools. The Government has invested in ICT, which is especially accessible through Teacher Net, and learning resources have been made available through the **National Grid for Learning**, which helps teachers in lesson-planned teaching. More than 100,000 teachers are participating in the Learning Schools Programme under the New Opportunities Fund ICT Teacher Training Initiative. Pilot schemes have been commissioned by the **Department for Education and Skills** (DfES) for the development of on-line material, e.g. in mathematics, Latin and Japanese, for 11-year-old pupils, where suitable resources did not previously exist. ICT has been compulsory for all pupils since the introduction of the **national curriculum**. Nevertheless, a survey commissioned by the DfES in 1999 showed that pupils still spend up to four times as long using computers at home as they do at school. (See also **Curriculum Online**)

initial teacher training (ITT) or initial teacher education and training (ITET)   For some years there has been a dispute about the most appropriate generic title for courses leading to **qualified teacher status**. Before the **Robbins Report** (1963) most **primary school** teachers and some **secondary** teachers were educated and trained at **teacher training colleges.** The Robbins Report recommended that the colleges be called **colleges of education**. Today entry to the teaching profession is almost entirely restricted to graduates, and some assume that their degree should have provided them with appropriate educational knowledge leaving a separate task of professional training to be completed before they become qualified teachers. Those professionally concerned with teacher education generally object to this simplistic distinction and prefer to call all kinds of teacher preparation 'teacher education and training', but they lost a major battle when the **Council for the Accreditation of Teacher Education** (CATE) was replaced by the **Teacher Training Agency** (TTA) in 1994. The debate is more than a verbal quibble because those who prefer 'teacher training' also tend to advocate a training regime consisting of outcomes or standards that can be ticked off when **competence** is demonstrated (See also **competency-based teaching, qualified teacher status**).

Initial Teaching Alphabet (ITA)   An alphabet of 44 characters, each representing a sound in the English language, devised by Sir James Pitman. It claims to bypass some of the difficulties encountered by young children learning to read using the ordinary alphabet.

Inner London Education Authority (ILEA) The Inner London Education Authority was established in 1964 when the London County Council merged into the Greater London Council as a result of the London Government Act (1963). It was the largest **local education authority**, and was Labour controlled for most of its existence. It was abolished by the **Education Reform Act** (1988) and its responsibilities were shared among the 13 inner London boroughs, each of which became a new local education authority.

in-service education of teachers (INSET) For many years one of the complaints about the teaching service has been the lack of provision of **continuing education** and training for teachers. It was alleged that many teachers took no courses after their initial qualification to update their professional skills or to broaden their educational horizons. The **James Report** (1972) was particularly concerned with the provision of professional courses for teachers throughout their careers. INSET is generally taken to include short courses run by the **Department for Education and Skills** or the local authority; short courses or day conferences at **teachers' centres** and secondment to study for diploma and higher degrees in education either on a full-time or a part-time basis.

Kenneth Baker, when Secretary of State in the 1980s, introduced five non-contact days in every school year (in addition to the 190 teaching days), which were to be used for in-service training. Inevitably, they became known as 'Baker Days'. Research by the **National Foundation for Educational Research** in 2001 found that many of the INSET days were used for giving out information or dealing with administrative matters, and that teachers would prefer individualised professional development where they could update their own specialist knowledge.

inspection and inspectors (See **Her Majesty's Inspectorate**, **local education authority inspectors**, **Office for Standards in Education**)

Institute for Learning and Teaching (ILT) A professional body launched in 1998 to maintain and improve standards and practice in **higher education** in the UK. There are two categories of membership of the Institute: an academic with at least five years teaching experience or who has successfully completed an ILT accredited programme can become a Member. The Associate category is for the academic with at least one year's teaching experience and who has successfully completed an accredited programme. The Institute works closely with 24 subject centres of the Learning and Teaching Support Network. Many colleges offer accredited programmes, leading to such qualifications as the Postgraduate Certificate in Learning and Teaching in Higher Education and the Diploma in Professional Development.

Institute for Public Policy Research (IPPR)   A left-of-centre think tank, founded in 1988 by Lord Hollick with support from Neil Kinnock's office. It has produced a series of 'education and training' papers, including: Number 1, *A British Baccalauréat: Ending the Division Between Education and Training* (1990); and, Number 3, *Markets, Politics and Education*, by David Miliband (1991).

Institute of Economic Affairs (IEA)   A right-wing think tank, founded in 1955 by Sir Antony Fisher to promote free-market economics. Its education committee has been run by Stewart Sexton.

Institutes of Education   Set up following the recommendations of the **McNair Report** in 1944, the Institutes of Education consisted of a federation of teachers, colleges or institutions in a particular region, with the university playing a major part. The Institutes, many of which appointed new staff, were recognised **Area Training Organisations** (ATO). Amongst their tasks were: the validation and award of education qualifications, such as **Bachelor of Education** degrees and diplomas; recommending to the **Department of Education and Science** the granting of **qualified teacher status** (QTS); providing research facilities for higher degree students; and the mounting of in-service courses.

instruction   A term sometimes used to indicate the same kind of process as 'teaching', but generally in a more limited and less ambitious sense. Thus, in English educational terminology, instruction is to training as teaching is to education.

instructor   A term for those not holding recognised teacher qualifications. The majority of these teach commercial studies, though there are instructors in **technology** and other subjects in secondary schools.

instrument of government   The 1944 **Education Act** (Section 17) laid down that every primary school should have an instrument of management and every secondary school an instrument of government, which set out the constitution for bodies of **managers** and **governors**. The 1980 Education Act made a number of changes in nomenclature. The term 'managers' was abolished and now both primary and secondary schools have governors. Similarly, both types of schools now have instruments of government and articles of government.

instrumental enrichment (IE)   Instrumental enrichment has nothing to do with music education. It is a set of techniques, to help children improve their thinking ability. In the USA, materials have been developed by Curriculum Development Associates Inc. to stimulate problem-solving skills in the classroom. They were originally designed for educationally retarded children in order to accelerate their learning and to enable them to be integrated into normal classes; but they have since been found useful for all kinds of children – usually high school students aged between 12 and 14 years. The materials have been used experimentally in the UK.

instrumental learning Instrumental in this sense implies not for its own sake but to achieve some other goal. An example of instrumental learning might be for an individual to learn a foreign language not because he or she found any pleasure in that learning but because it might be useful for travelling abroad. Most educationists would prefer **expressive** learning, i.e. the kind of learning where no external reward or motivation is needed, but where the learning process is valuable and satisfying in its own right. There would be a connection, therefore, between instrumental learning and extrinsic motivation; expressive learning and intrinsic motivation. (See also **intrinsic/extrinsic**)

integrated day The conventional school timetable is replaced, under an integrated day system, by a more flexible approach that enables pupils to explore resources and to work at their own pace. This approach is found mainly in **primary schools**.

integrated studies During the 1950s and 1960s various attempts were made, especially in **secondary modern** schools and **comprehensive** schools, to break down the existing subject barriers by planning courses across a wider range. In the primary school there had been a longer tradition of approaching teaching by way of projects rather than through subjects. One such approach was described as the 'integrated day' which virtually abolished the formal timetable and emphasised **topics**, **projects** and interest-based learning. (See also **interdisciplinary studies**)

integration Integration can be perceived as a slogan description of various educational procedures, ranging from social functions where children with special needs and 'normal' children are brought together from time to time, to the complete assimilation of disabled pupils into an ordinary school. Integration is seen as one aspect of the moves to 'de-institutionalise' handicapped persons; it has an even closer affinity with the USA concept of 'mainstreaming' children with special educational needs into ordinary classes and schools. Integration thus attempts to shift the emphasis of special services from handicapping conditions and problems to children's learning needs. (See also **special educational needs**)

intelligence A term that is widely used but often with insufficient clarity. It has been defined as 'general mental ability' or 'the ability to see relationships' or even 'what **intelligence tests** measure'. During the last quarter of the twentieth century the usefulness of the concept of intelligence was increasingly questioned, and Howard Gardner, a Harvard psychologist, produced evidence to show that it would be more useful to talk of **multiple intelligence** rather than to concentrate on the limited range of abilities usually covered by the word intelligence and assessed by **intelligence tests**. (See also **intelligence quotient (IQ), normal curve, spatial ability, verbal reasoning**)

intelligence quotient (IQ)   A measure of an individual's performance on a standardised intelligence test. Since tests were originally developed mainly for children it was convenient to express a child's score in terms of mental age (MA) rather than chronological age (CA); the score can be converted into a percentage using the following formula:

$$IQ = \frac{MA}{CA} \times 100$$

Thus a child with an average score will have an IQ of 100; a child above average will score more than 100. Tests are usually **standardised** so that two-thirds of the normal population will score between 85 and 115. (See also **age, chronological and mental, Gaussian curve, meritocratic education, normal curve, under-achiever**)

intelligence tests   Intelligence tests were first constructed in France by Alfred Binet (1857–1911) to assess children's educability in schools. Binet's intention was more specific than many later psychologists; he was also much more optimistic about the chances of 'teaching **intelligence**'. An intelligence test is **standardised** and a score given as an **IQ** or **intelligence quotient**. Intelligence tests have sometimes been criticised because they appear to favour certain social groups such as whites in the USA and middle-class children in the UK. (See also **Gaussian curve, Koh's blocks, meritocratic education, nature–nurture controversy, reliability, spatial ability, under-achiever, validity, verbal reasoning**)

intercultural education   (See **multicultural education**)

interdisciplinary studies   Studies in which two or more disciplines are studied together focusing upon common topics: e.g. politics and science (perhaps looking at problems of conservation or pollution of the environment). The essential aspect of an interdisciplinary study is that the disciplines are studied in such a way as to produce planned interaction. It is quite different from a multi-disciplinary approach in which several disciplines are employed to examine the same topic from their own separate perspectives. (See also **integrated studies**)

internal assessment   An arrangement by which candidates' work is assessed by their own teacher under assessment and moderation arrangements specified by the awarding body.

internal degree   A degree for which the student follows the formal course of instruction at an institution of **higher education** and takes the prescribed **examinations**.

internal examiner   (See **examiner, internal**)

International Baccalaureate (IB)   An examination designed for students in their last two or three years at secondary school in the UK and in international schools abroad, and intended to qualify them for entry to undergraduate courses not confined to British universities. Six academic subjects are covered in the course: two languages, mathematics, an exact or experimental science, a human science and a subject of the student's choice. Three of these are examined at a higher level and three at subsidiary level. At present it is being offered in 47 schools in England and Wales, and in schools in other countries. Some schools are considering taking it as an alternative to **A Levels**. (See also **Baccalauréat, Technological Baccalaureate**)

International Institute for Educational Planning (IIEP)   Established by the **United Nations Educational, Scientific and Cultural Organisation** (UNESCO) in 1963, in Paris, to act as an international centre for advanced training and research in the field of educational planning. It co-operates with training and research organisations all over the world and publishes reports.

intrinsic/extrinsic   Some theories of human motivation make a distinction between **motivation** to perform well or to engage in an activity for its own sake (intrinsic motivation), and the kind of motivation that operates for the sake of some external reward (extrinsic motivation). Most educators prefer students to be stimulated by intrinsic motivation, but on the way to that long-term goal various kinds of extrinsic motivation (e.g. a desire to please the teacher or to get good marks) may be employed.

invigilator   An official who supervises students whilst they are answering examination papers.

ipsative assessment   A system by which a student's performance *now* is compared with his/her earlier achievement, not with other members of a class or group.

item   A question or problem designed to be part of an item bank. An item bank is a collection of test questions. New tests can be composed not by creating new items but by making a new selection from the item bank. Item analysis is the process of studying students' responses to each item in order to improve the test, and then removing items that are seen as too difficult or too easy.

item bank   (See **item**)

J

James Report   The Committee of Enquiry into Teacher Education and Training under the chairmanship of Lord James of Rusholme reported in 1972. The Report outlined a completely new system of teacher education. It envisaged three cycles:

First cycle   Students were to be given the choice of taking a degree at a college or university or a diploma in higher education; the latter course lasting two years and located within the further education system.

Second cycle   A one-year course of professional studies and training. Successful candidates would become licensed teachers for the second year, and would be monitored by a professional tutor. After the second year of this cycle, teachers would be awarded a Bachelor of Arts (BA) (Education) degree.

Third cycle   Paid in-service training, consisting of one term every seven years, was an essential aspect of the scheme.

There was opposition to the concept of consecutive rather than concurrent training, which was clearly spelt out in the scheme. Teachers questioned the status of the proposed new degree and the **Diploma in Higher Education**. The suggested administrative structure of teacher education was also criticised. (See also **induction**)

Joint Council for GCSE   When the **General Certificate of Education** (GCSE) was introduced, the **examination boards** responsible for the new arrangements were required to form themselves into a Joint Council in order to facilitate comparability of procedures and standards. Gradually, successive governments insisted on more and more central control of examinations, including GCSE, through such bodies as the **School Curriculum and Assessment Authority** (SCAA) and, later, by the **Quality and Curriculum Authority** (QCA). The Joint Council was accordingly abolished in 1998, but some of its functions were taken over by the Joint Forum of Awarding Bodies.

Joint Council for General Qualifications (JCGQ)   The JCGQ was established in January 1999. Its members are the three unitary awarding bodies (Assessment and Qualifications Alliance (AQA), Edexcel and Oxford, Cambridge and **Royal Society of Arts** (OCR)) together with the Northern Ireland **Council for Curriculum, Examinations and Assessment** (CCEA) and the **Welsh Joint Education Committee** (WJEC). The JCGQ discusses matters of common interest in terms of policies and procedures on the following qualifications: **entry level**; **General Certificate of Secondary Education** (GCSE); **General National Vocational Qualifications** (GNVQ); **Vocational Certificate of Education** (VCE); **General Certificate of Education** (GCE); **Key Skills**; and **Advanced Extension Awards**. (See also **examination boards**)

Joint Council of National Vocational Awarding Bodies (JCNVAB)
In February 1995, the three major awarding bodies for vocational qualifications – the **Business and Technology Education Council** (BTEC), the **City and Guilds Institute of London**, and the **Royal Society of Arts** (RSA) – launched a joint council to co-ordinate aspects of work on the **General National Vocational Qualifications** (GNVQ). In 1992, JCNVAB was merged with the Joint Council for GCSE, and became the Joint Forum of Awarding Bodies.

junior school   Traditionally, a school catering for pupils between the ages of 7 and 11. From the time of the **Hadow Report** on the Primary School (1931), a distinctive educational philosophy based on enlightened approaches was advocated. The **Plowden Report**, *Children and their Primary Schools* (1967), for the most part adapted a similar stance. Many junior schools have now combined with **infant schools** under one headteacher. Where **middle schools** exist, the former junior school age range spans both the **first school** and the middle school itself.

junior technical school   From 1913, the Regulations of the Board of Education recognised a new type of day technical school, the junior technical. These schools prepared boys for trades within industry, such as engineering and building.

Keohane Report   A study group under Professor Kevin Keohane was set up by the Secretary of State for Education in April 1978 to consider the **Schools Council**'s proposals for a Certificate of Extended Education and to consider possible developments in the provision of relevant courses and examinations in schools and further education. In its Report, *Proposals for a Certificate of Extended Education* (1979), it recommended the development of non-compulsory vocationally oriented syllabuses and compulsory tests of efficiency in English and mathematics, with pupils able to select other aspects of their studies as appropriate. The proposal was rejected by the then **Department of Education and Science**.

key skills   Some examples of **curriculum** planning divide learning into **knowledge**, understanding and **skills**. This is an over-simplification, but may be found useful for some planning purposes. Another over-simplification is that skills are associated with **training** rather than education: the development of skills is an essential aspect of many kinds of educational learning such as reading. **Core skills** have been identified for several purposes in training and education: e.g., in 1989 an attempt was made to list core skills common to both academic **A Level** courses and to the vocationally oriented **General National Vocational Qualifications** (GNVQs). These core skills were listed under three headings: communication, application of number and information technology. They were later renamed key skills. The term 'key skills' is also used in other contexts, as in writing an essay or riding a bicycle, usually in an attempt to specify some crucial teaching and learning areas. Some key skills involve knowledge and understanding.

Key Stage (KS)   The national curriculum **Programmes of Study** (PoS) that pupils are required to follow are sub-divided into four Key Stages: KS1 (5–7); KS2 (8–11); KS3 (11–14); KS4 (14–16).

kindergarten   A system of education for infants based on the ideas of Froebel. Play is regarded as a natural means for children to learn, and games are used to develop body, mind and spirit. It has sometimes been pointed out that the 'kindergarten' (children's garden) metaphor is misleading, especially if applied to older children. Whereas plants may grow naturally in a garden, the processes of children's cognitive, social and moral development are much more complex than automatic 'growth'.

Kingman Report   The *Report of the Committee of Inquiry into the Teaching of English Language* (chaired by Sir John Kingman) was published in

March 1988. It provided useful background to discussions of the **English curriculum**. The Report was criticised by some right-wing politicians for failing to recommend that teachers of English should concentrate on formal grammar. (See also **Cox Report** and **Language in the National Curriculum (LINC)**)

knowledge   Knowledge is often contrasted with **skills**, and with **attitudes** and values, but this is sometimes unhelpful because knowledge overlaps with both those categories. Another distinction is between 'knowing how' and 'knowing that', the former being more closely connected with skills. A related issue is how human beings acquire knowledge. This was Piaget's major interest and formed the basis of his work on stages of development. The conventional pre-Enlightenment view of knowledge was that all knowledge was created by God and only discovered by human beings through the use of their reason. Traces of that view survive in some popular attitudes to education which tend to regard knowledge as a commodity to be collected by a pupil. Post-Reformation science encouraged a move away from a unified view of knowledge to a sub-division of knowledge into science, theology, law, and so on.

In the twentieth century the educational argument about knowledge frequently centred on the relation between the structure of knowledge and the content of the curriculum, particularly the subjects. In the USA, Phenix conducted influential work on 'realms of meaning'; in the UK, Hirst's 'seven forms of knowledge' approach was much discussed. The sociology of knowledge is concerned with the idea that the perception of reality is filtered through cultural constraints which differ from one society to another; and also that within any society an individual's view of knowledge and reality is related to his/her own social position. These ideas have generated a good deal of productive criticism, but they can also lead to an extreme form of relativism – the idea that one view of reality is as good as any other. In education, particularly in studies of the curriculum, the danger exists of moving from the recognition of class-based tastes and prejudices to statements that the whole of school knowledge is merely 'bourgeois'. Some Marxist writers such as Gramsci, however, saw that the future of education had to be concerned with making available to everyone those kinds of essential knowledge which had been part of elite education in the past. (See also **academic**, **culture**, **disciplines**, **encyclopaedism**, **essentialism**)

Knowledge about Language (KAL)   A term that has developed in the context of **national curriculum** English. The **Kingman Report** and **Cox Report**, as well as the **Language in the National Curriculum** project, recommended that pupils should study the structure of the English language, but not in the shape of exercises in formal grammar. Since 1997, knowledge about language has been incorporated into the **National Literacy Strategy** and the **literacy hour**.

Koh's blocks   A non-verbal **intelligence test** in which an individual has to construct from a number of coloured blocks certain patterns presented to him/her from a booklet.

L

labelling   A term much used in the sociology of education to indicate the tendency to classify an individual as a member of a category, and then treat him/her as a type rather than a person. The stereotypes that are particularly mentioned in this respect are 'slow learning child', 'culturally deprived child' or 'linguistically deprived child', and 'delinquent'. The obvious danger of teachers treating children in this way is that of **self-fulfilling prophecy**. (See also **mixed ability grouping**, **setting**, **streaming**, **Pygmalion effect**)

ladder of opportunity   A term associated with the meritocratic view of schooling and with selection in education. Use of the metaphor 'ladder of opportunity' assumes the existence of different levels of school so that an individual child can climb from one level (e.g. the pre-1944 **elementary school**) to a higher level (the **grammar school**). This view of education is objected to by many educationists since it appears to regard the majority level as inferior. Thus, in the early twentieth century, many Labour Party educationists as well as those in the Trades Union Congress proposed instead the 'broad highway' approach to education for all. (See also **Bryce Report**, **eleven plus examination**, **Secondary Education For All**)

laissez-faire   (1) The policy of non-interference by government in the activities of business and industry. It was particularly important in the history of elementary education in the UK, since advocates of *laissez-faire* did not believe that the State should provide, or interfere in, education. Although the doctrine of *laissez-faire* in education was apparently overcome by the middle of the nineteenth century, the attitude still survives, particularly in England where many parents who can afford to do so choose to send their children to fee-paying schools. Many politicians on the right believe this to be a much healthier attitude to education than State provision. (2) The teaching style that allowed pupils to work according to their own interests, with a minimum of direction and control.

language across the curriculum In 1975 the **Bullock Report** recommended that every teacher should be a teacher of English, all sharing responsibility for 'language across the curriculum'. Schools were recommended to develop systematic policies along these lines. In 1997, the new Labour Government advocated a more systematic and focused teaching of language, developing the **National Literacy Strategy** and the **literacy hour** in primary schools.

language colleges The 1988 Education Reform Act introduced a new category of school, **city technology colleges** (CTCs). The definition of such schools was later widened to include specialist schools in the arts, and in 1995 it was extended to provide for language colleges. (See also **specialist school**)

language deficit The theory that some children under-achieve at school because their language skills are inadequate. This theory is related to a view of society that suggests that certain kinds of homes – e.g. working-class and those of some ethnic minorities – do not equip children with adequate language skills to cope with the curriculum and other demands of the classroom. (See also **Bullock Report**, **compensatory education**, **disadvantaged**)

Language in the National Curriculum (LINC) A £21 million Education Support Grant Project (1989–92) intended to improve the teaching of **national curriculum** English, following on from some of the ideas in the **Kingman Report** and **Cox Report**. Successive Education Ministers refused to publish the report but eventually acquiesced to the proposal that some materials could be handled by commercial publishers. The result is available as: R. Bain, *et al* (eds), *Looking into Language* (Hodder and Stoughton, 1992); T. Wright, *Investigating English* (Edward Arnold, 1994); R. Cater (ed.), *Knowledge About Language and the National Curriculum: the LINC Reader* (Hodder and Stoughton, 1990).

language laboratory A specifically designed room equipped with electronic equipment for the teaching of languages. The laboratory consists of booths for the students and a console (a large control desk) for the instructor who communicates through a microphone with one or more students at a time. In more sophisticated installations tape-recorders (previously, record players) carrying programmes enable individuals to proceed at their own pace. Language laboratories became popular in the 1960s; but though common enough in higher education, they have almost disappeared from maintained secondary schools. (See also **direct method**)

language schools   Schools mostly aimed at overseas students who wish to learn English as a second language. A number of examinations that test efficiency at the end of the course are available. Many schools, which are privately owned, seek accreditation by becoming accepted as a members of the Association of Recognised English Language Schools (ARELS). (See also **English as a foreign language**)

late developer   Children develop physically, emotionally and intellectually at different rates. Late developers are those who realise their potential in some or all aspects of school work after the majority of their contemporaries. (See also **intelligence**, **intelligence test**)

lateral thinking   A technique of looking at a problem from many different points of view instead of following the one that is most obvious. In some respects, lateral thinking is related to **divergent** thinking. Lateral thinking is particularly associated with the work of Edward de Bono.

Launch Pad schools   An initiative announced in January 2002 by Estelle Morris, the **Secretary of State for Education**, by which 30 schools, both primary and secondary, are identified in order to carry out investigations into ways of reducing teachers' work loads. A sum of £5 million was to be provided for the purpose.

law of education   The law of education is enshrined in **Education Acts** such as that of 1944, which stated that education was to be organised in three successive phases: primary, secondary and further. Statutory law is complemented by common law; e.g. the teacher is said to be in *loco parentis* and is accountable to the Courts if there is a failure to fulfil this responsibility. Recent sweeping changes in education have been brought about by legislation. For instance, the Education Reform Act (1988) introduced the **national curriculum** into schools; the **Children Act** (1989) established a comprehensive legal framework for the care and upbringing of children which has extensive implications for education; the **Further and Higher Education Act** (1992) abolished the **binary system** and established a single framework for higher education; and the Education (Schools) Act (1992) provided for a new system of inspection which greatly reduced the role of **Her Majesty's Inspectorate** in this work. The 1994 Education Act, which set up the **Teacher Training Agency** (TTA), led to changes in the relation between the training institutions and the schools. The 1998 Schools Standards and Framework Act created new categories of schools and, in the same year, the Teaching and Higher Education Act led to the setting up of the **General Teaching Council**. (See also **Education Acts**, **Local Government Acts**)

lead body   (See **Industry Lead Body**)

Leadership Programme for Serving Headteachers (LPSH)   (See **headship training**)

league tables   *The Parent's Charter* issued by the Government in 1991 stipulated that parents should in future receive an annual written report which gives information about their children's performance in examinations and **national curriculum** tests. In addition, the report includes a comparison with those of children of the same age. The Department for Education and Skills publishes performance or league tables of examination results, national curriculum tests, **truancy** rates of pupils' destinations and other **performance indicators** of all schools. From 1997, primary schools have been included in league tables.

It is claimed that raw data of this kind needs careful interpretation; e.g. the school's intake and social background are important determining factors. For this reason, **value added** information is being introduced which will take into account the effect on a school's performance of such factors as class size, funding levels, and whether it is single- or mixed-sex. Another possible outcome of publishing league tables is that schools may concentrate on producing good examination results at the expense of a balanced education, and may also adopt undesirable selection policies. England is the only country in the UK that issues league tables.

learndirect   (See **University for Industry**)

learned journal   A publication in an academic discipline or field of study normally consisting of a collection of articles, written by authoritative figures. In education, all the foundation disciplines have such journals: e.g. *British Journal of Educational Psychology; Journal of Philosophy of Education.* Frequency of publication may vary from journal to journal.

learning   A permanent or lasting change in knowledge, skill or attitude that is the result of experience rather than maturation. (See also **active learning, computer assisted learning, conditioning, distance learning, individual learning, instrumental enrichment, learning theory, over-learning, passive learning, precision learning, programmed learning, rote learning.**)

Learning and Skills Council (LSC)   Established by the Learning and Skills Act (2000), which set out to modernise post 16 education and teaching. The Council came into being in April 2001 with a number of responsibilities, the main one being to plan and fund education and training throughout England. Forty-seven local LSCs, headed by a chairman and executive directors, replaced the **Further Education Funding Council** and **Training**

and Enterprise Councils. Their size differs according to population in the area. They operate within **local education authority** boundaries, thus making possible links with schools. The Councils consist of employers, local government representatives, trade unionists and people involved in the area who have recent and substantial business experience. The £6 billion grant received by the LSCs is allocated to four aspects of its work: the education and training of young people; raising skill levels for adults; local initiatives; and improving standards and administration. It will also aim at improving adult basic literacy and numeracy skills. It is envisaged that there will be some six million learners in this scheme. By 2010, young people and adults in England are expected to have the knowledge and productive skills to match the best in the world. (See also **Adult Learning Inspectorate, Centres of Vocational Excellence, Further Education Funding Council, Further Education National Training Organisation**)

Learning and Skills Development Agency (LSDA)   This Agency, formerly known as the **Further Education Development Agency** (FEDA), is a national body concerned with providing resources and research for improving the practice of post-school education and training. The Agency gives curriculum support and advice to schools, colleges and training organisations, and organises national programmes for vocational learning. It also mounts courses in basic skills and adult education in co-operation with the **National Institute of Adult Continuing Education** (NIACE).

Learning and Teaching Scotland   This was formed as the result of a merger in July 2000 between the Scottish Consultative Council on the Curriculum (CCC) and the Scottish Council for Educational Technology (CET). It seeks to improve the quality of learning in schools by providing advice and support to teachers and to encourage the use of **information and communications technology** in education and lifelong learning.

learning difficulty   Where a child has significantly greater difficulty in learning than most pupils of his/her age or where there are disabilities that prevent using the normal education facilities which are available. (See also **special educational needs**)

learning mentors   Under the **Excellence in Cities** scheme, every pupil in a designated area receives personal help in overcoming learning problems. Since September 1999, **secondary schools** have had professionally trained learning mentors and they will also liaise with local **primary schools** in order to identify pupils with special needs who will shortly enter secondary schools. Learning mentors assess the progress of every child at the end of their first year in secondary school and when he/she enters **Key Stage** 4.

From 2001 the **Department for Education and Skills** (DfES), with a national mentoring network, has paid close attention to quality and disseminating good practice through a funded pilot scheme. (See also **mentor**)

Learning Support Service   A system operated by many **local education authorities** that provides a central team of special needs teachers to help and advise schools on children with **learning difficulties**.

Learning Support Unit (LSU)   These units, which enable schools to deal with disruptive pupils, have been established in **Excellence in Cities** areas. In 2001 there were more than 450 LSUs. This total included 59 pilot primary LSUs that allow schools to deal with pupils without excluding them. The scheme reports many successes. The Green Paper *Schools: Achieving Success* (2001), envisaged that by 2002 the number will have grown to over 1,000 and every excluded full-time pupil will be receiving full-time education.

learning theory   Different schools of psychology explain learning in different ways: e.g. behaviourist psychology and Gestalt psychology propose different learning theories.

lecture   Presentation of a topic in oral form by a lecturer to students, who may take notes. It may be accompanied by visual aids and followed up with a **seminar**. The original meaning of 'lecture' was a reading of a text: before the invention of printing this was a useful practice. Some lecturers still read texts to students. (See also **tutorial**)

lecturer   (1) A post associated with **higher education** institutions. Above this position is senior and principal lecturer and **reader**. (2) A person who delivers a lecture.

left-handedness   In a predominantly right-handed environment, teachers tend to be less aware of the problems of left-handed children. Awkwardness in writing postures and in practical work are examples. To counter this, some schools successfully run clubs to give left-handed pupils a positive image and to act as a support group.

Leicestershire Plan   A two-tier system of schooling devised by Stewart Mason in 1959, then Direction of Education for Leicestershire, for the county (excepting the city of Leicester). Pupils between the ages of 10 and 14 attended **high schools**, formerly known as **secondary moderns**, and then transferred to **upper schools** (all but one of which had been created from former **grammar schools**), which catered for 14–18-year-olds. The Plan came into operation in 1969.

lesson (1) A period of time, usually between 35 and 50 minutes, into which the timetable is divided for teaching purposes. Traditionally, at secondary school level, some subjects are allocated double periods or more of lesson time: e.g. home economics and technology. (2) The smallest unit of **curriculum** planning, i.e. single planned learning episode which would normally form part of a sequential scheme of work. (See also **syllabus**, **timetabling**)

level description/descriptor After the **Dearing Review**, detailed **statements of attainment** for each **level of attainment** were abolished and replaced by a single description for each level indicating what pupils must know, understand, and be able to do.

levels Increasingly the word 'level' is used to refer to the **standard** of achievement within a pre-specified **curriculum** and assessment system. For example:

1. reaching one of the eight levels within an **Attainment Target** in the **national curriculum**.

2. **National Vocational Qualifications** (NVQs) are awarded at five levels.

3. The **Dearing Report** on Higher Education specified levels of achievement within higher education ranging from Certificate to Doctorate.

(See also **Quality Assurance Agency for Higher Education**)

levels of attainment In the **national curriculum** pupils are measured on an eight-point scale from the age of 5 to 14. It is assumed that they will progress through the eight levels at different rates: an average child should reach level 2 at age 7, level 4 by age 11, and level 5 or 6 by age 14. (See also **national curriculum**, **level descriptions**)

Lewis Report Set up during the First World War, the Departmental Committee on Juvenile Education in Relation to Employment after the War reported in 1917. It particularly concerned itself with young persons who required special training and those who could not find relevant work. The chairman was J. Herbert Lewis, MP. The report's main recommendations were that the **school leaving age** should be raised to 14 and that **day continuation schools** should be widely available. Although the first recommendation was adopted and was written into the 1918 Education Act, the second was only briefly and partially implemented.

liberal education The meaning of 'liberal' in this connection is associated with freedom. Liberal education is that kind of education that broadens and therefore frees the mind from narrow prejudices and preconceptions. Liberal education avoids premature specialisation. In England, sixth-form studies have attempted to be both specialised and 'liberal' by the strategy of general studies. Liberal education is frequently contrasted with **vocational** training by association with a nineteenth-century upper-class view of the correct form of education for Christian gentlemen: in the nineteenth century, the upper classes were regarded as needing liberal education whereas vocational training was more appropriate for the lower classes. (See also **general education**, **liberal studies**)

liberal studies   The curriculum followed by many students in **further education** is narrow and vocational. It was frequently thought that such students needed a liberalising element in their programme, and the teaching of liberal studies became a compulsory part of many further education programmes. 'Liberal studies' is derived from the medieval idea of liberal arts which consisted of the trivium (grammar, logic and rhetoric) and the quadrivium (arithmetic, geometry, music and astronomy). Modern liberal studies is, however, much more likely to be concerned with literature, social studies and, possibly, appreciation of film and television. (See also **liberal education**)

Library Association   The Association was founded in 1876 and received a Royal Charter in 1898. It is concerned with the professional education and raising the standards and working conditions of its members. The Association actively promotes the improvement of library services. The importance of the links between schools and the library service have long been recognised by the Association and Heads of Library and Information Services within schools. Chartered librarians have expertise in matters relating to information and information handling, learning resources and the library process. (See also **School Library Association**)

licensed teacher   The Licensed Teacher Scheme was introduced in 1991, together with the **articled teachers** scheme, to offer an alternative to the two established routes: the **Bachelor of Education** (BEd) and the **Postgraduate Certificate of Education** (PGCE). The Scheme was available to suitably qualified applicants, over the age of 24, including teachers with overseas qualifications not fully recognised by the then **Department of Education and Science**. The school in which a licensed teacher was employed was responsible, in consultation with the **local education authority**, for prescribing a course of study to complement the teaching experience being gained at the school; the school and local authority were also responsible for deciding whether the licensed teacher had satisfactorily completed such a course of study, in an institute of higher education or elsewhere. If the licensed teacher's performance was in all respects satisfactory, he or she became a qualified teacher after one year or whatever longer period might have been specified. The **Open University** was involved in preparing study materials for licensed (and articled) teachers. The scheme has now been discontinued and superseded by the **Graduate and Registered Teacher Programme** (GRTP). (See also **initial teacher training**)

lifelong learning   Many educationists have stressed the need for education to be differentiated from schooling: much learning takes place outside school and before and after compulsory schooling. Various terms have been used in this context such as **continuing education, recurrent education** and **permanent education**. Most writers also emphasise the need to see education as an integral part of life rather than something cut off from the real world.

limited grade examination   An examination, or a section of an examination, for which the range of grades or marks that may be awarded, is restricted. This may be achieved by insisting that candidates enter for a paper which only gives scores for the lower range, or – at the other extreme – confines scoring possibilities to the highest grades. For example, in some **GCSE** subjects candidates enter for one of three papers: the easiest paper would give access to grades E–G; the 'middle' paper to grades C–F; the difficult paper, A–D. An objection to this procedure is that if a candidate is entered for the difficult paper but fails to reach grade D, then no lower grade is possible.

limited-range syllabus   A syllabus where the entire range of content or skills is not covered. In the case of the **national curriculum** it would refer to a **GCSE** test where the range of possible awards covers only some of the grades. (See also **tiering**)

link course   A course run co-operatively by two or more institutions. Some courses, mainly vocational in character, for the 16–19 age group are run jointly by **secondary schools** and by local colleges of **further education**.

literacy   The ability to read and write at a conventionally accepted level. There is no universal standard of literacy, but within any given society it is possible to define **functional literacy** and then to arrive at figures for the number of illiterates in that particular society. Since 1997, the Labour Government has focused attention on literacy and **numeracy** in primary schools, and has developed policies for a **National Literacy Strategy** and a **literacy hour**. (See also **oracy**)

literacy hour   The literacy hour was introduced in 1999 as part of the **National Literacy Strategy**. It was an attempt to raise standards of reading and writing at **Key Stages** 1 and 2 in **primary schools** (later extended to **Key**

Stage 3 in secondary schools). The literacy hour specified techniques of teaching **phonics, spelling** and **grammar**. National materials were produced centrally to assist teachers, and schools were encouraged to associate the literacy hour with teaching and learning **targets** and **national curriculum tests**. An important aspect of this initiative was the involvement of parents.

loans, student   By the Education (Student Loans) Act (1990), a top-up loans scheme for full-time home students, except postgraduates in higher education, was introduced. The objective was to find a cost-effective scheme which would be reasonably economical to administer. Students were offered loans at a 'real interest rate of zero'. Students ceased to be eligible for social security benefits. Opponents of the scheme claimed that it deterred working-class youngsters from going on to **higher education**. Nevertheless, the scheme continued but some modifications were made by the Education (Student Loans) Act (1996). The Labour Government in 1999 extended student loans to include low-income, part-time students from the year 2000.

local education authority (LEA)   Local education authorities came into existence with the 1902 **Education Act**, replacing the **school boards**. Unlike the latter, the new education authorities were also responsible for **voluntary schools**; the county and borough councils were also given responsibility for secondary and technical education. One important feature of the system was that each local education authority had to appoint an education committee (Section 101, Local Government Act (1972)), consisting of elected councillors and co-opted members. The political party gaining a majority at a local election elects from its members a chairman of this committee.

Traditionally, education accounted for a large part of a local authority's budget. The situation changed with the introduction of education support grants in 1984, when grants were earmarked for specific education policies, and with the Interim Advisory Committee in 1987, which gave Secretaries of State for Education control over teachers' pay and conditions of service. There were also changes in methods of raising local authority finances, particularly rate capping. The Education Reform Act (1988), which introduced **local management of schools** and **grant maintained schools** further undermined the role of local education authorities. This has continued with the loss of **polytechnics** from local authority control and the independence granted to **further education**, tertiary and **sixth form colleges** under the **Further and Higher Education Act** (1992). Government education initiatives have additionally limited their role. However, the Green Paper, *Modernising Local Government Finance* (2000), recommended that LEAs were to retain responsibility for budget allocation, though a close watch should be kept on their spending priorities. In 2001 the DfEE published a policy paper called

The Role of the Local Education Authorities in Education, confirming their important role in supporting schools to raise standards. It proposed to delegate 90 per cent of funding to schools in place of the existing 85 per cent. This paper identified areas where schools alone should not attempt to provide services such as planning, the supply of school places in an area, the co-ordination of special education needs services, and home-to-school transport. LEAs also have an important role to play in implementing national initiatives such as post-16 adult learning and the **Connexions** Service for 13–19-year-olds. (See also **local education authority inspectors, Local Government Acts**)

local education authority inspectors   Employed by **local education authorities** to ensure that standards are being maintained. Until recently, the term 'adviser' was commonly used, but the change of name to 'inspector' indicates an important change in their functions. Under the **local management of schools**, their role has been further modified. In some authorities, the entire advisory budget has been given to schools, which will be able to buy in advice either locally or elsewhere. The Education (Schools) Act (1992) set up a system of four-year inspections which obliged governing bodies to consider two tenders for each inspection. Although 5,000 lay inspectors have been appointed under the Act, local authority inspectors still have the task of monitoring the implementation of the **national curriculum** but have lost the right to inspect. Governing bodies receive £70 million from funds formerly allocated to local education authorities. Under Section 14 of the Education (Schools) Act, local education authority inspectors are able to tender for inspection of **grant maintained** and **independent schools**, as well as schools in neighbouring authorities. (See also **Her Majesty's Inspectorate, Local Government Acts, Office for Standards in Education**)

Local Government Acts   Local government legislation from the last quarter of the nineteenth century has had a direct effect on the development of the education service in England. The 1888 Local Government Act set up county and borough councils and provided the administrative unit for education – entitled the **local education authority** – under the 1902 Education Act. Local education authorities then received greater powers under the 1944 Act. The system of percentage grants was swept away by the 1958 Local Government Act, to be replaced by a rate support grant.

There was a shake-up of local educational administration following the 1963 Government Act, which abolished the London and Middlesex County Councils; these were replaced by the Greater London Council, with education powers exercised by an **Inner London Education Authority** (ILEA) and 20 separate outer London boroughs. The 1972 Local Government Act, which came into effect on 1 April 1974, dealt with the remainder of the country, and reduced the number of local education authorities. Larger conurbations were divided into metropolitan districts and some county authorities disappeared, leaving shire counties responsible for education.

Traditionally, the cost of education has been shared between central and local government. Since the 1980s there has been a significant shift towards governmental control of local government finance. The Local Government Finance Act (1988) replaced domestic rates by the Community Charge, widely known as the Poll Tax; and another Act of 1992 again changed the system with the introduction of the Council Tax. The Local Government (Access to Information) Act (1985) gave the public the right to inspect the agendas, reports and minutes of council meetings and sub-committees. Four years later the Local Government and Housing Act (1989) removed the voting rights of non-elected education committee members including teachers' representatives. Compulsory competitive tendering for local authority services was introduced by the Local Government Act of 1988: this applied to aspects of education such as catering and the maintenance of school playing fields. The scope of competitive tendering was widened by the 1992 Local Government Act to include legal services, information technology and pay rolls. The Act also included provision for the **Audit Commission** to devise **performance indicators** for local government services, including education. (See also **law of education**, **revenue support grant**, **standard spending assessment**)

Local Government Association (LGA)   This Association, established in 1997, is a national organisation representing almost 500 local authorities. It encompasses three former local authority associations, the **Association of County Councils**, the Association of District Councils and the **Association of Metropolitan Authorities**. One of its tasks is to represent the **local education authorities** of England and Wales in all matters of concern. Amongst its recent initiatives are joint bids with private companies to help run education services in failing local authorities, and the establishment of a commission to investigate the structure of the school year. Although Wales is represented on the LGA there is also the Welsh Local Government Association (WLGA). London members also have the Association of London Government which deals with London matters.

local management of schools (LMS)   In 1987, when the Conservative Government was preparing what was to become the Education Reform Act (1988), it commissioned the management consultants, Coopers and Lybrand Deloitte, to produce a study of the implication of the financial delegation aspects of the Bill. The Report stated, 'The changes require a new culture and philosophy of the organisation of education at the school level. They are more than just financial; they need a general shift in management: we use the term *local management of schools (LMS).*'

One of the intentions of the Bill was to encourage competitiveness among schools and to stimulate parents to have a greater say, through an elected governing body, in their children's education.

Lockwood Report   (See **Schools Council**)

London Allowance   An extra annual sum of money awarded to teachers working in and around London to compensate for the high cost of living. The amount awarded depends on location. London is divided for this purpose into three zones. Teachers working in Inner London and six outer London Boroughs receive the most, followed by the rest of London and the fringe. (See also **teachers' salaries**)

London Chamber of Commerce and Industry (LCCI)   The LCCI was founded over a century ago with the aim of providing a unified representational voice for business that would enable commercial interests to influence government policy. The Chamber's role has expanded in recent years and it now offers its members practical assistance in the form of business services and information facilities. The LCCI Examination Board is one of the oldest and largest examining bodies in the field of business. It prepares for a broad range of business careers both in the UK and abroad. Examinations are offered at Certificate and Diploma levels in a wide range of managerial, secretarial and technological subjects. (See also **business education**)

London County Council (LCC)   The 1888 Local Government Act enabled the newly created county councils to be directly elected. London was dealt with in a different way from others, becoming an administrative county consisting of those parts of the Metropolis that were in Middlesex, Kent and Surrey. The LCC's education functions were limited, with the School Board for London (established 1870) continuing to carry out this work. The 1902 Education Act did not apply to London, but a London Education Act two years later transferred the whole range of education services to the LCC. The London Government Act 1963 resulted in the replacement of the LCC by the Greater London Council (GLC) from 1964, with an **Inner London Education Authority** (ILEA) responsible for the education service.

longitudinal study   A study over a period of time that is concerned with following through changes in an individual or a group of individuals, with reference, for example, to health and educational achievement. (See also **National Children's Bureau**)

Lord President of the Council　After the establishment of the **Committee of the Privy Council on Education** in 1839, the Lord President was a key member. He represented the Council, and later the **Education Department**, in the Lords. The educational aspects of the Lord President's work was transferred in 1900 to the **President of the Board of Education**.

lower school　Formerly a term used to refer to the first two or three forms of a **public** or **grammar school**, but now more commonly to **comprehensive schools** where, for organisational purposes, there is a lower, followed by a middle and an upper school.

M

Macfarlane Report　A Committee chaired by Neil Macfarlane, then Under-Secretary at the then **Department of Education and Science**, was set up in 1979, to examine the educational provision for the 16–19-year age group. Its Report, issued in January 1981, was a disappointment. No national policy was put forward though local authorities were urged to review their provision for this age group. It acknowledged the educational and other advantages of a break in schooling at 16 years of age in favour of **tertiary** or **sixth form colleges**; for financial and demographic reasons, however, such a course was not recommended.

magnet schools　From their election in 1979, Conservative politicians looked for alternatives to the alleged uniformity of comprehensive secondary schools. **City technology colleges** (CTCs) and **grant maintained schools** emerged from this search; but when Kenneth Baker, then Secretary of State, visited the USA in 1987 he was impressed by some of the magnet schools he saw.

The idea behind magnet schools is that they should specialise in some way: one well-known New York magnet school specialises, e.g. in the performing arts; others are concerned with science or technology. In addition to catering for special interests, magnet schools also provide a broad curriculum. Some magnet schools in New York and Washington are very popular, but their critics complain that they succeed by attracting the most motivated parents in a district, thus making the problems for other schools more severe. There have been some attempts to evaluate magnet schools in the USA, but without conclusive results.

maintained school   The correct term for what are generally known as 'State' schools – i.e., schools that are maintained from public funds.

maintenance grant   A sum of money awarded to students to meet day-to-day living and accommodation costs, as distinct from fees, for college courses. Many **local education authorities** have **discretionary** schemes for educational maintenance allowances to enable children to stay on at school or college after age 16. (See also **discretionary award**, **Education Welfare Service**, **entrance award**, **mandatory award**)

Man – A Course of Study (MACOS)   A **curriculum development project** based on the work of Jerome Bruner and developed by Peter Dow. The project included film and course materials for which teachers needed a course of training. It has been used to a limited extent in the UK as a social studies teaching kit. In some parts of Australia and the USA it was thought highly controversial and was sometimes banned.

manager   Historically associated with nineteenth-century **voluntary elementary** education, school managers were responsible for the control and supervision of school personnel and organisation as well as raising funds. After the 1870 Education Act, school boards appointed managers to their schools. The 1902 Act took away many powers from voluntary school managers: at the same time all county council schools were in future to have managers, though this was left optional for borough councils. It was not until the 1944 Education Act that it was made a requirement for all primary schools to have managers, whose powers and terms of office were stated in an instrument of management. Since the 1980 Education Act came into force, the use of the term 'manager' has disappeared, with all schools now having **governors**. (See also **instrument of government**)

mandatory award   Local education authorities have a duty under law to make grants to full-time students taking advanced courses if they are eligible under national regulations. For example, first degree courses and those for initial teacher training fall into this category. The award, covering fees and maintenance during term time, is means tested. (See also **discretionary award**, **entrance award**, **maintenance grant**)

Manpower Services Commission (MSC)   A national training agency set up in 1974 to co-ordinate the work of statutory training boards and to take over and expand the Government's own vocational training schemes. Later these included the **Training Opportunities Scheme** (TOPS), the **Youth Training Scheme** (YTS), the **Community Programme**, and the **Technical and Vocational Education Initiative** (TVEI). In 1988, the MSC became the Training Agency, which was superseded by **Training and**

Enterprise Councils (TECs) and the Training Enterprise and Education Department (TEED).

mark scheme   A specification detailing how credit is to be awarded in relation to an examination component. A mark scheme normally characterises acceptable responses to tasks and identifies the amount of credit each attracts.

mastery learning   A theory put forward originally by Benjamin Bloom and some of his colleagues that mastery of any kind of knowledge is theoretically possible for any learner given sufficient time and appropriate teaching. Part of the theory is that pupils differ not only in their pace of learning, but also in learning styles. Mastery learning is closely associated with **individualised learning**.

matching   A type of item in an **objective test** where the student has to choose from a set of pictures the one that matches a corresponding word (or vice versa).

matriculation   Candidates who achieved credit grades in five subjects including one at least from each of three groups – humanities, foreign languages, mathematics and science – at the **School Certificate** examination were given matriculation exemption by the majority of universities. The University of London, as early as 1858, offered a matriculation examination that could be taken by external candidates wishing to go on to **higher education**. The term originated with the ceremony of signing the role (matricula) on being admitted to a university. From 1951, matriculation came to depend on the passing of two **A Levels**.

Matriculation Diploma (MD)   The Matriculation Diploma was proposed as a new award in the Green Paper, *14–19: Extending Opportunities, Raising Standards* (2002). It was intended to be an overarching award to stimulate greater breadth and coherence for all learners aged 14–19. The MD would make use of existing qualifications such as the **General Certificate of Secondary Education** (GCSE), **National Vocational Qualifications** (NVQs), **A Levels**, and vocational awards, together with a recognition of wider interests including active citizenship and work-related learning. It was proposed in preference to other awards such as the **International Baccalaureate**. (See also **General Education Diploma**)

maturation   The physical, mental or moral changes that occur as part of an individual's 'natural' development: maturation is by definition the result of innate factors, not environmental ones. The work of Piaget is much concerned with the development, and thus the maturation of, certain innate abilities. (See also **Piagetian**)

mature students   Universities and colleges differ in the age they regard students as 'mature'; 25 used to be the norm but some now accept a lower age of 21 or 23. Mature students are often exempt from normal **entry requirements**. (See also **entry qualification, Open Tech, Open University, university entrance requirements**)

McNair Report   In 1942, a committee chaired by Sir Arnold McNair was appointed by the **Board of Education** to consider the supply, recruitment and training of teachers and youth leaders. Its Report was published in 1944.

Mechanics' Institutes   In 1799 Dr George Birkbeck began a series of evening lectures for workmen, at the Andersonian Institution in Glasgow, on natural and experimental philosophy. From this sprang his idea of a course of scientific instruction and in 1823 his *Proposals for a London Mechanics Institute* was published. The movement spread rapidly and by 1850 there were over 600 institutes. (See also **technical education**)

memory   An individual's inner record of his past mental and sensory experience. Memory may be made evident by the individual's ability to recall or recognise. Memory span is the technical term indicating the amount of information a person can remember either immediately after, or within a specified time, of having data presented. Some **intelligence tests** involve, e.g. the memorisation of unrelated digits. Certain psychologists have claimed that the ability to memorise a long series of unrelated digits is a good indication of general intelligence.

mental age   (See **age: chronological and mental**)

mentor   A trusted adviser – in education there are specific meanings according to context. For example, a newly recruited inspector of **Her Majesty's Inspectorate** has, as a mentor, an experienced inspector who will guide him or her for the first year of service; a **tutor** in a school who supervises trainees on **teaching practice** is sometimes called a mentor; in the field of nursing education, nurses supervising the work of student nurses are sometimes given the title of mentor.

meritocratic education   Meritocracy was a word invented by Michael Young in *The Rise of the Meritocracy, 1870–2033: An Essay on Education and Equality* (1961). This book satirised a society in which the status of a person is determined by 'merit', which is determined by the simple formula 'IQ plus effort equals merit'. Meritocratic education is that kind of education that concentrates on the identification of talent, preferably by means of **intelligence tests**, and then on separating the talented from the less talented into different schools and curricula. Meritocratic education is different from elitist education inasmuch as elitist education depends upon social selection, whereas meritocratic education depends on selection by **ability**. Michael Young's book demonstrated the folly of such a system very convincingly. (See also **ladder of opportunity**)

microteaching   A system used in some colleges and departments of education for developing specific teaching skills. Normally, the student-teacher would teach a small group for a limited amount of time, perhaps only ten minutes, concentrating on a specific objective. The lesson is then analysed with the help of the tutor and other students from a film or video tape recording. It is a technique that is usually regarded as having some value in **initial teacher training**, but is rarely used with all students. It is increasingly likely that its use will be confined to those with particular problems or difficulties. (See also **competency-based teaching**)

middle school   The shift to a comprehensive school system in the early 1960s without a stock of adequate buildings gave rise to the setting up of middle schools. In 1963 the West Riding of Yorkshire submitted plans to introduce schools for the 9–13 age range and in the following year the law was amended to allow **transfer** ages other than 11. A further impetus to the spread of middle schools followed with the Department of Education and Science Circular 10/65 which suggested middle schools as one way of establishing **comprehensives**. The **Plowden Report** also recommended an extension of the primary mode until age 12 or 13. The starting and leaving ages of pupils differ depending on the individual **local education authority**, with patterns such as 8–12, 9–13 and 9–14. Falling rolls and the changing pattern of sixth-form education has resulted in local education authorities returning to schools for the 11–16 age range, at the expense of middle schools. In 2002, there were 147 middle schools (primary) catering for 9–12-year-olds, and 316 middle schools (secondary) for 9–13 or 14–year-olds. (See also **junior school**)

Ministry of Education   The 1944 Education Act provided for a Minister of Education in place of a President and a corresponding change in the name of the Department from the **Board of Education** to the Ministry of Education. In 1964 the Ministry was replaced by the Department of Education and Science (DES); and in 1992 it became the **Department for Education**. From July 1995 it was changed to the **Department for Education and Employment** (DfEE), and in June 2001 it became the **Department for Education and Skills** (DfES).

minority group   Refers to a group in any society that can be identified usually by reason of religion, race, nationality or special needs. (See also **sub-culture**)

mission   Part of the **accountability** language of the 1980s and 1990s. Every educational institution should have a mission – i.e. a list of **aims** and strategies for achieving them which could be expressed as a 'mission statement'.

mixed-ability grouping   The grouping of pupils in such a way that each class in a year group has a roughly equal range of attainment. A survey undertaken by **Her Majesty's Inspectorate** and published in a report entitled *Mixed Ability Work in Comprehensive Schools* (1978) stated that only in a very small number of the schools visited were pupils learning at an appropriate level and pace in classes organised in this way. Other criticisms made were that bright pupils were not being extended and that too much emphasis was put upon social **objectives**. A third of all comprehensive schools in the sample were undertaking some mixed-ability work that was found largely in the first three years of school. Since this survey there has been a decline in mixed-ability grouping. (See also **labelling**, **setting**, **streaming**, **unstreaming**, **workcards**)

mock examination   An internal examination taken by candidates preparing for a public examination such as the **General Certificate of Secondary Education** (GCSE) or **A Level**. It is designed to give candidates 'examination experience' some months before taking the final exam; it may also be used to judge whether candidates are likely to be successful and to estimate the final **grade**.

moderation   The process of aligning standards – often between teachers responsible for the assessment of their own candidates. The methods of moderation fall into two broad categories: (1) Statistical moderation, which involves some form of **scaling** or alignment against performance in an externally assessed component. (2) Moderation by inspection, which involves candidates' work being inspected by an external moderator, or by peer group moderation through an agreement trial.

The most appropriate form of moderation will depend on the nature of the assessment being moderated.

Modern Apprenticeship   A development in work-based training introduced in 1995. Its aim is to attract able 16–17-year-olds to work-based training where people learn in a working environment, on and off the job, in order to achieve an **NVQ** at Level 3 within three years. In addition, an accelerated Modern Apprenticeship is intended for 18–19-year-olds who are likely to have achievements at advanced **GNVQ** or **A Level**. Such entrants can achieve an NVQ 3 in 18 months. (See also **national traineeships**)

'Modern Greats' The final honours degree course at Oxford University in philosophy, politics and economics (PPE). (See also **Greats**)

modular course When the normal Bachelor's degree course consisted of the study of one subject or discipline, the mode of assessment tended to be a series of final examination papers taken at the end of the course. During the last 20 years or so several developments have taken place: more and more courses consisted of a mixture of subjects organised in units or **modules** (some or all which would be 'chosen'); and it became convenient to examine each module or group of modules year by year rather than waiting for the end of the whole course. The trend has now spread into the school system so that **General Certificate of Secondary Education** (GCSE) and **A** and **AS Level** courses can be 'modularised'.

module A relatively short, self-contained unit which forms part of a modular syllabus. **National Vocational Qualifications** (NVQs) and **General National Vocational Qualifications** (GNVQs) are organised in modules. For the NVQ a module is defined in terms of an area of competence and the standards by which the competence is assessed.

monitorial system The monitorial or mutual system of education is associated with an Anglican clergyman, Andrew Bell, and a Quaker teacher, Joseph Lancaster, at the beginning of the nineteenth century. Both arrived at a similar plan for mass education: one master aided by a number of boys (monitors) supervised large numbers of pupils in the **three Rs**.

monitoring Systematically studying the work of pupils, teachers, schools or even **local education authorities** in order to assess levels of performance. During the 1970s, the phrase 'monitoring standards' became commonly used especially in connection with the work of the **Assessment of Performance Unit** (APU).

Montessori schools Maria Montessori (1870–1952) was the first woman in Italy to qualify as a doctor. Instead of joining a practice she spent two years as an assistant at the Psychiatric Clinic of the University of Rome where she was responsible for the care of mentally handicapped children. Montessori became interested in educational theory and travelled to Paris and London to study teaching methods. She was unimpressed by a good deal of what she saw, although the writings of Seguin influenced her own theories. In 1907 she directed the first *Casa dei Bambini,* a school for poor children of pre-school age in a slum area of Rome. Montessori aimed at designing a scientific method of education, using specially designed didactic apparatus. A Montessori Society was founded in 1912 in England, and her work led to the establishment of many Montessori schools.

moral development, moral education   Moral development is some-times confined to **maturation** or the innate development of a child's moral thinking; more commonly, it is used to refer to the combination of maturation and experience including moral education. Moral education is the conscious attempt to contribute to a child's moral development. In the UK, various attempts have been made to base moral education on sound psychological and philosophical criteria, and to distinguish moral education from religious education.

Moser Report   Since 1997, when Labour came to power, the Government has been developing a new framework for **lifelong learning**. This includes a review of Adult Basic Education carried out by Sir Claus Moser and a consultative group. Its Report (1999) recommended a National Adult Basic Skills Strategy. The Government responded in November 1999, accepting the recommendations in principle and the need for funding.

The main recommendations of the Moser Report were: a national strategy for adult basic skills with ten elements – i.e., national targets; an entitlement to learn; guidance, assessment and publicity; better opportunities for learning; quality; a new curriculum; a new system of qualifications; teacher training and improved inspection; new technology; and planning of delivery. The national targets suggested included: reducing the percentage of those with poor basic skills by 50 per cent by the year 2010; doubling the number of those receiving help to 500,000 by 2002; and the expansion of trained teachers from 4,000 to 15,000 full-time equivalents. (See also **adult literacy**, **Basic Skills Agency**)

multicultural education   England and Wales, like many other modern industrial societies, are now multicultural societies. It is usually accepted that even if children live in an area where there are no ethnic **minorities**, schools still have a duty to include in the curriculum topics that will help pupils to understand the concept of **culture** and to appreciate the variety of cultures that now exist in the UK, not least to promote better race relations. (See also **Rampton Report**)

multidisciplinary studies   (See **interdisciplinary studies**)

multilateral school   A school that catered for all the **secondary education** of children in a given area and included provision for **grammar**, **technical** and modern courses on one site. Unlike children in **comprehensive** schools, those in multilateral schools remained in separate courses during their secondary school life. This type of school was advocated by the Trades Union Congress (TUC) from the 1920s as a first step to breaking down class distinctions in education. (See also **secondary education for all**, **tripartite system**)

multiple choice test   A form of **assessment** where the candidate is presented with a number of alternative answers to questions posed. Responses are usually denoted by ticks. Multiple choice tests are now common in many public examination papers in addition to essay type questions. (See also **open-ended**)

multiple intelligence   Howard Gardner, an American psychologist, has criticised traditional one-dimensional views of intelligence on the grounds that intelligence should be divided into at least seven sub-categories. (See also **intelligence** and **intelligence test**)

Munn Report (1977)   A Scottish Committee under the chairmanship of Dr James Munn considered the appropriate curriculum for third- and fourth-year secondary school pupils. A **core curriculum** was favoured, based on a 40-period week; and 14 'non-core' periods were recommended for two additional optional activities which were available. An important point made by the Committee was that assessment should be geared to educational **objectives** in the curriculum, rather than the curriculum being controlled by the assessment system. This might be achieved by schools making their own assessment on a range of subjects. Further consideration of assessment procedures was undertaken at this time by the **Dunning Committee**. (See also **Scottish Education Department**)

museum education   The educational value of museums has long been recognised. The appointment of education officers in national and some local museums to liaise with schools is now quite usual. Museums cater for groups of pupils who may be preparing for examinations, engaged on topic work or making a visit in connection with some aspect of the school curriculum.

N

N and F Levels   In 1973, the **Schools Council** put forward a proposal to replace **A Levels** with a two-tier five-subject system entitled N (Normal) and F (Further) Levels. It was planned that students would take three N levels (each equal to half an A Level) and two F Levels (each equal to three-quarters of an A Level). Although there was agreement on the need for change, the proposal encountered opposition and was eventually dropped. The recommendation of **Curriculum 2000** – that students aged 16–18 should take five subjects at **AS Level** and three at **A Level** – is clearly related to the reform debated in the 1970s. (See also **examination boards, Q and F Levels**)

National Advisory Body (NAB)   The National Advisory Body for local authority higher education was formed by the Government in December 1981. Its main task was to advise on the present and future provision of higher education in the non-university sector at a time when available resources were shrinking. The Board was replaced by the Polytechnics and Colleges Funding Council (PCFC) in 1988, which in turn was disbanded and became the **Higher Education Funding Council** (HEFC) in 1992. (See also **polytechnics**)

National Advisory Council for Education and Training Targets (NACETT)   (See **National Targets for Education and Training**)

National Advisory Council on Education for Industry and Commerce (NACEIC)   The NACEIC was established in 1948 following the recommendations of the **Percy Report**. During its 29 years, it issued a series of important reports. The first, *The Future Development of Higher Technological Education* (1950), led to the setting up of the National Council of Technological Awards, later the **Council for National Academic Awards**; and others dealt with such areas as **business studies, sandwich courses** and **day release**. The Council was disbanded in 1977. (See also **business education**)

National Assembly for Wales (NAW)   The NAW took over responsibility for education from the **Welsh Office** in 1999 following the **Government of Wales Act** (1998).

National Association for Gifted Children (NAGC)   The aim of the Association, a registered charity which was founded in 1966, is to enable gifted children to achieve their full potential both at home and at school. Membership comprises parents, teachers and interested adults. Where branches exist, there are usually meetings once or twice a month to provide activities for children and parents. The Head Office at Milton Keynes also organises educational consultancy, in-service education of teachers, counselling and network support. Direct support is given at two levels. For the 3–10-year-olds, there is an online area for children and parents which is linked with resources. The 11–18-year-olds have a Youth Agency and Youth Café with a password-protected website for youngsters. Funded by the **Department for Education and Skills**, the National Lottery Charities Board and the Potential Board, the scheme offers a counselling service and provides a forum where ideas and creative work can be shared. (See also **giftedness**)

National Association for Primary Education (NAPE)   This Association, with over 200,000 members, consists of parents, teachers, governors,
inspectors, educational officials and school communities. Its main concern
is to provide high quality primary education for children between birth and
13 years of age and is in regular contact with appropriate official bodies and
agencies.

National Association for Special Needs   The Association promotes
the development of children and young people with **special education needs**
and represents those who work with them. The present membership in
the UK is over 11,000. It runs two joint projects with the **Department
for Education and Skills** (DfES), publishes policy documents on such
topics as **inclusion** and partnership with parents, and organises regional
conferences.

National Association of Career Guidance Teachers (NACGT)   All
secondary schools have a careers co-ordinator, and the Association, which
has some 2,000 members, provides a forum for them. One of its aims is to
provide careers education as a core element of the **national curriculum**.

**National Association of Educational Inspectors, Advisers and
Consultants (NAEIAC)**   Formerly the National Association of Educational
Inspectors, Advisers and Consultants, this Association represents 2,500 local
authority advisers, OFSTED inspectors and private consultants.

National Association of Governors and Managers (NAGM)
Launched in 1970, this pressure group was constituted for the purpose of
reforming governing bodies by involving parents, pupils, teachers, the local
community, and the local authority. This philosophy was later endorsed by
the **Taylor Committee** in its report (1977). The Association, which is
non-political and financially independent, has played a leading part in the
debate on the duties and responsibilities of **governors** and governing bodies
since the **Education Reform Act** (1988), it has also set up training courses
for governors. Whereas the **National Governors' Council** draws its
membership from schools as a whole, the Association consists of individual
members.

National Association of Head Teachers (NAHT)   Established in
1897, it now has a membership of over 40,000, which represents the interests
of **heads** and **deputy heads** in both primary and secondary sectors in England
and Wales. More than 75 per cent of primary heads and over 60 per cent of
secondary heads are members. (See also **headteacher**, **teachers' unions**,
Secondary Heads Association)

National Association of Schoolmasters/Union of Women Teachers (NAS/UWT)   The second largest teachers' union since the amalgamation of the two separate bodies in 1976. At the present time there are more than 250,000 members, with twice the number of men to women. It is now the largest teachers' union in Northern Ireland and is the only English union represented on the Scottish national negotiating body. (See also **teachers' unions**)

National Association of Teachers in Further and Higher Education (NATFHE)   This body represents lecturers and academic related staff in post-school education. It was formed in 1976 through a merger of the Association of Teachers in Technical Institutions (ATTI) and the Association of Teachers in Colleges and Departments of Education (ATCDE). The Association has some 68,000 members, about two thirds of whom are in further education colleges and a third in higher education, mostly in post-1992 'new universities'.

National Children's Bureau   Founded in 1962 as the National Bureau for Co-operation in Child Care, it has addressed itself to research into the care, development and education of children. Its purpose is to identify and promote the interests of all young people and to improve their status in a diverse and multicultural society. The Bureau membership ranges from local and health authorities, to professional and voluntary organisations, to universities and other teaching bodies. It is perhaps best known for The National Child Development Study, a **longitudinal** study based on subjects born in one week in March, 1958, and followed up by the Bureau when they were aged 7, 11, and 16 years. Since its inception, the Bureau has undertaken many research projects. Present ones include evaluating a curriculum for pre-school children and examining the services offered by three multiracial nurseries in London.

National College for School Leadership (NCSL)   The College, launched in November 2000, provides a major resource for schools for **headship training** at three different levels and took over full responsibility for this function from the **Department for Education and Skills** (DfES) in April 2001. It also gives professional support to **deputy heads** and school leaders. In January 2002, the College launched a pilot programme of training for school **bursars.** The College buildings in Nottingham are supplemented by a 'virtual' College, NCSL Online, which provides access to seminars, course materials and research papers. In September 2001, Wales launched the Professional Headship Induction Programme (PHIP), similar to the **Head Teachers Leadership and Management Programme** (HEADLAMP).

National Commission on Education (NCE)　The refusal of the Government to set up a Royal Commission on education led to the establishment by the **British Association for the Advancement of Science**, with the active support of the Royal Society, the British Academy and the Fellowship of Engineering, of a National Commission on Education in May 1992. Sir Claus Moser was a prime mover in the matter. The terms of reference are to consider educational goals, policies and practice to meet both the country's needs and those of individuals throughout their lives in the light of the opportunities and challenges that will face the UK over the next 25 years. The NCE produced a report, *Learning to Succeed: A Radical Look at Education Today and a Strategy for the Future* (1993). In June 1995, a follow-up report, *Learning to Succeed: The Way Ahead*, appraised developments in education and training since the 1993 Report.

National Confederation of Parent–Teacher Associations (NCPTA)
Parent–Teacher Associations (PTAs) exist in many schools and are mainly concerned with local issues. The NCPTA, formed in 1954, provides a national organisation to which PTAs can affiliate. A non-political body, it holds annual conferences and raises issues of concern with government departments. At one stage it was dominated by teachers, but at its 1987 conference, the constitution was changed to give parents a two-thirds majority. (See also **parent power**)

National Council for Educational Technology (NCET)　A registered charity funded by the government, the Council promotes and develops the use of educational technology in all areas of education and training. For example, it produces resource packs for primary school teachers working on plans to incorporate **information and communication technology** into history and geography at **Key Stage** 2, as well as for teachers involved in implementing **Attainment Targets** of the technology curriculum.

National Council for Vocational Qualifications (NCVQ)　The Council was established in 1986 to monitor vocational awards and qualifications, particularly **National Vocational Qualifications** (NVQs). It was not itself an examining body. It devised a national framework for vocational awards based on four **levels** that defined the skills needed by industry. The **Dearing Review** (1996) recommended the merger of the NCVQ and the **School Curriculum and Assessment Authority** (SCAA): this was implemented in 1997 when the **Qualifications and Curriculum Authority** (QCA) was established, having responsibility for academic and vocational awards. (See also **National Vocational Qualifications**)

national criteria   In February 1980 the Government announced its proposal for a single system of examining at 16 plus, recommending that national criteria should be established for syllabuses and assessment procedures 'to ensure that all syllabuses with the same subject title have sufficient content in common, and that all Boards apply the same performance standards to the award of grades'. The **General Certificate of Education** (GCE) and **Certificate of Secondary Education** (CSE) examination boards were invited to draft the criteria for some 20 subjects for the examination later called the **General Certificate of Secondary Education** (GCSE). The Secretary of State for Education provided guidelines for the work.

national curriculum   A national curriculum for children aged 5–16 in all **maintained schools** in England and Wales was introduced by the Education Reform Act (1988). Ten subjects were specified as compulsory: English, mathematics, science, technology, history, geography, art, music and physical education, with a modern foreign language for 11–16-year-olds. The first three were prioritised as **core subjects**. In Wales, the Welsh language was an additional **foundation subject** either as a first or second language. Originally each foundation subject was organised into sets of objectives called **Attainment Targets** (ATs), setting out what pupils should know and be able to do at each **Key Stage**.

   At the end of each **Key Stage** (i.e. 7, 11, 14 and 16) it was intended to test pupils by means of **Standard Assessment Tasks or Tests** (SATs). The first tests, for 7-year-olds, were taken in 1991, followed by 14-year-olds in 1992. Had these plans been carried out in full, the national curriculum with its testing programme would have made England and Wales the most tightly controlled system in the world.

   However, the first testing proved to be far too detailed in its requirements, presenting almost impossible paperwork demands on teachers, especially at Key Stages 1 and 2. The result was a boycott of the testing arrangements by all the teacher unions. Sir Ron **Dearing** was given the task of slimming down the testing and curricular requirements. Even this slimmed-down version of the national curriculum did not prove to be entirely satisfactory and further changes have been made. Eventually the **Qualifications and Curriculum Authority** (QCA) carried out a consultation on the revised proposals for a national curriculum in May 1999. Once again, the intention was to reduce prescriptive content and to bring the curriculum up to date. The revised national curriculum became statutory from August 2000, with some exceptions such as **citizenship**, which was delayed until August 2002. One feature of the national curriculum was an explicit statement setting out values, aims and purposes underpinning the curriculum. It was also intended that schools might take action to meet pupils' individual needs and requirements. Sections on learning across the curriculum set out ways in which the national curriculum can contribute to spiritual, moral, social and cultural development as well as mentioning **key skills**, thinking skills, financial capability and education for sustainable development.

Religious education remains compulsory, but locally defined. A very important addition was a new foundation subject in citizenship, which is non-statutory at Key Stages 1 and 2 (being linked to **personal, social and health education** (PSHE)), but compulsory at Key Stages 3 and 4 from 2002. To support the PSHE and citizenship curriculum, a National Healthy School Standard was launched by the **Department for Education and Employment** (DfEE) and Health Ministers in October 1999. This standard encourages a school culture and environment to support PSHE and citizenship; it also sets criteria for sensitive issues such as drug education and sex education. Another radical change to the original idea of a national curriculum is that at Key Stage 4 there is now a range of vocational qualifications available for 14–16-year-old students, which might be seen as an alternative to the more academic aspects of the national curriculum.

National Curriculum Council (NCC)   The NCC was established in 1988 as a result of the **Education Reform Act** (1988). It conducted statutory consultation on the subjects of the **national curriculum**, and received remits from the Secretary of State. It also provided advice to a wide range of interests on the implementation of the national curriculum; advised the Secretary of State on curriculum research and development; kept the curriculum of maintained schools under review; and disseminated information about the curriculum. In 1993, the NCC, together with its partner body the **School Examinations and Assessment Council** (SEAC) merged to become the **School Curriculum and Assessment Authority** (SCAA). In 1997, the SCAA merged with the **National Council for Vocational Qualifications** (NCVQ) to become the **Qualifications and Curriculum Authority** (QCA).

National Education League   A Nonconformist pressure group established in 1869 to ensure that State education should be secular, free and compulsory. Some of the aims of the League were achieved by the 1870 and 1876 Education Acts. (See also **free education**, **National Education Union**)

National Education Trust   Founded in 1972 with the title the National Council for Educational Standards because it was felt that rising expenditure on education was not leading to any proportionate improvement in standards. The Trust aims at influencing and alerting public opinion through its conferences and twice-yearly *Bulletin*. Many of the contributors to the latter have also written for the **Black Papers**. (See also **pressure groups**, **standards**)

National Education Union   The Union was formed in the same month as the **National Education League** 1869 by supporters of the **voluntary schools** in order to counteract the League. It promoted denominational teaching in schools. The 1870 Act admitted the principle of a **dual system**. (See also **school board**)

National Extension College (NEC)   Founded in 1962, the College was established in order to give adults a second chance in education. It is an independent organisation and conducts its work by means of **distance learning** courses, and preparing many of its students for the **Open University**.

National Foundation for Educational Research (NFER)   Established in 1946 by **local education authorities**, with the co-operation of the **Ministry of Education**. The NFER's task was to investigate those 'practical problems arising within the public system of education as are amenable to scientific investigation'. Its research programme ranges from the pre-school stage to higher education. It is an independent body and carries out research projects commissioned by a wide range of organisations. It is divided into three departments. The Department of Assessment and Measurement has developed tests and assessment for the **national curriculum**, and analyses examination results and develops test material. The Department of Evaluation and Policy Studies deals with cross-curricular areas including careers education, **vocational education** and training, school improvement and **value added** issues. The Department of Professional and Curriculum Studies is concerned with topics such as curriculum development evaluation, **truancy**, professional development, teaching strategies and **special educational needs**. The Head Office is in Slough with a northern office based in York and a Welsh Unit in Swansea.

National Governors' Council (NGC)   Formed in 1994, the Council represents the concerns of governing bodies at national level. Unlike the **National Association of Governors and Managers** (NAGAM), it is composed of governing bodies rather than individual governors. The Council consists of independent associations of governing bodies, based on **local education authority** areas and is active in more than half the country. Associations that are independent of their local education authority, and represent at least half of the governing bodies in their area, are eligible to became full members of the Council. As an independent body, it acts on behalf of its members in relation to appropriate organisations and serves on most governmental education working groups. The policy of the Council is determined by the members' meeting, held twice yearly.

National Grid for Learning (NGfL) This Government scheme provides resources for improving the use of **information and communications technology** (ICT) by giving schools access to the Internet. More than 20,000 schools – representing 88 per cent of the total number – were connected to the Internet by April 2000. A commitment by **local education authorities** to achieving the baseline of a minimum threshold of access to information and communications technology by August 2002 was a condition of grant. The Grid also assists serving teachers to become competent in teaching and using ICT, and provides information for governors on-line as well as providing activities for children. In addition, the **Department for Education and Skills** encourages parents to understand the benefits of the Internet. (See also **Curriculum Online**)

National Institute of Adult Continuing Education (NIACE) A national organisation founded in 1949, promoting co-operation, dissemination of information and the general advancement of adult education in England and Wales. It receives support and finance from **local education authorities**, universities, residential colleges and the **Department for Education and Skills**. The NIACE works in partnership with Scottish and Northern Ireland adult education. Since 1 July 2000 the functions of the Institute in Wales has been under the supervision of the NIACE Dysgu Cymru/Learning Wales, which is concerned with the development of lifelong learning in Wales.

National Learning Targets The National Learning Targets were launched in October 1998 by the Education Secretary, David Blunkett, to provide a focus for raising attainment and participation in education and training for the stages at 11, 16, 19, 21, and later in adult life. The 11 targets were intended to underpin the Government's education and employment priorities: i.e. a competitive economy, and a society where everyone has an equal chance to realise their potential.

The National Learning Targets (England) for 2002 were: 80 per cent of 11–year-olds to reach the expected **literacy** standard for **Key Stage** 2; 75 per cent to reach Key Stage 2 standard in **numeracy**; 50 per cent of 16–year-olds to gain five **General Certificate of Secondary Education** (GCSE) Grades A–C; 95 per cent to gain at least one GCSE at any Grade; 85 per cent of 19–year-olds to gain five GCSEs (A–C or equivalent); 60 per cent of 21–year-olds to gain two GCE **A Levels** or equivalent; 50 per cent of adults to have two GCE A Levels or equivalent; 28 per cent of adults to have a degree or equivalent; a 7 per cent reduction in non-learners; 45 per cent of medium or large organisations to be recognised as Investors in People; and 10,000 small organisations to be recognised as Investors in People.

National Literacy Strategy (NLS)   The plan to establish a NLS with a daily **literacy hour** was announced in 1996. The NLS emphasised traditional teaching methods in reading, writing and spelling. The **Office for Standards in Education** (OFSTED) inspected and reported on the NLS in 1998, generally in favourable terms; the **National Foundation for Educational Research** (NFER) also published an evaluation.

National Numeracy Strategy (NNS)   The NNS was launched in 1999 as an elaboration of the National Numeracy Project set up by the **Department for Education and Employment** (DfEE) in September 1996. The focus of NNS was on daily lessons in primary schools emphasising basic skills. (See also **targets**)

National Nursery Examination Board (NNEB)   The Board is the main provider of the nationally recognised child-care qualification for **nursery nurses**: the NNEB diploma in Nursery Nursing. This diploma qualifies the holder to work in hospitals, schools and day nurseries, and private homes. The diploma course, run mainly by local colleges of **further education** and **Sixth Form colleges**, consists of two years' full-time or five years' part-time study. In addition, practical experience is gained in different age groups up to the age of seven. (See also **nursery classes**)

National Professional Qualification for Headship (NPQH)   See **headship training**

national qualifications framework   All qualifications accredited by the **Qualifications and Curriculum Authority** (QCA) must fit into the national qualifications framework, which is intended to clarify the relations between qualifications and to identify broad equivalencies and progression routes.

There are three types of qualification:

1. General qualifications (e.g., **GCSE** and **A Level**).
2. Vocationally-related (e.g., **Vocational A Levels**, previously known as Advanced **GNVQs**)
3. Occupational (**National Vocational Qualifications** (NVQs)).

There are also six levels, ranging from **entry level** to Level 5 (Postgraduate).

National Record of Achievement (NRA)   Developed in the 1970s as a result of widely voiced dissatisfaction with the educational examination pattern, which did not take into account or encourage the wide range of pupil attainment. It is a record of a young person's achievements which, together with portfolios of evidence, will help that person to decide his/her next steps either in education, training or employment, with governmental desire for course skills to be included in both academic and vocational post-16 courses. In 1990, the **Department of Education and Science** records of achievement were 'the means by which achievement across the **national curriculum** and beyond can be most effectively reported to a range of audiences'. From 1993, the scheme was made compulsory. The **National Council for Vocational Qualifications** (NCVQ) is responsible for its management. A review in 1996 (chaired by Sir Ron **Dearing**) of qualifications for 16–19-year-olds, recommended a change of name from NRA to **Progress File**. This was followed by a three-year period of monitoring of guidance materials. At the time of writing, it is still being evaluated by ten funded projects. (See also **record of achievement**, **school records**)

National Society   The National Society for Promoting the Education of the Poor in the Principles of the Established Church was founded in 1811 as a result of the success of the non-sectarian **British and Foreign School Society**.

National Targets for Education and Training (NTET)   In the 1995 White Paper, *Competitiveness: Forging Ahead*, the proposed revised national targets for the year 2000 were accepted.

national traineeships   Since the Second World War various attempts have been made to revive improved forms of the **apprenticeship** system. One of them was the national trainee programme, which in 2000 became part of the Foundation Modern Apprenticeship Project. (See also **Modern Apprenticeship**)

National Training Organisations (NTO)   Introduced in 1997 to rationalise the provision of education and training. There were 73 training organisations, led by employers, to oversee the training for manufacturing and service industries, to set standards, to identify and improve skills needs, and to promote a qualified work force. NTOs received public funds of £10 million per annum, and they varied greatly in size, from a workforce of 4 million to 20,000. These were replaced in 2002 by Sector Skills Councils, backed by a central **Sector Skills Development Agency**. The Councils will support vocational training from **General Certificate of Secondary Education** (GCSE) level to **foundation degrees**. (See also **Learning and Skills Council**)

National Union of Students (NUS)   Founded in 1922, the NUS was initially intended for university students only, but now includes most institutions in further and higher education in the UK. The NUS is a federation of the autonomous students' unions, each of which sends delegates to the twice annual conference. There is an elected executive body which carries out the decisions made at the conferences. The main aim of the union is to promote and maintain the educational, social and general interests of students. Membership consists of one-and-a-half million members at 850 institutions. (See also **Students' Union**)

National Union of Teachers (NUT)   The largest and oldest of the teachers' associations with a membership of over 294,000. Originally called the National Union of Elementary Teachers, when it was founded in 1870, it dropped 'elementary' from its title in 1889. The local associations, of which there are more than 400, elect delegates at the annual conference, where policy matters are debated. (See also **teachers' unions**)

National Vocational Qualification (NVQ)   The **National Council for Vocational Qualifications** (NCVQ) was established in 1986 to reform and rationalise vocational qualifications. NVQs are designed to meet the needs of employers and employees and indicate **competence** at work. There are five levels of NVQ:

Level 1 – competence in a range of work activities;

Level 2 – competence in more complex activities, e.g. teamwork;

Level 3 – competence in a broad range of activities, including supervisory work;

Level 4 – complex technical or professional work;

Level 5 – similar to vocationally related postgraduate qualification.

The NCVQ envisaged that NVQs would eventually be used to grade every occupational postholder. The NCVQ adopted a **competency-based** model for the specification of the qualification, with 'statements of competence' for each particular vocational area. In Scotland there is a different framework. (See also **Scottish Qualifications Authority**)

National Youth Agency (NYA)   The NYA aims to advance youth work, to promote the personal and social development of young people, and to promote their voice in society. It is funded primarily by the **Local Government Association** (LGA) and various government departments. It provides resources to improve work with young people and supports the leadership of organisations involved. The NYA has a team of specialists who work alongside the **Youth Service** and has a collection of resources on work with young people available.

natural wastage The process of achieving a smaller teaching staff, either in schools or in universities and other institutions of higher education, by allowing members of staff to leave either on retirement or by resignation, without them being replaced. Many institutions have preferred to pursue the policy of 'natural wastage' rather than invoke redundancy. The problem of such policy is, however, that this frequently results in very unbalanced staffing and a patchy curriculum since retirements and resignations tend to be completely haphazard rather than falling equally across all subject areas. (See also **falling rolls**)

nature–nurture controversy For a number of years psychologists, sociologists and others have debated, sometimes bitterly, about whether aspects of an individual's personality are mainly inherited genetically or are due to environment, in particular, learning. The argument has been pursued on both sides of the Atlantic. In the UK, advocates of the genetic point of view have included Sir Cyril Burt (whose work has been partly discredited) and Professor H. Eysenck; in the USA the best-known advocate of heredi-tarianism was Professor Arthur Jensen, who felt that there was evidence to suggest that black children and working-class children were genetically inferior in terms of **intelligence** scores.

neighbourhood school (1) A school that draws its pupils from a clearly identifiable 'neighbourhood' in the sense of a **catchment area** which is both homogeneous and compact. (2) The view that schools should identify closely with neighbourhood people and neighbourhood interests. Some **comprehensive schools** would be classified as neighbourhood schools, whereas **grammar schools** often draw their pupils from a much wider area. (See also **community school/college**)

new deal The new deal is part of the Welfare to Work policy for those over 18. It gives the unemployed, disabled, lone parents and some others, the chance to develop knowledge and skills and to find work. This scheme began within the **Department for Education and Employment** (DfEE) but was transferred to the Department for Work and Pensions after the General Election in 2001.

New Education The name given to reformers active from the end of the nineteenth century who were opposed to the traditional, instrumental education of the time. There was no conscious 'school' united under one banner, and the views of individual reformers often differed widely. One group, the 'practical educationists', advocated manual training as a means of promoting educational values. Another, the 'social reformers', placed more emphasis on ways of improving the physical well-being of children. The 'naturalists' expounded the theories of **Froebel** and Pestalozzi, whilst others looked to Herbart's teachings. There were also the 'scientific educationists' who based their work largely on psychological research, as well as those who looked to moral education as a replacement for religious instruction. The ideas of the New Educationists helped to provide a basis for the later progressive education movement. (See also **progressive education**, **progressive schools**, **New Education Fellowship**)

New Education Fellowship (NEF)   An organisation designed to promote various aspects of progressive, non-authoritarian education in schools. It was launched by Mrs Beatrice Ensor at the Calais Conference in 1921. The journal *The New Era* was part of the early work of the NEF and is still published. In 1966, the NEF became the **World Education Fellowship**. (See also **New Education**, **progressive education**, **progressive schools**)

New Opportunities Fund (NOF)   The New Opportunities Fund was established in 1998 to make grants from lottery funding to education, health and environment projects. Many grants programmes focused on promoting social inclusion. The Government provides the Fund with policy directions, setting out the amount of funding available and a framework for programmes. The Fund's Board then allocates funding in accordance with its mission statement. Programmes are intended to complement funding available from other sources. The New Opportunities Fund supports local, regional and national strategies in England, Scotland, Wales and Northern Ireland.

Newbolt Report   One of the **Prime Minister's Reports**. The Departmental Committee on the position of English was appointed in 1919. Its Report, which was published in 1921, made English central to the curriculum and advocated that 'every teacher is a teacher of English'. (See also **Bullock Report**)

Newcastle Report   The Newcastle Commission was set up in 1858 'to inquire into the present state of Popular Education in England, and to report what Measures, if any, are required for the extension of sound and cheap elementary instruction to all classes of people'. The chairman, the Duke of Newcastle, reluctantly agreed to undertake this task. The Report, issued in 1861, was a comprehensive survey of all types of education available for the poor in England as well as its provision in continental countries. It drew attention to the unsatisfactory state of the curriculum and the low standard of achievement in the basic subjects. The recommendations included concentration on the **three Rs** and a system of '**payment by results**', which was introduced in 1862.

newly qualified teacher (NQT) On attaining **qualified teacher status** (QTS), the teacher undergoes a period of **induction** over a period of three terms in an educational establishment. During this time the newly qualified teacher receives an individual Support Programme. If the NQT has met the **Induction Standards,** the **induction tutor** and/or the head informs the NQT's employer of the successful completion of the period. From June 2001, all NQTs had to register with the **General Teaching Council** in order to be able to teach in **maintained schools**.

Newsom Report The **Central Advisory Council for Education** (CACE), under its chairman John Newsom, was asked in 1961 to consider the education of pupils aged 13–16 of average or less than average ability. The Report, entitled *Half Our Future*, was published in 1963. It recommended raising the school leaving age to 16.

Newsom Report (on Public Schools) In 1965, following Circular 10/65, a Public Schools Commission chaired by John Newsom was established to explore ways in which **public schools** could be integrated into a system of **comprehensive schooling**. A Report was published in 1968 with far-reaching proposals which were not acted upon. In 1968 the Commission was reconstituted. (See also **Donnison Report, Fleming Report**)

Normal College The Normal Schools of France, Switzerland and Prussia, where teachers were trained on lines laid down by Philipp von Fellenberg, were admired in England in the early nineteenth century. When Dr Kay was appointed First Secretary of the **Committee of the Privy Council on Education** in 1839 he gave priority to the foundation of Normal Training Colleges. (See also **training college**)

normal curve A bell-shaped curve on a graph that shows the distribution that is expected to occur when the number of people obtaining each score follows the distribution that occurs for height in the adult population. There are very few people who are very tall and very few who are extremely short, but the curve rises to the highest point midway between the two extremes, showing that the majority are around average or medium height (hence the bell-shaped curve). Psychologists involved in constructing **intelligence tests** make the assumption that intelligence follows the normal distribution and therefore construct tests so that a normal population will have the same kind of distribution. Not all social scientists accept this assumption.

norm-referenced testing Where a pupil's performance is compared with the performance of other pupils: the pupil's grade is therefore dependent on the average performance of the candidates as a whole. Norm-referenced testing is contrasted with **criterion-referenced testing**.

Northern Ireland Act (1998)   This Act established the **Northern Ireland Assembly** which was intended to have full powers of legislation within its delegated areas of responsibility, including education.

Northern Ireland Assembly   (See **Northern Ireland Act (1998)**)

Norwood Report   A Committee of the **Secondary School Examinations Council** (SSEC) was appointed in 1941 to consider changes in secondary school curriculum and examinations. Chaired by Sir Cyril Norwood, the Committee reported in 1943. Like the **Spens Report**, it supported the notion of a **tripartite** division of secondary schools.

Nuffield Science   In 1962 the Nuffield Foundation, a body concerned with funding curriculum research and development, attempted to encourage the development of curricula in school science. More than 20 were projects in science and mathematics were produced and published over the next two decades, including **General Certificate of Education O and A Level** syllabuses. This work was regarded as an important precursor to the **national curriculum** science **programme of study**, but the Nuffield Foundation has now withdrawn from the world of curriculum development, concentrating its funding on other aspects of education. (See also **curriculum development project**)

numeracy   The Crowther Report (1959) introduced the concept of numeracy, defining a well-educated man as one who was both literate and numerate. Numeracy includes the need to think quantitatively and have an understanding of the scientific approach to the study of phenomena – observation, hypothesis, experiment and verification. Later, the **Cockcroft Report** (1982) proposed a more modest definition: that an individual should be sufficiently familiar with mathematical skills to cope with everyday life. In 1998, the School Standards and Framework Act revived the debate about numeracy, and the **National Numeracy Strategy** was introduced. (See also **graphicacy**, **literacy**, **oracy**)

nursery classes   For children between the ages of two and five, these classes form part of an infant **primary school** (unlike **nursery schools**, which are free-standing institutions). (See also **playgroups**, **pre-school education**)

nursery nurse   An assistant to qualified teachers in **nursery schools** and classes who holds the Nursery Nurses' Examination Board Diploma.

nursery school   Caters for children of pre-school age, usually between the ages of two and five. There are both State and private schools, though the former invariably have qualified staff. State schools have a recommended staff:child ratio of 1:13. The school day usually begins at about 9.00 a.m. and normally ends at 3.30 p.m. In September 2001, a curriculum for three-year-olds, to the end of the reception year, called the **Foundation Stage** was introduced. (See also **nursery classes**, **playgroups**, **Plowden Report**, **positive discrimination**, **pre-school education**)

O Level   (See **Ordinary Level**)

objectives   There are number of different interpretations of this word in an educational context. **Behavioural objectives** are concerned with the desirable changes in behaviour of pupils to be brought about by formulating specific objectives at the beginning of a course. Such an approach is criticised on the grounds that it is too deterministic, that the outcomes may be trivial, and that it is not applicable to the arts and humanities. One writer, Elliot Eisner, therefore suggested the additional need for **expressive objectives**, in some aspects of the curriculum, where the predicted terminal behaviour is not fixed in advance. It is important, too, for teachers to distinguish between the short-term and the long-term objectives they wish to achieve. (See also **aims**, **objectives teaching**)

objectives teaching   The objectives model of teaching seeks to evaluate pupil performance in any **curriculum** area against an agreed list of curriculum objectives. It implies that the teacher has already formulated, clarified and written down objectives which he or she wishes to attain, and is the medium through which the recording and evaluation of pupil performance takes place.

objective test   A test designed so that all examiners agree on the scores achieved by candidates. There is no room for interpretation on the part of the tester. Objective tests take several forms: **multiple-choice** questions, or filling a blank with a single word or short phrase. Some objective tests may be marked by computer.

object lessons   Stemming from Pestalozzi's teaching that the educator must work in accordance with natural laws that are discoverable by observation, object lessons consisted of lessons where objects were analysed – under such headings as qualities, parts and uses – by first-hand examination.

This system was popularised in England by the publication of a series of textbooks in 1830 by a disciple of Pestalozzi, Elizabeth Mayo, entitled *Lessons on Objects*. Object lessons remained popular in elementary schools for the rest of the century and were often badly taught.

Observational Research and Classroom Learning Evaluation
(See **ORACLE**)

occupational group   A group of jobs centred on the same basic discipline, e.g. production engineering, within which the recruitment qualifications overlap.

Office for Standards in Education (OFSTED)   In 1992 the Education (Schools) Act introduced a new system of inspection following the complete reorganisation and reduction in size of **Her Majesty's Inspectorate** (HMI). The grade of Senior Chief Inspector was abolished and the new head was given the title of Chief Inspector of Schools in England. He is assisted by HMI and other staff. An inspection is carried out by a team of inspectors led by a **registered inspector**. Each team also has a lay member. Contracts for inspection are put out to tender and inspectors are self-employed. Every inspection leads to a published report. Inspectors are required to have an education to degree level, and a minimum of five years recent successful teaching experience, or two or more years at senior management level in schools or colleges, or of working with schools in an advisory role. OFSTED also began inspecting all 150 **local education authorities** in January 1998 in order to identify where improvements needed to be made. Inspection of private and funded nursery schools, primary and secondary schools, initial teacher training courses, sixth form colleges, further education colleges and youth work is now within the remit of OFSTED. Since September 2001, OFSTED also inspects all early years child care and education. The Welsh school inspection service is called ESTYN. (See also **Early Years Directorate**)

open admission   The policy of allowing students into a university (or other institution) irrespective of their possession of normal **entry qualifications**. In the USA, a few universities operate an open admission system (or open access, open enrolment or 'open door' policies). In the UK, the **Open University** is the only institution of **higher education** that operates on this basis, although many other universities have admission systems (for **mature students**) that are more permissive but not completely open – in other words, access would be by means of alternative methods of assessment such as interview or essay writing rather than **A Level** results. (See also **Open College**, **Open Tech**)

Open College The Open College was set up by Lord Young (then Secretary of State for Trade and Industry) in 1987 to help retrain Britain's workforce for the 1990s. The College's original intention was to attract individual learners through an extensive network of local colleges, but this has now been transformed into catering for individual learners via customised contracts with several hundred corporate customers. The College updates employee skills, e.g. by running supervisory management courses for the staff of superstores. (See also **Open Tech, Manpower Services Commission**)

Open College of the Arts (OCA) The College, situated near Barnsley, was founded by Lord Young of Dartington in 1986. It provided **distance learning** arts courses at higher education level for more than 5,000 students. Individual tuition is made available by a national network of 300 tutors who are practising artists and craftsmen. Like the **Open University**, to which it is affiliated, there are no entry qualifications and the College attracts mainly **mature students**. Courses include creative writing, art and design, music, singing, the history of art, interior design, and calligraphy. Optional graded assessment is offered on many courses, and successful completion carries with it a **credit accumulation** transfer scheme (CATS), units of which can be used towards a degree or similar qualification.

open day An occasion when a school or college opens its doors for visitors to view aspects of its work. There are usually displays of students' work and demonstrations of activities. (See also **parents' evening**)

open-ended An item on a test where the candidate is encouraged to answer the question in his or her own words, and where a variety of responses is possible. This is a very different technique from a **multiple choice** item in which only one of the alternatives is correct. Open-ended questions avoid the danger of guesswork and enable candidates to express themselves more fully. Marking and scoring are, however, much more complex and less 'objective'.

open enrolment The policy, strongly encouraged by the Education Reform Act (1988), of insisting that schools admit pupils to the maximum capacity if that is the wish of parents, even if there are other local schools with spare places.

open-plan school Open planning recognises the link between progressive educational methods and the need to break down the class or form into several working groups. This flexibility is achieved in a number of different ways and there is no one standard pattern. Ten per cent of all **primary schools** are of open-plan design, but this is much less common in the secondary sector. (See also **progressive education**)

Open Tech   A government-sponsored body, set up in 1981 by the **Manpower Services Commission** and involving both the then Department of Employment and the **Department of Education and Science**. It consisted of 14 members from industry and education and was charged with the task of creating a system to help people of different ages to learn technology and to enable adults to retrain for different jobs. (See also **Open College**)

Open University (OU)   A university established in Buckinghamshire in 1966 to provide degree and other courses for students of 21 years and over. The OU is 'open' in the sense that it operates an **open admissions** policy – i.e. it does not insist on normal entrance qualifications such as two **General Certificate of Education** (GCE) **A Levels**. The University arose out of the idea of a 'university of the air' much favoured by Harold Wilson when he was Prime Minister. However, the courses now provided are more like well-planned **correspondence courses** with supplementary tuition by means of television, radio and **information communications technology**. Tutorial advice on a local basis is also usually available. Students pursue their courses at home for about 12–15 hours a week, 30 weeks in each year.

Each undergraduate course is planned as a year's (part-time) study on this basis, and a degree is awarded after successful completion of six courses (or eight courses of suitable standard for an honours degree). Courses are available in arts (humanities), social sciences, law, mathematics, science and technology, as well as education. Professional qualifications in medicine are not available. Many students follow undergraduate courses; others are involved in MA units, PhD theses and special short-courses or various forms of **continuing education**. (See also **academic year**, **developmental testing**, **foundation course**, **universities, history of**)

options   Some courses at school and university are designed on the 'core plus options' system. This means that a certain amount of the learning required is laid down as a compulsory 'core', but beyond that a student may be free to choose from a number of alternatives. To some extent it might be argued that some **national curriculum** subjects are organised on this principle, although the word 'core' in the national curriculum has a different meaning – prioritising English, maths and science over the other compulsory subjects.

ORACLE (Observational Research and Classroom Learning Evaluation)   A project funded by the **Social Science Research Council** and carried out by members of the University of Leicester School of Education on **primary school** children's behaviour and progress when working with different types of teachers. The conclusion of the ORACLE project was that **teaching styles** had a large effect on achievement.

oracy   A term invented to indicate that speech is just as important educationally as reading and writing. Oracy is the ability to understand and communicate fluently in speech. In the **national curriculum** the importance of oral communication is indicated by the fact that 'speaking and listening' is an **Attainment Target** alongside reading and writing. Some of the ideas behind oracy have also been included in the **National Literacy Strategy** and the **literacy hour**. (See also **graphicacy**, **numeracy**)

oral examination   A form of **examination** in which the candidate is assessed on her/his performance in response to an examiner's questioning. Examinations in music and modern languages often contain an oral component. (See also **viva**)

Order in Council   An Order made by the Queen 'by and with the advice of Her Majesty's Privy Council' for the carrying on of government business. The Order may be either in virtue of the Royal Prerogative, such as declaring war, or under statutory authority. The latter category, often termed subordinate legislation, is widely used by governments to give force to administrative regulations. (See also **statutory instrument**)

Ordinary Level   The **General Certificate of Education** (GCE) Ordinary (O) Level examination was intended, when it replaced the **School Certificate Examination** in 1951, as a test for brighter pupils who had completed a full secondary school course up to the age of 16. The minimum age limit was abandoned in 1953. The **O Level** pass was equivalent to the credit grade of the former Schools Certificate and was originally intended for potential **higher education** students and those entering the professions, although **O Levels** were always more widely demanded by employers. Unlike the School Certificate, it was a single-subject examination and was offered by eight different examining boards. The introduction of the **Certificate of Secondary Education** (CSE) in 1965 for the ability range below those thought capable of achieving O Levels raised questions of comparability between the two examinations – a CSE Grade 1 was accepted as equivalent to O Level Grades A–C. There was pressure to move towards a common system of examining at 16 plus, and this was eventually achieved in 1988 when O Level and CSE were combined to form the **General Certificate of Secondary Education** (GCSE). (See also **examination boards**)

Ordinary National Certificate (ONC)   A post-school vocational award of two-year part-time duration which may be replaced by **National Vocational Qualifications** (NVQ) awards. (See also **Business and Technology Education Council** (BTEC))

Ordinary National Diploma (OND)   A post-school vocational course that existed prior to **National Council for Vocational Qualifications** (NCVQ) criteria. Eventually all vocational awards will be accommodated to **National Vocational Qualifications** (NVQ) levels. (See also **Business and Technology Education Council** (BTEC))

Organisation for Economic Co-operation and Development (OECD)   Established in Paris in 1961 as successor to the Organisation for European Economic Co-operation (OEEC), the OECD aims to promote economic and social welfare by assisting its member governments in the formulation of such policies. As a result, co-ordination of policies might be achieved. There is worldwide membership, consisting of 24 countries. The Council consists of one representative from each country, and decisions and recommendations are adopted by mutual agreement of all members. There are more than a hundred specialised committees and working parties including one on education. Much of the educational work is carried out by the **Centre for Educational Research and Innovation** (CERI). The OECD publishes reviews of national policies for education of its member countries.

organised games   Activities, involving teams or classes, such as rugby, cricket, hockey and netball, which are timetabled as a regular feature of the school **curriculum**.

organised science school   The term given by the **Science and Art Department** to schools and colleges which from 1872 organised science classes (day or evening), and presented candidates for the Department's examinations.

orienteering   An outdoor activity which combines cross-country running, map-reading, and locating check points with the assistance of a map and compass. Orienteering is sometimes (but not always) organised as a race in which contestants follow a pre-planned course in much the same way as drivers in a car rally. The educational merits of orienteering are considered to be the development of map-reading skills, enjoyment of the environment and the practical application of physical fitness.

out-of-school activities   The **Department for Education and Skills** issues advice on school visits and the supervision of pupils. The Health and Safety at Work Act (1974) requires **local education authorities** and governing bodies to ensure the health and safety of pupils who are off premises, both at home and abroad. The **Children Act** (1989) states what is considered reasonable for teachers' actions in emergency situations in promoting pupils' welfare. Recent unfortunate incidents have raised the whole question of pupil safety outside of school.

outcomes   National Vocational Qualifications (NVQs) are assessed on outcomes or specific kinds of **competence**. The compulsory curriculum for **initial teacher training** as modified in Circular 4/98 was also expressed in terms of outcomes or lists of competencies.

outreach   Originally an American term, but one which is increasingly being used to describe certain programmes/activities in the UK where it is an advantage for staff to go out into the community rather than wait for young people to come into the college or university. In some projects, outreach workers are employed to make contact with the kind of young person not otherwise attracted to further education. Outreach staff are also employed by the **Youth Service** and in **adult education**.

over-learning   A technical term in psychology to indicate that learning continues in the process of practising a **skill** or piece of **knowledge** that has already been superficially learned. The theory behind over-learning is that short-term retention of knowledge or skills may be possible after a certain period, but if the need to recall the knowledge or recover the skill is required over a longer period, then it will be necessary to continue practising beyond a time when the skill has apparently been acquired.

Overseas Trained Teacher (OTT)   Teachers trained in another country need to gain **qualified teacher status** (QTS) before they can be employed on a permanent basis in England. From April 2001 new arrangements were introduced by the Government to help OTTs to gain QTS. If they hold a degree equivalent to one from the UK, they may present themselves for assessment for QTS without further training. If in addition the candidate has at least two years' full-time teaching experience and is judged to have met the **Induction Standards as** well, he/she may be exempt from serving the **induction** year.

Oxbridge   A colloquial name given to the ancient universities of Oxford and Cambridge, as distinguished from the later nineteenth- and twentieth-century creations. (See also **universities, history of**)

pacing   It is sometimes suggested that a good teacher carefully matches the rate of material presentation with the pupil's abilities and attention span. He/she paces his/her teaching carefully.

paradigm   In 1970 the American writer on the philosophy of science, Thomas Kuhn, wrote *The Structure of Scientific Revolutions* in which he suggested that science did not develop in a linear fashion, but by a series of revolutions in which the dominant paradigm was replaced by a new paradigm. Since then, the word paradigm has been much used in the sociology of knowledge to indicate a set of perspectives or assumptions that may be dominant at one time, but which is eventually replaced suddenly by a new paradigm. In the sociology of education, the traditional paradigm that took for granted official statistics and positivist methodology was replaced by the new wave sociology described by Michael Young in his book *Knowledge and Control* (1971). Kuhn's view of the development of science and the application of that view of social sciences has been challenged a good deal since the 1970s. The use of the word 'paradigm' has been particularly criticised for its ambiguity.

parametric statistics   Statistical procedures based on the assumption that a sample is appropriate because the parent population was 'normal', i.e. it had a normal distribution. If that assumption cannot be made safely, then non-parametric statistics are recommended. In mathematics, a parameter is a constant occurring in the equation of a curve, by the variation of which the equation can represent a whole family of curves. In other words, some kind of regularity can be assumed from the existence of a curve. Difficulties exist in educational experiments in terms of whether a population can be regarded as falling into a normal curve or not. (See also **Gaussian curve**, **normal curve**)

parent governor representative (PGR)   Parent governor representatives are **parent governors** elected by fellow governors to provide a voice for all parents in their area in local decision-making. They work with **local education authorities** who must provide voting and speaking rights for representatives on committees concerned with education. Starting in summer 2000, there are now approximately 320 representatives throughout England (about 2–5 in each authority). The **National Foundation for Educational Research** (NFER) runs a support network for parent governor representatives. Local education authorities receive a grant from the **Department for Education and Skills** (DfES) to cover induction and training.

parent governors   By the Education Act of 1986 parents were given equal representation with **local education authorities** and now constitute a quarter of the membership of the governing body of a school. Parent governors are elected for four years by secret ballot, the candidates list being sent by post. Given the wide-ranging nature of the responsibilities of school governors, and the expertise needed in curriculum and other matters, parent governors require appropriate training courses. (See also **Education Acts**)

parent power   Parents are increasingly becoming involved in educational decision-making. They are responsible for children of compulsory school age receiving a full-time education and attendance at school or equivalent. For instance, they must be informed on school progress through the **annual parent meeting**, can act as **parent governor representatives**, have rights on **school admissions,** and participate through the **parental partnership** service with **local education authorities**, who cater for parents of children with **special educational needs**.

parental partnership   The Green Paper, *Excellence for all Children: Meeting Special Educational Needs* (1998), stressed the importance of **local education authorities** providing a parent partnership service. This would include access to information and advice on **special educational needs** procedures, provision and support and dispute resolution procedures. Local education authorities are obliged to recruit and train Independent Parental Supporters (IPS).

Parent–Teacher Association (PTA)   An association, consisting of members of staff and parents of pupils in a particular school, for discussing educational issues, raising funds for the school and organising social functions that lessen the division between home and school. Much depends on the enthusiasm or otherwise of the headteacher for the success of such an association. There is a **National Confederation of Parent–Teacher Associations** which puts forward policies reflecting the views of its membership. (See also **Home and School Council**, **parent power**, **pressure group**)

Parent's Charter   The new rights and responsibilities in education for parents in the government's Citizen's Charter were stated in a booklet *The Parent's Charter: You and Your Child's Education*, issued in July 1991. The Charter included plans for annual written reports on children's progress; regular reports by independent inspectors on each school's strengths and weaknesses; published **league tables**, which made possible comparison between the performance of local schools; and independent assessors on panels, which would hear parents' appeals if they were unable to get the school of their choice for their children.

parents' evening   An evening arranged for parents at their children's school in order to discuss progress and other aspects of their children's performance. The frequency of open evenings varies from school to school but they are held at least once a year. (See also **open day**)

Parliamentary Papers   Documents ordered to be printed by the House of Commons for its own use or delivered to the House for the information of MPs, and listed in the daily Votes and Proceedings of the House. Many are subsequently printed by Her Majesty's Stationery Office (HMSO). They include Bills, reports of **Royal Commissions**, **Select Committees**, and **Departmental Committees**, **White Papers**, and some **Green Papers**, as well as about 40 per cent of Statutory Instruments (which can include **Orders in Council**). Before 1921, virtually all important official reports and documents were issued as Parliamentary Papers. (The nineteenth-century term for Parliamentary Papers was 'Blue Books', but since that date many have appeared outside the Parliamentary Paper series.) Documents delivered to or printed by the House of Lords are also Parliamentary Papers.

participant observation   Research in the field of social psychology in which the researcher takes part as a member of the group being observed and records the behaviour of the group. See, e.g. Ervin Goffman's fieldwork on the social world of the hospital inmate, published as *Asylums* (1968). (See also **case study**, **triangulation**)

participation rate   (See **age participation rate**)

part-time education   Refers to courses in further and higher education which students take on a part-time basis. Courses may range from those of a recreational nature to PhDs. Many part-time students combine these courses with other occupations.

passive learning   Some educational psychologists and other educationists make a distinction between **active learning** and passive learning. In a passive learning situation, a pupil is given no opportunity to make any contribution and is simply expected to learn pre-digested information which is presented to him/her by the teacher or lecturer. (See also **learning**)

passive vocabulary   Words that an individual can recognise and understand when used by others, although they may not be part of that individual's **active vocabulary** (i.e., the vocabulary that he actually uses himself). Active and passive vocabulary may be confined to speech or may also be measured in terms of reading and writing.

pass mark   The minimum grade or mark fixed by examiners which candidates are required to obtain to be successful.

pass rate   The ratio or proportion of candidates who are successful in an examination or assignment.

pastoral system   During the 1960s it became common in some local authorities for **comprehensive schools** to divide the responsibilities of teachers into academic and 'pastoral care'. In such schools there were two hierarchies of teachers and senior staff: one academic and the other pastoral.

This system of separating academic from pastoral was sometimes referred to as the 'pastoral system'. Pastoral care is seen to have a dual role: on the one hand it serves as a support system to pupils in academic aspects of the school's work, and on the other, it serves as a 'pastoralising agent' for those pupils who do not appear to benefit from what the school offers. Pastoral systems tend to be structured into Year or House groupings, with **tutors** attached, responsible to a pastoral leader, called head of house or head of year, for the guidance of a number of pupils.

pay spine   Most teachers with **qualified teacher status** are paid according to their position on the qualified teachers' pay spine (or scale). The spine has nine points, and teachers normally progress by one point each year until they reach the maximum when they become eligible to cross the **performance threshold**. Teachers performing exceptionally well may be awarded two points in one year and reach the performance threshold more quickly. (See also **teachers' salaries**)

'payment by results'   The **Newcastle Report**, published in 1861, was concerned with the cost of extending sound and cheap instruction to all classes. As a result, Robert Lowe, then Vice-President of the Council, introduced a revised code in the following year. Grants hitherto payable to certificated teachers were abolished. A school's finances were dependent on the annual examination of children in the **three Rs** (with plain needlework for girls) by **Her Majesty's Inspectorate** (HMI) ('payment by results'), coupled with the fulfilment of a minimum number of attendances. The grant earned by the school was paid direct to the managers. Opposition to the revised code delayed its introduction until 1863, but its effects on elementary schools were felt until after the close of the century. More recently, some politicians have revived the notion that teachers' pay should be linked to their pupils' tests and examination results. (See also **homework, performance related pay**)

pedagogy   Defined by Brian Simon as 'a science of teaching embodying both curriculum and methodology'. ('Why no pedagogy in England?', in B. Simon and W. Taylor, *Education in the Eighties* (Batsford, 1981).)

Pelham Report   Following the recommendations of the **McNair Report** that **training colleges** after the Second World War should recruit well-qualified staff, a Committee on staff salary scales was appointed, and reported in 1945. The Report, signed by its acting chairman, Sir Henry Pelham, a former civil servant, suggested an enhanced salary scale. This was accepted and remained in operation until superseded by the **Houghton Report**'s findings in 1975.

percentile   A statistical term used for many educational tests. A percentile indicates the point in a set of scores or marks that exceeds a given percentage. For example, the 40th percentile is the point below which 40 per cent of all the candidates score. The term percentile rank is used to indicate the relationship to all other scores. Thus a person might score 59 per cent on a test, but if that score was better than 70 per cent of all other candidates he would be said to have the percentile rank of 70.

Percy Report   A Special Committee set up by the **Minister of Education** 'to consider the needs of higher technological education in England and Wales and the respective contributions made thereto by universities and technical colleges'. In its report published in 1945, the Committee envisaged a complete reshaping of higher technological education. The Minister of Education accepted the report and many of the Committee's main recommendations were implemented. (See also **Robbins Report**)

performance contracting   During the **accountability** debate in the USA in the 1970s, some states employed commercial organisations to provide instructional services to a school district on the basis of a fee being determined by success rates measured by performance of students on criterion tests. Such schemes were closely scrutinised by teachers' professional organisations who were delighted to report those occasions when the organisations failed, or where maladministration amounting to fraud was reported.

performance criteria (GNVQ)   Within GNVQs performance criteria make clear the requirements against which the student's performance will be assessed, and set the level of acceptable performance; they specify required **outcomes**.

performance indicators (PIs)   A series of indicators that are postulated in order to judge whether a school or other institution is **effective**. PIs originated from economics, where it was applied to 'value for money' and cost-effectiveness. They are seen as a way of monitoring the work of a school. Lists of PIs show differences in approach. *The Parent's Charter* (1991) mentions the construction of performance tables which will include examinations, **national curriculum** tests and **truancy** rates. Others prefer the quality of the teaching/learning experience, good management, the level of care offered by the school, and a shared sense of mission by the staff, which would include leadership. Problems arise from the difficulty of collecting different types of indicator, the interpretation of raw data, and the effects on school intakes of the publication of the results, and the need to differentiate school performances in terms of their physical location.

By the **Education (Schools) Act** (1992), the Department for Education proposed three categories of indicators: **GCSE** and **A/AS** examination results, **national curriculum** assessment results, truancy figures and a matrix of destination data for each of the 15-, 16-, and 17-year age groups. (See also **league tables**)

performance related pay (PRP)   The Labour Government after 1997 was interested in improving the performance of teachers by relating pay to their classroom performance. This was opposed by the profession but the Government forced through a compromise measure in October 2000. Teachers with nine years' teaching experience, or good honours graduates with seven years' teaching experience, could apply to be judged according to a set of quality standards and thereby 'cross the performance threshold'. Most teachers who applied in 1999–2000 were successful. The scheme was heavily criticised as being too costly to administer and too time-consuming for heads, and as having little detectable impact on the standard of teaching. (See also **teachers' salaries**)

performance test   (1) The kind of test in which the candidate is required to demonstrate a practical skill rather than write about it. (2) A test that requires a candidate to perform certain tasks specified as a means of **selection**. (3) A test of actual **ability** and/or attainment rather than an indication of possible future potential. (See also **aptitude test**, **attainment test**)

performance threshold   A qualified teacher normally progresses along the nine-point pay scale (referred to as the **pay spine** since 2000) until reaching the maximum. At this point teachers are eligible to apply to cross the threshold onto the upper pay range. Successful applicants receive an immediate increase of £2,000 in 2001 and become eligible for four additional increments on the upper pay scale. Passing the performance threshold depends on effectiveness as a teacher, not on undertaking additional management responsibilities or extra duties.

peripatetic teacher   A teacher, usually in subjects such as languages and music, who is not attached to any one particular school, but visits various schools in a **local education authority** for a number of sessions with pupils.

permanent education (*l'education permanente*)   A term more frequently used in Europe than in the UK, but one which is gaining ground. Permanent education is an ideal that aims for the availability of education throughout an individual's life, not ending with the completion of **compulsory schooling** or a further period of **higher education** or **further education**. The **Council of Europe** has committed itself to the ideal of permanent education and has produced a large number of reports on this subject. Permanent education overlaps but is not identical with either **recurrent education** or **continuing education**. (See also **adult education**)

Personal Advisor (PA)   One important aspect of the **Connexions** Service is the Personal Advisor, who is intended to give extra help to young people with barriers to learning, or those who are at risk of dropping out. Advice might include information on learning and career options, either in a group setting or as one-to-one support over a prolonged period. PAs should raise awareness about available options and help to formulate career goals.

personal and social education (PSE); personal, social and health education (PSHE)   One of the problems of the **national curriculum** was that it consisted of a list of discrete subjects. Yet some of the most important aspects of development do not fall neatly into any one subject area. One such area is the whole question of personal and social education, or how to come to terms with the individual 'self' and with others in society. This kind of development, together with **moral education** and **health education**, is recognised as important, but in the past, little systematic attention had been paid to it. In a review of the national curriculum in 1998–99, David Blunkett, then Secretary of State for Education, advised by Professor Bernard Crick, added **citizenship education** to the national curriculum, which was linked to PSHE, especially in primary schools.

phonic method   A technique used in the teaching of **reading**. It is based on the sounds of letters rather than the names of letters. Most teachers combine this method with 'looking and saying', that is by reading aloud. (See also **Gestalt**)

phonics   The teaching of **reading** is one of the disputed areas within the **English curriculum**. The phonic method attempts to teach children the rules of reading and spelling by splitting each word into discrete consonant and vowel sounds: 'c-a-t spells cat'. Those who advocate the phonic method, excluding all other approaches, ignore the fact that about 30 per cent of words in English – including some of the most common – do not follow the rules. The phonics method was included as part of the **National Literacy Strategy** and the **literacy hour**, introduced in 1998.

Piagetian   The adjective referring to the work of Piaget, in particular the stages of development approach. Piaget's theory was that children, by a process of maturation, progress through four stages of development: (1) the sensory motor stage; (2) the pre-operational stage; (3) concrete operations; and (4) formal operations. (See also **enactive**)

pilot scheme; pilot study   Many **curriculum development projects** involve a 'pilot stage'. This usually involves trying out experimental materials in a small number of 'pilot' schools. The object is either to improve the materials at this stage, or possibly to reject them completely as inappropriate. In more general terms, a pilot study is one that precedes a main study. (See also **feasibility study, induction scheme**)

playcentre   Introduced in London in 1898 by Mrs Humphry Ward, play-centres offer a range of leisure activities for children of **primary school** age after school, in term time, as well as full time for an extended age range in the school holidays. Playcentres are situated in schools near to the children's homes and may be staffed either by teachers or outside helpers. Since the abolition of the **Inner London Education Authority**, a large number of playcentres have been closed. Similar schemes exist in many **local education authorities**.

playground   An area normally within the precincts of a school where pupils may play either before, during, or after school hours. The official morning and afternoon breaks in the **primary school** day are often called 'playtime'. The playground is also frequently used for outdoor physical education and games. It is regarded as much more important in England than elsewhere.

playgroups   Introduced in 1960 after the refusal of the **Ministry of Education** to give preference in State **nursery schools** to teachers' own children. A playgroup has a minimum of six children aged between 2½ and 5 supervised by leaders who do not have to hold teaching qualifications. Sessions usually last for a morning or an afternoon in premises that have been passed by the Social Services Department. There is a national body that looks after the interests of its members, the **Pre-School Learning Alliance**. A survey by the Association in March 1992 showed that most of Britain's 15,000 playgroups were being run on a small budget and advocated a comprehensive system for resourcing their work. (See also **Children Act (1989)**)

playing field   An area for school children where sporting or physical activities – such as football, rugby or hockey – can be carried out. Because of financial constraints, a growing number of education authorities have been selling off playing fields. Between October 1998 and June 2001, 159 applications for selling off playing fields were approved by the **Department for Education and Employment**, with only five applications refused.

Plowden Report   The Report of the **Central Advisory Council** (England) entitled *Children and their Primary Schools* was published in 1967. The

Council's terms of reference were 'to consider primary education in all its aspects, and the transition to secondary education'. This aspect of schooling had not been examined since the two **Hadow** committees in the 1930s. Under the chairmanship of Lady Plowden, the Council made a number of important recommendations for the amelioration of social disadvantage. **Positive discrimination**, in the form of educational priority areas (EPAs) where extra staffing and resources could be allocated, was suggested. Better nursery education provision was needed nationally, but especially for EPAs. The structure of primary education was to be changed. Instead of the existing pattern of infants (5–7) and junior (7–11), there should be a first school (5–8) and then a middle school (8–12). The starting age for children was to be more flexible. Continuity between the stages was recommended, including the secondary stage. The Report also stressed the need for more co-operation between home and school: as the focus of the community, the school should welcome parents to participate in school activities. The Report, the last of those produced by the Central Advisory Council, has recently come under attack from right-wing educationists who attribute to it the decline in educational standards. The statement at the beginning of Chapter 2 'At the heart of the educational process lies the child', has been interpreted as an advocacy of **progressive education**, i.e. encouragement to neglect the **three Rs**, and a deterioration in teaching methods.

political literacy   The alternative word 'politeracy' (in keeping with numeracy etc.) has never caught on. Many curriculum theorists feel strongly that understanding political terminology and institutions is an essential aspect of secondary education that is neglected in the **national curriculum**. (See also **citizenship education**)

polytechnics   In 1965, the then Secretary of State for Education, Anthony Crosland, made his famous Woolwich speech calling for a distinct system of higher education with the establishment of polytechnics. The 1966 White Paper, *A Plan for the Polytechnics and other Colleges* (Cmd 3006), described the polytechnics as regional centres that linked with industry and business. University validation was largely replaced by the **Council for National Academic Awards** (CNAA) though institutions would continue to be financed by local authorities. In 1969, eight polytechnics were created in England and Wales and the number later expanded to 30. After 1973, a number of colleges of education were absorbed into the existing polytechnics, bringing with them additional expertise in the arts and humanities. The 1988 Education Reform Act (ERA) gave the polytechnics their independence from local government from 31 March 1989. A new Polytechnics and Colleges Funding Council (PCFC) was responsible for their funding. Within two years, in May 1991, a White Paper, *Higher Education: A New Framework*, abolished the distinction between universities and polytechnics and the PCFC and the **University Funding Council** (UFC) would merge to become a single funding structure. The 1992 **Further and Higher Education Act** abolished the CNAA and allowed polytechnics the power to award their own taught courses and research degrees. From 1992, the 34 polytechnics in England and Wales, and the five in Scotland, with the approval of the Privy Council, changed their designation to university.

positive discrimination   The provision of resources to mitigate educational or other disadvantage caused by social and/or economic deprivation. This is often known as **compensatory education**. The **Plowden Report** recommended the identification of inner city districts which were to be recognised as educational priority areas (EPAs) for this purpose. Much of the emphasis is on pre-school facilities, nursery schools, the involvement of the parents with teachers and the development of community education. The issue is a political one and there are different views on the causes of inequality. As a result, the Plowden philosophy has not been fully translated into resources. (See also **Head Start**)

postgraduate   A person studying for an award above that of a first, i.e. a Bachelor's, **degree**. This might take the form of a diploma or a higher degree, either at the master's or doctorate levels.

Postgraduate Certificate of Education (PGCE)   (See **Professional Graduate Certificate of Education**)

praxis   A term used by many Marxist educationists, but especially Paulo Freire (1972). For Freire, real education comes through an individual's interaction with his environment. The task of a teacher is not to pass on a package of **knowledge** (the banking concept of education), but to go with the pupil and explore the relationship between experience and knowledge in a practical way. Praxis is, therefore, more than the opposite of theory. It is the exploration by an individual (or a group) of the environment in a way that produces 'real' knowledge rather than theoretical or second-hand knowledge.

precision learning   (See **objectives teaching**)

prefect   Pupils who occupy posts of special responsibility in a school, usually chosen from the upper forms. They assist in various ways with the smooth running of the school. The term itself dates back only to 1865 in this sense. Although the prefect system is retained in many **independent schools**, only a minority of state schools now have one. Many different schemes exist which allow pupils to show leadership qualities and participate in the decision-making process. One example is where each class selects representatives for year-group meetings, which in turn select representatives for the **school council**, where a wide range of maters can be discussed. (See also **head boy/girl**)

preparatory school   Often abbreviated to 'prep school', these are **independent schools**, either of the day or boarding type, which prepare their pupils for either the **Common Entrance Examination** at 13 plus or, where it still exists, the 11 plus examination. Some **public schools** retain their own preparatory schools, but most are independent of them. Where the target is the Common Entrance Examination, the curriculum includes Latin and French. While these schools are not required to follow the **national curriculum**, many have introduced the **Key Stage** 2 tests for 11-year-old pupils.

pre-school education   All education provision for children below the statutory school-starting age of five, organised by local authorities or voluntary organisations. Although educationists are divided on the benefits to children of lowering the statutory school-starting age, in 1997 the Labour Government introduced a system for providing a funded pre-school place for children the term after they reached four years of age. More primary schools are now offering full-time education for four-year-olds in reception classes. The Education Secretary announced in October 2000 that every three-year-old will have access to five two-and-a-half hour school sessions per week by 2004.

Pre-School Learning Alliance (PSLA)   In February 1995 the Pre-School Playgroups Association (PPA) formed themselves into a new corporate identity – the PSLA. They provide playgroup facilities for the under-fives.

President of the Board of Education   The Board of Education Act (1899) created a single body to superintend educational development in England and Wales. Its head was a President, a Government minister. In 1944 the Board of Education became the **Ministry of Education**.

pressure group   Like-minded people who band together to press their claims on a particular issue or a set of issues to affect or modify the behaviour or actions of a body holding power. Since the 1960s, they have become a familiar part of the education scene. An early example was in the field of **pre-school education**, where the National Campaign for Nursery Education, formed in 1965, succeeded in persuading the government to make wider provision available. A number of groups have sprung up in recent years which have marked views on the need to bring about change in schools, such as the Campaign for Real Education, the **National Education Trust** and Parental Alliance for Choice in Education. Some pressure groups have a national organisation but rely on local branches to provide the momentum, such as the Campaign for Comprehensive Education and the **National Confederation of Parent–Teacher Associations**.

pre-test (post-test)   In some experimental situations used in education a test is given to a student before starting a course or using experimental materials, and again at the end of such a course. The pre-test results are then compared with the post-test results and an estimate made of the effectiveness of the course or teaching programme or materials involved. The procedure seems to be a plausible one, but in practice all sorts of contaminating influences work to the detriment of simple interpretations or results.

pre-vocational education   A number of attempts have been made to improve the kind of education suitable for those who intend to proceed to work rather than to university after the age of 16. For example, in 1976, a **Certificate of Extended Education** (CEE) was established on an experimental basis, but did not meet with official approval. This was abolished in 1983 and replaced by the **Certificate of Pre-Vocational Education** (CPVE), which soon gave way to the **Diploma of Vocational Education** (DVE). In 1986 the **National Council for Vocational Qualifications** (NCVQ) was established to co-ordinate vocational courses. It was merged into the **Qualifications and Curriculum Authority** (QCA) in 1996.

primary school   Prior to the reorganisation following the **Hadow Report** of 1926, most **elementary schools** were divided into two parts – infants, taking in children from 5 to 7, and then boys' and girls' departments, from 7 to 14. The Hadow Report's suggestion – that 11 years of age was a more suitable time for the **transition** to **secondary education** – produced a distinctive unit, the primary school, consisting of an infants department, as in pre-Hadow times, and a junior department, with children of 7–11. By the 1944 Education Act, the elementary school finally disappeared, and was officially replaced by the primary school. This system still exists in most **local education authorities**, except where **middle schools** have come into existence.

A report by Professor Robin Alexander and two colleagues issued in January 1992 stressed the need for primary teachers to focus more firmly on the outcomes of their teaching and to have more specialist knowledge of their subjects. The first **Standard Assessment Tasks**, **Key Stage** 1, were taken by 7-year-olds in 1991.

Prime Minister's Reports   Early in 1916, H. H. Asquith, then Prime Minister, had presided over a Reconstruction Committee, consisting of seven Cabinet colleagues, which later decided to investigate questions of public interest such as the neglect of science and the place of modern languages in education. The political upheaval caused by the accession of Lloyd George in place of Asquith in December 1916 led to the removal of the Reconstruction Committee to *ad hoc* bodies, thus lessening the impact of their recommendations.

primer   Originally having a religious connotation – a 'book of prime' (or hours) – the word now covers any book that deals with the elements of a subject. (See also **reader**)

principal   Holder of the post of chief officer of a university, college or school. The title of the office varies from one university to another. In London, the post is largely administrative, as there is also a **vice-chancellor**. (See also **Committee of Vice-Chancellors and Principals**)

prison education   The Youth Justice Board, which is responsible for the under-21 justice system, supervises the education of the 2,800 offenders in its care. **Literacy** and **numeracy** present major problems. The Youth Literacy and Numeracy programme aims to improve standards. The Prisoners' Learning and Skills Unit was set up in April 2001 to review prison education A minimum of 30 hours' education and training is now stipulated, with daily literacy and numeracy hours. There is a director of learning and skills in every institution who reports directly to the governor.

Private Finance Initiative (PFI)   A partnership between **local education authorities** and private companies that allows the latter either to build, finance and maintain schools or redesign existing schools. In return for this investment, the local education authority pays an annual fee under a long-term contract. The PFI initiative was highlighted in the Green Paper, *Schools: Building on Success* (2001), as one of the means of transforming education. (See also **Public Private Partnership**)

private school   (See **independent school**, **public school**)

probation   In order to obtain **qualified teacher status** (QTS) trained teachers are required to undergo a one-year period of **induction**, occasionally referred to as probation.

problem solving   A style of teaching or learning where the aim is to encourage pupils to acquire **knowledge** and **skills** in the process of solving problems rather than simply learning about how other people have solved such problems.

Professional Association of Teachers (PAT)   This Association, which has over 34,000 members, is best known for the pledge of its members never to go on strike. It also seeks a professional code of conduct for teachers. The Association claims to be non-party political. (See also **teachers' unions**)

professional body An association incorporated for the purposes of seeking **standards** for those who practise in a profession or occupation, of advancing knowledge related to the profession and of protecting the interests of its members. A professional body may set examinations to its own syllabus or approve and monitor educational institutions to carry out examinations on its behalf.

professional development of teachers (See **continuing professional development**)

Professional Graduate Certificate of Education (PGCE) A certificate taken by graduates, either immediately after their first **degree** course or (increasingly frequently) a few years later after some work experience. It is normally a one-year full-time course involving a considerable amount of practical work in schools under supervision. The certificate was renamed in 2002–3 (from **Postgraduate Certificate of Education**) in order to fit in with the requirements laid down by the **Quality Assurance Agency**'s national framework.

professor Traditionally, the highest-ranking teacher in a field of learning at a university. A professor may hold either an established post, carrying with it a named chair in a named faculty, or a personal title, awarded on the basis of the holder's academic standing. **Polytechnics** had appointed professors from 1969, but not necessarily based on the same criteria as universities. Generally, the title was confined to senior staff and carried with it extra salary. From 1992, when the two sectors of **higher education** were merged, similar criteria for professorships began to be exercised.

The term is also used for senior staff at specialist institutions such as the Royal College of Surgeons, Cranfield, and the London Music Colleges. (See also **universities, history of**)

profile An attempt to provide an alternative form of **assessment** to school reports for pupils. Whereas the conventional report concentrates on performance in particular subjects, profiles assess a range of pupils' qualities, attitudes and behaviour, so that a much fuller picture of each individual may be given. It is claimed that they are particularly appropriate in the upper secondary school, for potential employers, and were included in the criteria for the **Technical and Vocational Education Initiative** (TVEI) extension programme as well as schemes for **records of achievement**. Criticisms are directed at the ethical and technical difficulties of profiles, at the place of teachers' value judgments in assessments, and at their value if confined only to those who achieve few examination successes. It should be noted that profile schemes can be pupil-controlled as an alternative to teacher-based judgments: this involves the pupils in recording their experiences and achievements.

profile component (PC)   In the **Task Group on Assessment and Testing** Report a profile component was a cluster of **Attainment Targets** within one of the **national curriculum** subjects. It was dropped after the **Dearing Review** in 1995.

programmed learning   Programmed learning is based upon self-instructional materials. They are designed to allow pupils to progress at their own pace, step-by-step, through carefully structured sequences. The programmes may be either linear or branching, or a mixture of the two. They are normally presented in the form of a programmed text or in a teaching machine. More recently, programmed learning has been associated with computer-assisted instruction or **computer assisted learning** (CAL). Some programmed learning is associated with the **behavioural objectives** school and/or the work of B. F. Skinner. (See also **individual learning, Skinnerian**)

Programmes of Study (PoS)   Defined in the **Education Reform Act** (1988) as 'The matters, skills and processes which are required to be taught to pupils of different abilities and maturities during each Key Stage'. There is a description of Programmes of Study for each subject with reference to appropriate **Key Stages**.

Progress File   The Progress File is a set of guidance and working materials intended to help students aged 13–19, as well as adults, to record, review and present their achievements, to set goals, and to mark progression in learning and in work. The Progress File was designed particularly to help students plan and review their learning transitions. In February 2002, Progress File materials were in use in about one third of **secondary schools**. (See also **individual learning plan**)

progression   A desirable feature of any planned system of **curriculum** and **assessment** is that pupils should be enabled to make progress at their own pace in any subject and that this progress is measurable. (See also **differentiation**)

progressive education   One of the most ambiguous terms in the whole of educational literature. For some, 'progressive' meant no more than a reaction against the nineteenth-century harsh discipline and unimaginative teaching methods. The reaction (at the end of the nineteenth century and more particularly at the beginning of the twentieth century) usually took the form of schools that did not use **corporal punishment**, that treated children as individuals, and that moved away from **rote learning** as the main system of acquiring **knowledge**. After the 1944 Education Act, however, the word 'progressive' began to be used by those who supported **comprehensive schools** rather than the traditional **tripartite system**. Comprehensive school supporters were described as progressive, while those who wished to retain the **grammar schools** would be labelled traditional. This was particularly confusing since one strand in the English progressive education movement was the group of **independent schools** associated with the **New Education Fellowship**.

In the late-1960s and early-1970s, progressivism in education was attacked in the **Black Papers**. This attack was on so-called progressive methods in **primary schools**, which usually consisted of an **integrated** approach to the curriculum rather than a subject-based timetable; and in **secondary schools**, where a more **child-centred** approach was attacked. In primary and secondary schools, the alleged lack of **'discipline'** was deplored. The abolition of the 11 plus system in primary schools and the liberalising of examinations at 16 plus in secondary schools was also criticised by the writers of the Black Papers. In the 1990s, these were probably still the major issues separating 'progressives' from traditionalists, but the label is sometimes applied indiscriminately. For example, an educationist might be a strong advocate of comprehensive schools, but someone who wishes to retain traditional examination. 'Progressive' is a term now best avoided unless carefully defined. (See also **New Education**, **progressive schools**)

progressive schools First pioneered by Cecil Reddie at Abbotsholme in 1889, the English progressive school movement was based on the notion of social reform through education. **Independent schools**, many of which are mainly boarding in character, represented miniature societies; Reddie and others looked to a reformed and enlightened system of schooling which eliminated **corporal punishment**, furthered team-spirit rather than individuals, was co-educational in composition, and democratic in its day-to-day running. This movement received a second impulse after the First World War and again in the 1930s. Well-known schools associated with the movement include Bedales, Dartington Hall, King Alfred School and Summerhill. (See also **New Education**, **progressive education**)

project (1) An educational activity often based on pupils' interests, centred on a particular problem or issue. This method emphasises co-operative learning between pupils and teachers. W. H. Kilpatrick, a colleague of John Dewey in the USA, was instrumental in popularising this approach after the

First World War. (See also **assignment**, **problem solving**, **team teaching**, **topic work**) (2) A name given to a small- or large-scale research programme, carried out by one or more persons, in some aspect of education. (See also **curriculum development project**)

proprietary school   A type of joint-stock company **public school** which became popular with the middle classes from the earlier part of the nineteenth century. Some of the early ones, such as University College School, London, and the Liverpool Institute, founded in the 1820s, were essentially **day schools** with a broad curriculum but without religious teaching. Later, with the coming of the railways, **boarding schools** became common, and resulted in a growth of such schools as Marlborough (1842), Wellington (1859), Clifton (1860), and Malvern (1862). (See also **Woodard schools**)

prospectus   All State schools are legally obliged to produce a prospectus setting out basic information for parents. The prospectuses vary from glossy brochures to much more modest efforts and can be combined with the governors' **annual report**. School prospectuses must contain information on **admissions** and **special educational needs** policies. They give details of **national curriculum** results, the religious education provided and, in secondary schools, a summary of public examination results. Prospectuses are published during the school year preceding the admission school year. Copies of secondary school prospectuses are also sent to the local careers service.

Public Private Partnership (PPP)   An inexact phrase, but it includes the contracting out of services by **local education authorities** to private companies. This can vary from minor aspects of education to private firms acting as consultants to several education authorities. (See also **Private Finance Initiative***)*

public school   In England, an independent fee-paying school, of which there are about 200, most of whose heads are members of the **Headmasters' and Headmistresses' Conference**. The majority of them are boarding schools. The origins of this type of school are complex and varied. Many were the result of the endowment of pious founders and were indistinguishable from **grammar schools**. Eton, Winchester and Westminster are typical examples. By the eighteenth century, a number of 'great schools' had emerged, including Harrow, Rugby, Sherborne, Canterbury and Shrewsbury. The **Clarendon Report** of 1864 named nine public schools as the object of its investigations and thus marked off these institutions from other endowed schools. Some have close links with universities under the terms of their founders: e.g. Henry VI established King's College, Cambridge, for Eton scholars and similarly, William Wykeham, founder of Winchester, endowed New College, Oxford. These schools are now called **independent schools**. In the USA and many other countries the term public school means State school.

punishment, corporal (See **corporal punishment**)

punishment, psychology and philosophy of A good deal of work has been done by educationists on both the psychology of punishment and the philosophy of punishment. Much of the work on the psychology of punishment has been carried out from a behaviourist point of view and sees punishment as a way of discouraging certain kinds of behaviour and encouraging alternative preferred behaviour. In the philosophy of punishment, distinction is made between punishment as a means of reform and as a means of retribution. (See also **corporal punishment**, **Society of Teachers Opposed to Physical Punishment**)

pupil (See **student**)

pupil referral unit (PRU) Schools have always faced the problem of how to deal with pupils who do not 'fit in' with the rules and other demands of school life. The traditional **independent school** solution was **expulsion** or permanent **exclusion**, but **maintained schools** operate within the context of every child having a right to education. Exclusion from maintained schools therefore tends to be very short-term, and if the period of exclusion needs to be longer then the **local education authority** has the responsibility for providing education either by means of a **home tutor** or in referral units with specialised staff trained to find ways of educating children, using methods different from those in schools. The main aim of PRUs is to return students to mainstream education as soon as possible. Pupil referral units have much more favourable **staff–student ratios** than normal schools.

pupil–teacher ratio (PTR) The majority of **local education authorities** approach the allocation of teaching staff to schools at all levels by the use of a pupil–teacher ratio (PTR). At the primary level, schools are staffed on the basis of numbers of children and size of school; at the secondary level, local authorities have moved from a single PTR for all pupils to age-specific PTRs which take account of the higher staffing demands imposed by older pupils. Special factors are increasingly taken into account. A major concern for parents is the size of classes of more than 30. Whilst educationists are not unanimous on the importance of small classes, **independent schools** regard this as an essential basis for good teaching.

Pygmalion effect (See **self-fulfilling prophecy**)

Q and F Levels   In 1969, the Standing Conference on University Entrance and the **schools council** put forward proposals to replace **A Level** examinations. This would have consisted of two stages: a Qualifying examination (Q), based on one year's study of five subjects beyond GCE **O Level**, and an F or Further examination, corresponding to one year's work beyond Q in not more than three subjects. The proposals did not meet with favour and were replaced by **N** and **F Levels**. No reform to **A Levels** took place until **Curriculum 2000**.

quadrivium   The **curriculum** in the Middle Ages consisted of the 'seven liberal arts'. The first three – grammar, logic and rhetoric – formed the **trivium**, and the other four – music, arithmetic, geometry and astronomy – made up the quadrivium. The whole made a course of seven years' duration. The term 'quadrivium' dates back to Boethius (AD 470–525). (See also **liberal studies**)

Qualifications and Curriculum Authority (QCA)   A public body set up under the 1997 Education Act to supersede the **School Curriculum and Assessment Authority** (SCAA) and the **National Council for Vocational Qualifications** (NCVQ). The Authority has a wide remit, being responsible to the Government for advice on the **curriculum** for those under five years of age; the **national curriculum** for 5–16-year-olds; national tests for 7, 11 and 14 year olds; and **General Certificate of Secondary Education, A Levels** and vocational qualifications. It accredits and reviews all externally awarded qualifications, except those from higher education institutions. There are separate bodies for Wales – the **Qualifications, Curriculum and Assessment Authority for Wales** (QCAAW); for Scotland – the **Scottish Qualifications Authority** (SQA); and for Northern Ireland – the **Council for the Curriculum, Examinations and Assessment** (CCEA).

Qualifications Curriculum and Assessment Authority for Wales (QCAAW)   This Authority, also known as the ACCAC (Awdurdod Cymwysterau, Cwricwlwm ac Asesu Cymru), is the principal advisory body for the **National Assembly for Wales** on all aspects of the school curriculum, examinations, assessment and vocational qualifications. Its functions are similar to those of the **Qualifications and Curriculum Authority** (QCA) in England, but it has particular responsibility for the **national curriculum** in Wales, especially the Welsh language, and the Welsh dimension of the whole curriculum.

qualified teacher status (QTS)   Although there are now several different routes into the teaching profession, all new entrants must reach national standards for the award of qualified teacher status. In England, trainees must pass a small but compulsory component, i.e. computer-based skills tests in numeracy, literacy and information and communications technology, organised by the **Teacher Training Agency** (TTA), and held at designated centres, before QTS can be awarded. (For an account of the routes, see also **Bachelor of Education**, **Fast Track**, **Graduate Teacher Programme**, **Overseas Trained Teacher**, **Professional Graduate Certificate of Education**, **Registered Teacher Programme** and **teacher training skills tests**)

quality assurance   A term introduced into the official language of education in the White Paper, *Higher Education: A New Framework* (1991). Quality assurance is a general term that includes two more specific aspects of quality: **quality control** that is carried out by the institutions themselves; and quality audit that is an external check on internal controls (probably by means of an **Academic Audit Unit**).

Quality Assurance Agency for Higher Education (QAA)   The QAA was established in 1997 to provide an integrated quality assurance service for UK **higher education**. It is an independent body funded by subscriptions from universities and colleges of higher education and through contacts with higher education funding bodies. The QAA reviews the quality and standards of UK higher education by auditing the way in which each **university** and college manages the overall quality and standards of its provision, and by reviewing academic standards and the quality of teaching and learning in each subject area. The QAA reviews result in reports available to the public. It also publishes a **code of practice**, a national framework for higher education qualifications and statements of subject **benchmark** standards. (See also **benchmarking academic standards**)

quality control   The aspect of **quality assurance** that is concerned with maintaining **standards** of teaching and student **performance**. Quality control is normally carried out by the institution itself.

quango (quasi-autonomous non-governmental organisation)
A term of abuse developed in the 1970s to attack a particular kind of bureaucratic structure. Some quangos were educational organisations, and a few of them were very important. The overall number of quangos was reduced in the early 1980s and a number of educational organisations disappeared. This did not, however, prevent the Government from creating new quangos such as the **Council for the Accreditation of Teacher Education** (CATE).

quota system   (1) A scheme operated by the then **Department of Education and Science** until 1975: **local education authorities** were allocated a quota of teachers as a means of ensuring fairness during a period of teacher shortage. (2) In order to link student numbers in **initial teacher training** with the quality of provision, the **Teacher Training Agency** (TTA) operated a quota system that encouraged 'good' providers to keep up their numbers or to expand, whilst restricting or eliminating the numbers of students in poorer quality institutions.

R

Race Relations (Amendment) Act (2000)   This Act was not primarily concerned with education but with Home Office Regulations for racial equality. Nevertheless, the Act has several implications for schools and other educational institutions. The Act places a positive duty on public authorities actively to promote equality and to take steps to avoid race discrimination before it occurs. Public bodies are required by the Act to set out their arrangements for avoiding discrimination, for monitoring their effectiveness and publishing the results. Education bodies will be required to have a written policy on race equality and to assess the impact of the policy on ethnic minority pupils, staff and parents. There is a particular emphasis on the attainment of ethnic minority pupils. **Local education authorities, Office for Standards in Education** (OFSTED) **and the Learning and Skills Council** (LSC) all have responsibilities under the Act.

ragged schools   Schools, aimed at street children, which were pioneered by John Pounds (1766–1839), a Portsmouth cobbler. The Ragged School Union, which was formed in 1844 under the presidency of Lord Shaftesbury, provided schools for the very poor. Religious teaching figured prominently in the curriculum. Ragged schools developed various agencies for employment, the best known being the Shoeblack Brigade.

raising of the school leaving age   (See **ROSLA**)

Rampton Report   One of the results of the discussions during the 1970s about the under-achievement of certain **ethnic minorities** was that a Committee of Enquiry was set up under the chairmanship of Mr Anthony Rampton in March 1979. Its Report was published in 1981 and became very controversial. Soon after the publication of the Interim Report, Anthony Rampton was replaced as chairman by Sir Michael Swann. (See also **multicultural education, under-achiever**)

range   In **National Vocational Qualifications** (NVQ) terminology range indicates the contexts in which the activity in the **element** is to be undertaken and the extent of the **knowledge**, understanding and **skills** that are to be demonstrated.

range statement   An addition to an **element** indicating the range of application of the element.

rank, ranking, rank order   Ranking is the process of arranging individuals in order of achievement (e.g. **reading ability** or **intelligence** or performance on arithmetic tests). The highest rank is given to the person with the highest score and this person is numbered 1, the second highest 2, and so on. (In the USA, ranking is sometimes reversed so that 1 is the lowest rank.) If a list of marks is published in this way (rather than alphabetically) the list may be described as a rank order.

readability   Since it is important that material presented to young pupils is not too 'difficult' for them, a number of educationists have attempted to develop measures of 'readability' which indicate the ease with which a passage or even a whole text may be read. Sometimes **reading ages** are assigned to texts in this way. The measures most frequently employed are length of words and sentences, but the familiarity of the language used and the style are also important. It is rarely possible to give an exact indication because two other factors are also very important and they are much more difficult to measure: the first is the number of abstract words and examples given; the second is the author's ability to motivate the child. It has been found that children can read 'above their reading age' if they find the subject matter sufficiently interesting. (See also **reading, readiness**)

reader   (1) A volume consisting of extracts of the works of various authors on a particular theme. (2) A university title, in status between that of senior lecturer and a **professor**.

readiness   A concept described by Jerome Bruner as a 'mischievous half truth'. The idea of readiness is that pupils should not be forced to learn certain **skills** (particularly **reading**) until they have reached a certain maturational stage, and are ready to embark upon that particular learning skill. Critics of the concept point out that it might encourage some teachers to avoid teaching children until they were 'ready', when they ought to be making them ready by teaching them the prerequisite abilities.

reading   The teaching of reading has become an ideological issue in two respects: first, how it is taught (See also **phonics**, **real books**, **graded readers**); second, what pupils are encouraged or required to read (See also **canon**).

reading age   A pupil's competence in **reading** measured against the average competence of children for his/her age. An eight-year-old pupil who was advanced in his/her reading ability might have a reading age of ten, whereas a less advanced eight-year-old might only have a reading age of six or seven. (See also **intelligence quotient**)

reading recovery   An intervention programme assisting early readers who encounter problems. There was an extensive research programme in New Zealand in the 1970s under the direction of Professor Marie Clay who came to England in 1991 to direct a project at the Institute of Education, University of London. The method is described in M. Clay, *The Early Detection of Reading Difficulties* (Heinemann, 1972).

real books   This is a preferred method of teaching **reading** by some teachers (for some children); it emphasises the enjoyment of reading real books rather than **graded readers** and **phonics**.

received pronunciation   The form of spoken English that is associated with educated classes in the South of England. It should not be confused with **standard English**.

reception class   The class reserved for five-year-old new entrants into the infant section of a **primary school**.

record-keeping   **Maintained schools** are required to keep records of all pupils' academic progress, including the results of **national curriculum** assessment at age 7, 11 and 14.

record of achievement   A method of summarising a pupil's attainments and activities in school so that they can be passed on from teacher to teacher and from school to school. (See also **National Record of Achievement** (NRA), **school records**)

recurrent education   A policy based on the view that **compulsory education** should be regarded as the first stage in the educational process, followed if not by **further education** or **higher education**, then by a series of returns to courses of education throughout the period of adult life. Recurrent education can be vocational or professional or entirely non-vocational, but there tends to be an association of recurrent education with the idea of updating professional skills. (See also **adult education, continuing education, in-service education of teachers, permanent education**)

'redbrick' university   Name coined by Bruce Truscot (pseudonym of F. Allison Peers) in his book, *Redbrick University* (1943), to describe the characteristics of seven of the English civic **universities** established in the late-nineteenth and early-twentieth centuries. The term has now passed into general usage and is contrasted with **Oxbridge**. (See also **universities, history of**)

redeployment   Voluntary or compulsory transfer of staff to another teacher post in another school. Because of **falling rolls** in schools, this practice has become more common.

reductionism   A belief held by some psychologists and others that it is possible to explain a complex phenomenon by breaking it down into smaller parts and explaining the individual constituents. Behaviourist psychology is said to be reductionist because it claims to explain the whole of human behaviour in terms of the two concepts – stimulus and response. Similarly, the **behavioural objectives** approach to **curriculum** planning is said to be reductionist because it reduces the learning process to a series of behavioural changes which can be measured. In psychology, an opposite point of view is held by **Gestalt** psychologists. In curriculum studies, the opposite point of view would be taken by those describing themselves as humanistic. (See also **behaviourism, objectives**)

reflective practitioner   A term association with Donald Schon – see *The Reflective Practitioner* (1983) – and not confined to teaching. According to this view, being a good teacher involves reflecting on (thinking about) what works in the classroom, why and to what purpose.

register (linguistic)   A variety of language associated with a specific context or purpose: e.g. medical language, or language used in advertising, or the language of horse racing. English syllabuses at **General Certificate of Secondary Education (GCSE)** or **A Level** sometimes specify understanding the concept register or being able to use the vocabulary and style appropriate to different registers. The concept of 'register' was also incorporated into the **National Literacy Strategy** and the **literacy hour** in a simplified form.

register (of attendance)   A record of pupils' attendance at school, including figures for lateness. Class teachers are required to keep accurate registers of attendance. (See also **truancy**)

registered inspector   A leader of **Office for Standards in Education** (OFSTED) inspections who has had previous substantial inspectorial experience, and has had responsibilities in an 'associate' team leader role. Prospective registered inspectors are nominated by contractors to OFSTED, who have an assessment programme for applicants. Some 1,500 out of the total OFSTED force of 7,500 inspectors are registered inspectors.

Registered Teacher Programme (RTP) This is similar to the **Graduate Teacher Programme** (GTP), but designed for trainees with at least two years' experience of **higher education** who do not possess a degree. Candidates train and work in schools while studying for a degree at a higher education institution. Trainees follow a programme which normally takes two years but those who have almost finished their degree or already have teaching experience may be able to train in as little as a year. (See also **Bachelor of Education**, **Professional Graduate Certificate of Education**, **initial teacher training**)

registrar A senior post in a college or **university** whose holder is responsible for students' enrolment, student records, examinations, academic administration, and the oversight of committees. Some institutions have both an academic registrar (concerned with enrolment) and a registrar with more general responsibilities.

registration of independent schools Since the 1944 Education Act, all **independent schools** providing full-time education for five or more pupils of compulsory school age have been obliged to register with the **Department of Education and Science** (now the **Department for Education and Skills** (DfES)) or the **Welsh Office**. After a school has been given provisional registration by **Her Majesty's Inspectorate** (HMI), visits are made to satisfy the Department on the suitability of the premises, accommodation, staffing and instruction; as a result final registration may be granted. The **Children Act** (1989) requires the proprietors of **boarding schools** to safeguard and promote the welfare of their pupils. Since 1977, **independent schools** have not been able to apply to be registered as efficient. The Independent Schools Joint Council have a system of **accreditation** of schools based upon inspection.

regius professor University chairs that were endowed by the Crown. The first, at Oxford in 1497, was the professorship in divinity. There followed other chairs at Oxford and Cambridge in divinity, law, physics, Hebrew and Greek, and in other fields. These chairs are confined to **Oxbridge** and Scottish universities. Although the Crown may nominate candidates for these chairs, appointments are, in fact, made on the advice of the Prime Minister or the Secretary of State for Scotland. (See also **professor**)

regression (1) A term derived from psychoanalysis, but which has become common in educational and counselling circles. Regression occurs when an individual returns (regresses) to behaviour typical of an earlier stage of his/her emotional or intellectual development. Regression is said to tend to occur when an individual encounters a situation that is extremely painful. (2) Regression is a statistical technique for analysing relationships between two or more variables in order to predict or estimate values. (See also **regression to the mean**)

regression to the mean   A phrase that is often found in discussions of intelligence and other desirable qualities. Where parents are tall (or intelligent) there is a tendency for children of those parents to be tall (or intelligent), but not as tall or intelligent as the parents – in other words, there is a tendency for offspring to be somewhere between the parents' score and the average score. This is, of course, a tendency and not a general rule. The same process applies to unintelligent parents: their children are likely to be below average, but closer to the average than their parents. (See also **regression**)

reification   A term much used in sociology of education. It refers to the tendency of individuals, including social scientists, to treat 'ideas' as if they existed as 'things'. For example, the class structure is 'man-made' or socially constructed, but it is often referred to as if it had an independent existence. More controversially, some sociologists have suggested that **knowledge** is reified and that subject barriers are taken for granted when they ought to be questioned.

reliability   A technical term which must be distinguished from **validity**. Reliability means the extent to which a test or an individual test item will give the same result on different occasions. For example, an individual test of **intelligence** should give the same result for a given individual on a number of separate occasions. If it does this, it could be said to be a 'reliable test' even if there were some doubts as to whether or not it was measuring real intelligence – i.e., a question of the validity of the test.

remedial education   Such education tends to be of relatively short duration and limited to specific objectives, particularly remedying failures or the difficulty in learning some school subjects (especially in basic education). Schools differ in their method of providing such education. In the **Warnock** conception of a range of alternative forms of special provision in ordinary schools, the remedial teacher would be part of a school's response to children with **special educational needs**.

report   Most schools have kept parents informed of their children's progress by means of one or more reports during the year. These included the results of internal examinations and/or classwork throughout the year together. From summer 1992, schools were required to send a written report to all parents at least once a year, to include information on achievements in the **core subjects** of the **national curriculum** and the results of **Standard Assessment Tasks** (SATs) taken at 7, 11 and 14; also, results in other examinations or tests taken during the year; how the child's results in the Standard Assessment Tasks tests compare with those of other children of the same age; and the child's general progress and his/her attendance record. Parents are also encouraged to explore with the school ways in which they can help to improve their children's performance. (See also **National Record of Achievement**, **school records**)

research and development (R and D)   A style of research activity that focused on practical issues and where the intention was to produce results of a practical improvement kind as part of the research programme. It is closely related to the style of research described as **action research**. In **curriculum** studies one style of innovation is described as R, D and D (research development and dissemination). This is based on a concentric model of dissemination with an expert at the centre doing the research, pilot schools carrying out the development and, finally, the good news being disseminated to other schools. The model is now regarded as generally too simple to be of practical use in a curriculum development programme.

Research Assessment Exercise (RAE)   Every four years universities are invited to submit their research work for scrutiny by the appropriate **Higher Education Funding Council** (HEFC). The HEFC determines on a method of assessing the quality of the research and negotiates the assessment exercise with individual universities, department by department. The university, or the department, has to decide which of its academic staff are 'entered' and then each department is graded from five stars (very good) to one star (poor). Each department is awarded a research grant on the basis of its grade (e.g. five) and its multiplier (the number of researchers entered). A very small number of universities or higher education institutions do not enter, and therefore receive no share of the research grant from their HEFC.

Research Fellow   An individual, holding a post in an institution of **higher education** for a specific period of time, who is employed to investigate a particular topic or range of topics. Many of these posts are sponsored by bodies outside the institution.

research grant   A sum of money made available to an individual or an institution in order to carry out research into a topic. The outcome is usually presented in the form of a report.

research project   A systematic inquiry of some kind of limited duration designed to produce new knowledge or to test new materials or methods, or in some other way engage in scientific discovery or problem solving. The **Economic and Social Research Council** (ESRC) annually promotes funded research for a number of educational inquiries. The **National Foundation for Educational Research** (NFER) also engages in a series of such projects. (See also **curriculum development project**)

revenue support grant (RSG)   (Previously called the rate support grant.) This is a grant from central government towards the cost of services for which a local authority is responsible – including education. The RSG is fixed as a result of negotiations between government and local authorities. In November/December the government issues **standard spending assessments** (SSAs) to all local authorities, including a specific SSA for education. (See also **Local Government Acts**)

review of results   A process through which awarding decisions at **GCSE** or **A Level** are checked to ensure that candidates' results reflect their achievements fairly.

Revised Code   (See '**payment by results**')

'rising fives'   By law, parents are obliged to send their children to school at the beginning of the term after which their children reach the age of five. **Local education authorities** may admit them to schools if there is sufficient accommodation before the statutory age. Such pupils are called 'rising fives'. (See also **nursery classes**, **nursery schools**)

Robbins Report   A committee on higher education appointed by Harold Macmillan, the then Prime Minister, and chaired by Lord Robbins to review the existing patterns of **higher education** in Great Britain, and to advise whether there should be any changes in that pattern and whether any new types of institution were desirable. This enquiry stemmed from the growing numbers of sixth formers who were eligible for advanced education. The Report, published in 1963, assumed as an axiom ('the Robbins Principle') that courses 'should be available for all those who are qualified by ability and attainment to pursue them and wish to do so'.

Several important recommendations were made. University first degree courses should be broadened and increased in length to four years, and more provision made for research and advanced courses. The status of **teacher training colleges** was to be raised by closer links with universities and the introduction of an appropriate degree. The Report recommended that they should be renamed **colleges of education**. The need to attract a higher proportion of first-class talent to technology was to be recognised by an expansion of postgraduate research and training. Colleges of advanced technology were to be granted charters as technological universities and the

Report recommended the setting up of six new universities and the advancement to university status of ten other colleges.

The Report was immediately accepted by government; £650 million was made available for capital expenditure; colleges of advanced technology were promoted to university status; and some technological universities were created. The policy was a success: between 1965 and 1975, university numbers doubled and the number of **polytechnics** increased by almost 50 per cent. Expansion continued into the 1980s and 1990s, culminating in the granting of university status to polytechnics in 1992. (See also **universities, history of**)

ROSLA (raising of the school leaving age)   During the academic year 1972–73 the statutory minimum leaving age was raised from 15 to 16, as was envisaged in the 1944 Education Act and specifically recommended by the **Newsom Report** (1963). The 'extra year' caused many **secondary schools** to rethink what they were doing and to mount, in some cases, special courses for pupils who had previously left at age 15. To some observers it seemed that schools could be divided into two categories: those who regarded the extra year as a challenge and an opportunity to provide a full course of **secondary education** for all their pupils; and those schools who regarded the extra year as a problem and began talking of courses for 'ROSLA pupils'. (See also **school leaving age**)

rote learning   Learning facts mechanically 'by heart', by a process of practice and repetition. A style of teaching that indulges in a good deal of rote learning without any attempt at understanding the material will now be criticised as old-fashioned.

Royal Commission   Royal Commissions are appointed by the Queen in Council and are charged with the duty of reporting in terms of their order of reference. Eminent people are invited to be members for their knowledge of the topic to be investigated. The Commission's Report is published as a **Parliamentary Paper**. Their recommendations may form the basis for legislation. Evidence taken is usually printed as a non-Parliamentary Paper by Her Majesty's Stationery Office.

The great age of Royal Commissions in education was the second half of the nineteenth century. Before this time, **Select Committees** were the chosen instrument. With the **Bryce Commission** on secondary education in 1895, the series of Royal Commissions came to an end because of the comparatively lengthy time which they took to report. From the founding of the **Board of Education** in 1900, the work of the Commission was given first to consultative committees and later still to **Central Advisory Councils**. (See also **Parliamentary Papers**)

Royal Society of Arts (RSA)   Founded in 1754 'for the encouragement of Arts, Manufactures and Commerce' and incorporated by Royal Charter in 1847, the Society, an independent and self-financing body, carries out a number of functions and has long shown a close interest in education. For many years it offered examinations in a wide range of subjects in vocational areas, such as languages, information technology, business and administration, and retail and basic skills. The RSA Examinations Board, which was a separate company with charitable status, is no longer affiliated with the Society. It has merged with the Oxford and Cambridge Examination Boards to form OCR (the Oxford, Cambridge and RSA Examinations Board). (See also **examination boards**)

rubric   A set of instructions and other items of guidance provided for candidates on an examination paper.

Ruskin College   An **adult education** college established in Oxford in 1899, offering full-time courses up to two years in length. Many of the students are actively involved in trade unions. At a ceremony to mark the opening of a hall of residence, in October 1976, the then Prime Minister, James Callaghan, launched the **Great Debate** on education, calling in his speech for the improvement of **standards** in schools and the introduction of the concept of teacher **accountability**. (See also **Yellow Book**)

Russell Report   A Committee of Inquiry under the chairmanship of Sir Lionel Russell was appointed in 1969 to review the provision of non-vocational **adult education** in England and Wales and to consider the appropriateness of existing educational, administrative and financial policies. Its report, issued in 1973, and entitled *Adult Education: A Plan for Development*, was an ambitious one. It recommended the commitment of central government funds to assist local authority financing of adult education and assumed a doubling of student numbers between 1973 and 1978. The recommendations were not implemented.

Rutter Report   A study, following a comparative survey of ten-year-olds in London and the Isle of Wight, of 12 inner London non-selective secondary schools which attempted to measure success by reference to pupils' behaviour both in and out of school, their academic achievements, and attendance rates. The team of researchers, led by Professor Michael Rutter, published their findings in 1979 in a book called *Fifteen Thousand Hours*. The Report concluded that schools could significantly affect children's achievements, compared with home and other influences. Schools with good attendance tend to have well-behaved pupils who perform well in examinations. The ethos of the school was found to be an important factor. Where teachers set good standards, provided good models of behaviour, and gave praise and responsibility to pupils, and where lessons were well prepared and organised, were all indicators of a good school. It is claimed that the schools selected were untypical, that some of the statistics were wrongly analysed, and that it over-estimated the extent to which schools can overcome social influences. Nevertheless, the study raises a number of important issues especially on the relationship between life in schools and factors affecting achievement. (See also **effective schools**)

S

S Level   An examination which may be taken by above average **GCE A Level** candidates who wish to go on to **higher education**. The standard is high and the result is taken into consideration only if the candidate has done sufficiently well in the **A Level** papers.

sabbatical   A period of paid leave for private study or research, varying in length from one term to one year. In the original sense of the term, a sabbatical year should occur once every seven years, but institutions differ widely in their practices. Sabbatical leave is commonly available in **higher education** institutions but much less so in schools. From 2001, teachers in England can apply for a paid six-weeks' sabbatical, funded by the **Department for Education and Skills**. As part of their professional development, successful candidates are expected to follow a programme of study that enhances their learning and effectiveness. (See also **study leave**)

Samuelson Report   The terms of reference of the Royal Commission on Technical Instruction chaired by an industrialist, Bernhard Samuelson, were 'to inquire into the instruction of the industrial classes of certain foreign countries in technical and other subjects for the purpose of comparison with that of the corresponding classes in this country; and into the influence of such instruction on manufacturing and other industries at home and abroad'. The Commission was appointed in 1881. Its second report in 1884 outlined a programme for developing **technical education**. Many of the recommendations were implemented after the passing of the **Technical Instruction Act** (1889) and a Local Taxation Act in the following year. (See also **Devonshire Report**)

sandwich course   A course consisting of a mixture of full-time studies and full-time work. Many **university degree** courses combine these two elements in such areas as engineering and **business studies**. The sandwich element can be either 'thick', with full-time employment of a year, or 'thin', consisting of two or three periods of time each lasting up to half a year.

scaling   The process of converting scores from one scale to another. Different procedures are used in different circumstances, e.g.:

1. The conversion of scores for a particular examination component from one scale (e.g. 0–60) to another (e.g. 0–100) to accord with the **weighting** of the component.
2. The adjustment of a set of scores to give the set a different mean and **standard deviation** (thus altering its weighting).
3. The adjustment of an individual examiner's scores to bring them into line with an agreed **standard**.

schema (*plural* schemata)   A technical term used by Piaget and other developmental psychologists to refer to a conceptual structure that is used to interpret information in the external world perceived by the senses. A schema is, therefore, a kind of hypothesis set up in the brain to make sense of reality. When a child (or adult) encounters a new situation that does not fit in with an existing schema, the individual will either be puzzled or adapt the schema or schemata to try to make better sense of reality.

scheme of assessment   A set of examination components – including terminal **examinations** and **coursework** – through which candidates' attainments on a particular syllabus are determined.

schemes of work   Designed by panels of subject specialists from the **Qualifications and Curriculum Authority** (QCA) and practising teachers, schemes of work are intended to help teachers to turn **Programmes of Study** into teaching programmes. They are accompanied by a teachers' guide which demonstrates how links across subjects may be established as well as with different **Key Stages** within the same subject. Schemes of work are not compulsory but serve as a useful lesson planning resource.

scholarship   (1) **Knowledge** and **skills** of a high standard in an **academic** field. (2) An **entrance award**, carrying with it a sum of money, for students embarking upon **higher education**, who are regarded as worthy of exceptional support.

scholastic/scholasticism   Scholasticism was the medieval theological system that attempted to integrate Christian doctrine with Platonic and

Aristotelian philosophy. 'Scholastic' can now mean: (1) pertaining to schools, universities or colleges; (2) pedantic or quibbling over detail.

scholastic agency (or agent)   An employment agency for private schools which also provides advice for parents wishing to choose such a school.

Scholastic Aptitude Test (SAT)   In the USA, batteries of **multiple choice** tests lasting about three hours are set at the end of high school courses to assist in the process of **selection** for colleges and universities.

school   (1) Most commonly refers to an institution where children of school-age are taught. (2) At Oxford, may describe a course of study leading to an examination for a first degree (e.g. philosophy, politics and economics), or more widely to describe all persons working in a subject (e.g. chemistry school). It also appears as part of a title of a college in other universities, for example the London School of Economics and Political Science. In the University of London, a school is a semi-autonomous college, as distinct from a Senate institute.

school adjudicator   Section 25 of the School Standards and Framework Act (1998) allowed the appointment of school adjudicators by the Secretary of State. They have two main functions: to deal with issues relating to **maintained school** admissions; and to make decisions on proposed change to school organisation. There is a Chief Schools Adjudicator assisted by a team of 14 adjudicators. Where ten or more parents of children of **primary school** age object to the selection procedures for entry to a **secondary school**, the school adjudicator can make a decision on the case. Proposed changes to school organisation are sent to the adjudicator where a **school organisation committee** either cannot reach a unanimous verdict or when the promoters of the proposal request the adjudicator to scrutinise the plan. **Foundation** and **voluntary aided schools** are allowed to challenge local proposals. Although the adjudicators' decisions are binding, they are still subject to judicial review.

school admissions   School admission procedures are governed by the School Standards and Framework Act (1998). A complicated appeal procedure was also introduced by the Act with the appointment of **school adjudicators**. There has been a sharp rise in the number of appeals. In the school year 1999–2000, one in ten parents appealed against decisions not to give their children places at preferred schools.

school board   The 1870 Education Act had two aims: to induce children to attend schools and to provide good schools throughout the country. This latter aim was to be achieved by filling up the gaps in the voluntary system then prevailing. Where there was a deficiency in the accommodation provided by voluntary effort, a school board was elected by the district. The board's duty was to build new schools from rate aid or to help existing ones. Normally, school fees were required (where parents could pay), and boards were empowered to frame by-laws for compulsory attendance for children between 5 and 13 years of age. The Act contained a **conscience clause** for board schools, individual boards determining the form of religious instruction given. The Act proved to be a success, with some 300 boards being formed by the end of 1871. This system of elementary education, together with those from denominational organisations, continued until they were abolished by the 1902 Education Act. (See also **free education**, **National Education League**, **National Education Union**)

school categories   The School Standards and Framework Act (1998) stipulated that there should be three categories of **maintained schools: community, foundation** and **voluntary**, divided into **voluntary aided,** and **voluntary controlled**. These replaced **county, special agreement** and **grant maintained schools**.

school-centred initial teacher training (SCITT)   During the 1980s and 1990s there was a tendency to criticise traditional forms of **initial teacher training** (ITT) – such as the **Postgraduate Certificate of Education** (PGCE) and the **Bachelor of Education** degree – for being too theoretical. One suggested remedy was to reverse the normal relationship between **higher education** institutions and schools by basing the training of teachers in a school or group of schools which would then contract higher education institutions or others to provide whatever theoretical backing was considered necessary. A few schemes were developed as school-centred initial teacher training units, but they produced comparatively few teachers and many have been criticised by the **Office for Standards in Education** (OFSTED). (See also **qualified teacher status**)

School Certificate   Introduced by the **Secondary School Examinations Council** in 1917, the School Certificate was an examination taken by pupils at the end of a four-year **secondary school** course of study, usually at 16 years of age. No certificate was awarded unless passes in five subjects were obtained. Credits in five subjects bestowed **matriculation** exemption on successful candidates. It was replaced by the **GCE O Level** examination in 1951. (See also **General Certificate of Education, Higher School Certificate**)

school closure   See **Section 12 notice**

school council   A council of students who are either elected or nominated within a school. It expresses views on school matters, though its terms of reference are normally laid down by the headteacher and staff. Such councils do not exist in all schools.

School Curriculum and Assessment Authority (SCAA)   The 1992 White Paper, *Choice and Diversity*, recommended that the **National Curriculum Council** (NCC) and the **School Examinations and Assessment Council** (SEAC) should be replaced by a School Curriculum and Assessment Authority (SCAA). This was carried out as part of the Education Act (1993). In 1997, it merged with the **National Council for Vocational Qualifications** (NCVQ) to become the **Qualifications and Curriculum Authority** (QCA).

School Curriculum Development Committee (SCDC)   When the **Schools Council** was abolished in 1982, it was replaced by two less powerful bodies: a **Secondary Examinations Council** and a **School Curriculum Development Committee**.

school day   The length of time a school is open for pupils and for which pupils of compulsory school age are obliged to attend. The Education Reform Act (1988) (Section 115) gave power to governing bodies to determine the length of the school day and to decide how the sessions should be organised (i.e. the length of lessons). Pressures arising out of the **national curriculum** may encourage a longer school day. The number of hours covered by the teachers' contract (in **maintained schools**) is 1,265 per annum.

school development plans (SDP)   A concept intended to encourage schools to plan for future developments rather than to react to changes imposed upon them. SDPs should give schools more autonomy and control, but **accountability** demands that eventually they will be expected to demonstrate progress in accordance with their SDP.

school effectiveness   (See **effective schools**)

School Examinations and Assessment Council (SEAC)   One of two statutory bodies established under the **Education Reform Act** (1988) to give advice to the Secretary of State on the **national curriculum** (the other being the **National Curriculum Council** (NCC)). In 1993 SEAC was abolished and, together with the NCC, was replaced with the **School Curriculum and Assessment Authority** (SCAA).

school funding   A distinction has to be made between the funding of **independent schools**, which are self-financing, and **maintained schools**, which receive funding from their **local education authority** or indirectly from the Government through another agency. Strictly speaking, it is incorrect to talk of **State schools** because the State has avoided direct ownership and control of schools, although the Government contributes the majority of the finance for most schools. (See also **local management of schools**)

School Health Service   Three official reports at the beginning of the twentieth century – those of the Royal Commission on Physical Training in Scotland (1903), the Interdepartmental Committee on Physical Deterioration (1904), and the Interdepartmental Committee on Medical Inspection and the Feeding of School Children (1905) – revealed the extent of ill-health and malnutrition amongst school children. As a result, in 1907 the Government established a School Medical Service (renamed the School Health Service in 1945). The 1907 Education (Administrative Provisions) Act made **local education authorities** (LEAs) responsible for providing for the medical inspection of pupils in **elementary schools**. The 1944 Education Act requested local education authorities to provide for medical inspection of children from time to time on school premises. By the National Health Service Reorganisation Act (1973), the School Health Service passed from local education authorities to the Secretary of State for Social Services.

school improvement   A movement concerned to improve primary and secondary schools by studying the characteristics of successful schools and how these features may be developed in other schools. (See also **effective schools**)

school leaving age   Under the 1870 Education Act, the newly formed school boards were required to draw up by-laws for the purpose of securing attendance of pupils between the ages of 5 and 13. The 1880 Act required unconditional attendance between 5 and 10 years and with exemption on the grounds of proven proficiency for those between 10 and 13. In 1893, the minimum leaving age was raised to 11, and in 1899 to 12 years of age. The 1918 Education Act raised the leaving age to 14; it was further raised to 15 in 1947, and to 16 in the academic year 1972–73. Section 47 of the 1997 Education Act gives **local education authorities** responsibility for providing suitable education at schools or otherwise for children who, for a range of reasons, including illness or **exclusion**, do not attend. (See also **Education Otherwise, ROSLA**)

School Library Association (SLA)   The Association promotes the development of school libraries and the use of books and other resources. It was founded in 1937 and its members include representatives of all levels of education, as well as publishers and public libraries. A joint board comprising representatives of the School Library Association and the **Library Association** validates courses for the Certificate in School Library Studies.

school meals   The poor physical condition of potential recruits for the Boer War led to the setting up of an Inter-departmental Committee on Physical Deterioration in 1904. Amongst its recommendations were the feeding of necessitous children and the establishment of school medical inspections. Accordingly, another Inter-departmental Committee the following year, headed by the President of the Board of Education, Lord Londonderry, examined these two aspects with special reference to the **elementary school**. In its report, the Committee asked for better co-ordination of existing organisations providing food. However, in 1906 an Education (Provision of Meals) Act went further in stating that the **local education authorities**, not voluntary societies, should be responsible for provision. Local authorities were empowered to levy a rate of half a penny in the pound for this purpose. Both World Wars increased the demand for such a service. The 1944 Education Act made it obligatory for local education authorities to provide a school meals service. The 1980 Education Act removed this obligation, though the need for provision for pupils whose parents were in receipt of supplementary benefit or family income supplement was acknowledged. Nutritional standards were also abolished by the Act. Nine years earlier when Mrs Thatcher was Secretary of State for Education the free school milk scheme was withdrawn. The local authorities' school meals service was replaced by competitive tendering. Concerned at the lack of healthy eating in schools, the Secretary of State, in the School Standards and Framework Act (1998), was given powers to make regulations stating compulsory minimum nutritional standards for school lunches. The new standards were introduced in 2002. Free meals must be provided for pupils of parents on certain income benefits. (See also **School Health Service**)

School of Education   (See **university department of education**)

school of industry   A type of school for pauper children advocated by John Locke in 1697 so that they would be kept 'in much better order, be better provided for, and from infancy be inured to work, which is of no small consequence to the making of them sober and industrious all their lives after'. Children worked up to 12 hours a day at, e.g., spinning, winding and knitting or strawplaiting, and received payment. Reading and writing lessons were given at a charge. The products of such schools usually found work in factories or became domestic servants. (See also **factory school**, **industrial school**)

school organisation committee   Since September 1999, school organisation committees have been set up in each **local education authority** (LEA) to consider plans for changes in proposed opening and closing of schools, and planning for the provision of places. By 1 June each year the LEA must provide an updated draft five-year rolling plan setting out how it proposes to remedy any excess or insufficiency of school places, and how they intend to provide for children with **special educational needs**. The committees are statutory bodies and not committees of the local authorities. They consist of up to six groups, each with between one and seven members, and who serve for three years. Membership consists of representatives of the local education authority, the Anglican and Roman Catholic Church and those reflecting local minority interests. Within the governors' group, there must be a representative from either a primary, middle, secondary or special school. Unless decisions are unanimous, they are referred to a **school adjudicator**.

school organisation plan   **Local education authorities** have a responsibility for ensuring that there are sufficient pupil places in its schools to accommodate present and future needs. By 1 June every year the LEA must provide an updated draft five-year rolling plan – the school organisation plan – setting out how the LEA proposes to remedy any excess or insufficiency of school places and also how they intend to provide for children with **special educational needs**. The school organisation plan then draws conclusions about the need to add or remove school places in specific areas. Copies of the plan must be sent to the governing body of every maintained school in the LEA. Any person can make objections to the plan. The LEA school organisation committee then considers the draft plan alongside any objections. In the event of disagreement, the plan is referred to the **school adjudicator** for consideration.

school phobia   Some children develop such anxieties about attending school that they feel that they cannot leave home or be separated from a parent. It is difficult to distinguish between dislike of a school and a neurotic condition, so much so, that estimates of school phobia numbers varies from about 7,000 in England and Wales (0.1 per cent of the school population) to twice that number. Some schools and **local education authorities** do not accept the existence of school phobia. An organisation has been set up to help genuine cases of school phobia: the Children's Home-based Education Association (CHEA). It produced a booklet, *School Phobia – How to Attack It* (1989), which provides helpful advice, including the option of educating children at home. (See also **Education Otherwise**, **school refusal**)

school psychological service   Educational psychologists are usually employed by **local education authorities** to provide psychological support services to ordinary schools, **special schools** and units, to other agencies like health and social service assessment centres, and to parents. Psychologists have recognised initial and **postgraduate** qualifications in psychology and many are experienced teachers. Psychologists specialise in areas of treatment such as family therapy or behaviour modification, and may act in consultative and advisory roles. They are mainly occupied with children with learning problems and maladjustment in ordinary schools and work closely with remedial services and child guidance clinics.

school records   Confidential records should be kept of all pupils in maintained schools. They contain details of academic achievement and other relevant details which are passed on when pupils change school. In recent years there has been a tendency to make the content of school records more available to parents. (See also **Parent's Charter**, **record of achievement**, **National Record of Achievement**)

school refusal   The condition of a child – a school refuser – whose dislike of school is so intense that he or she refuses to attend. It is often indistinguishable from **school phobia** although the neurotic anxiety of that condition may not be present.

school report   An assessment of pupils' progress in written form, usually subject by subject, for the information of parents. Reports may be issued on a termly, half-yearly or yearly basis. The traditional report has been attacked mainly on the grounds that it does not give a rounded picture of a pupil. **Profiles** have been suggested as an alternative. (See also **school records**, **National Record of Achievement**)

school self-evaluation   Schools are encouraged to carry out rigorous self-evaluation based on standards achieved by pupils, the quality of teaching, and the effectiveness of management. In this way, heads can more easily identify steps which are necessary for improvement. Many schools achieve this by heads and governors setting targets on a yearly basis as part of a strategic plan. A number of **local education authorities** have set out guidelines for their schools and there is also an **Office for Standards in Education** (OFSTED) framework for self-review between inspections.

school uniform   (See **uniform, school**)

Schools, Froebel   (See **Froebel schools**)

Schools, Montessori   (See **Montessori schools**)

Schools Council   In 1962, David Eccles, the then Minister of Education, established a small curriculum study group to give advice on the school **curriculum**. After some hostility from **local education authorities** and

teachers' unions, a Working Party on Schools, Curricula and Examinations, chaired by Sir John Lockwood, produced a Report in 1964 which reaffirmed the importance of the principle that schools should retain the responsibility for their own work, but that a Schools Council for Curriculum and Examinations was necessary for **research and development**. The Council took over the functions of the Curriculum Study Group and the Secondary School Examinations Council.

The Council funded many curriculum projects and published working papers and research reports. In March 1981 the Secretary of State for Education and Science announced that Mrs Trenaman had been invited to review the Schools Council and to make recommendations. Her Report (1981) concluded that the Council should continue with its present functions. It outlined a number of changes which should be made and recommended that the Council should not be the subject of any further review for the next five years. In April 1982 the Secretary of State announced his intention to disband the Council and replace it with two separate bodies – a **Secondary School Examinations Council** and a **School Curriculum Development Committee** – appointments to both of which would be made by the Secretary of State. These arrangements were changed as a result of the **Education Reform Act** (1988), which created a **School Examinations and Assessment Council** (SEAC) and a **National Curriculum Council** (NCC). These were in turn replaced by the **School Curriculum and Assessment Authority** (SCAA) in 1993.

Science and Art Department   The Department was created after the Great Exhibition of 1851 in order to encourage industrial skills. In 1852 a Department of Practical Art was established and in the following year a Science Division was added. The Department, situated at South Kensington, administered parliamentary grants in the field of science and art. By the 1890s, it had assumed the role of a central authority for **technical education**. The Department was eventually absorbed into the new **Board of Education** at the end of the century. (See also **organised science school**, **technical education**)

Science Research Council (SRC)   A council set up by the **Department of Education and Science** to allocate funds for approved scientific research. Members of the Council were appointed by the Secretary of State for Education and Science and met regularly to scrutinise research proposals and to allocate funds to what they considered to be the most deserving projects. In 1992 when the Department of Education and Science was replaced by the **Department for Education**, the Science Research Council ceased to be the responsibility of the Secretary of State for Education.

Scotland Act (1998)   This Act established the **Scottish Parliament**, with the first elections taking place in May 1999. It has full powers to legislate within its delegated areas of responsibility, including education. The functions performed by the **Scottish Education Department** (SED) were taken over by the **Scottish Executive Education Department** (SEED), which is now responsible to the Scottish Parliament.

Scottish Credit and Qualifications Framework (SCQF)   Unlike the English national qualifications frameworks, that produced by the **Scottish Qualifications Authority** (SQA) is a comprehensive framework covering schools, colleges and **higher education** at 12 levels, six for higher education (Doctorate, Masters, Honours Degree, Ordinary Degree, HND and HNC), and six below that level (Higher, Credit Standard Grade, General Standard Grade, Foundation Standard Grade, Access 2 and 1). The framework in Scotland was designed to encourage **credit transfer** between institutions and different types of learning, both academic and vocational.

Scottish Education Department (SED)   The SED was established at the time of the 1872 Education (Scotland) Act, which transferred the administration of schools from church to lay authorities, through locally elected school boards. The SED was set up as a central controlling and co-ordinating body for education. A Secretary (since 1926, Secretary of State) for Scotland was appointed in 1885 and since then has been responsible for the development of the system. After the Scottish Parliament Act (1998), the Department was replaced by the Scottish Executive Education Department. (See also **Dunning Report, Munn Report**)

Scottish Executive Education Department (SEED)   After the Scottish Parliament Act (1998), the **Scottish Education Department** (SED) was replaced by the SEED, which retained all the responsibilities of the SED.

Scottish Parliament   Since its establishment in May 1999, the Scottish Parliament has considerable powers, including education. The **Scottish Executive Education Department** (SEED), responsible to the Scottish Parliament, took over all aspects of education that were formerly carried by the **Scottish Education Department** (SED).

Scottish Qualifications Authority (SQA)   The SQA is roughly equivalent to the **Qualifications and Curriculum Authority** (QCA) in England but with some important differences: whereas the English Authority is mainly an advisory and regulatory body, the SQA combines those functions with those of an **examination board**. (See also **Scottish Credit and Qualifications Framework**)

Scottish University for Industry (SUfl)   Like its English counterpart, the **University for Industry** (UfI), it is a 'virtual' university providing a radical new approach to learning for industry and business, making full use of **information and communication technology**. The providers included learning centres, colleges and universities, trade unions and business advisers. The service is delivered through learndirect scotland.

screening   A process of identifying children with **learning difficulties**, especially in reading and mathematics. There are many tests available for assessing or diagnosing **special educational needs** associated with various disabilities such as impaired vision or hearing.

Secondary Education for All   The title of a Labour Party policy document issued in 1922, largely the work of R.H. Tawney. It advocated a wider curriculum for all pupils at the **secondary school** stage. This sentiment was echoed in the **Hadow Report** (1926) and provided for in the 1944 Education Act (Sections 7 and 8). (See also **Butler Act, comprehensive school, eleven plus examinaion, ladder of opportunity**)

Secondary Examinations Council (SEC)   When the **Schools Council** was abolished in 1982 it was replaced by two less powerful bodies: a **Secondary Examinations Council** and a **School Curriculum Development Committee**.

Secondary Heads Association (SHA)   Set up in 1976, from the former **Headmasters' Association** and the **Association of Headmistresses**, the Association's 9,500 members include heads and **deputy heads** from both the **maintained** and the **independent** sectors. All the major **public schools** are represented. The Association makes pronouncements on matters of common concern to both sectors, such as examination and **curriculum**, and is non-political in character. (See also **teachers' unions**)

secondary modern school   The **Hadow Report** on *The Education of the Adolescent* (1926) recommended the division of secondary education into two types: the **grammar** school, for the most intellectually able pupils, and the secondary modern school, which would cater for most adolescents between the ages of 11 and 15. The **curriculum** to be offered in the latter was to concentrate initially on offering a good broad education, but in the later years of schooling a more practical bias was to be introduced into the curriculum. The White Paper on Education Reconstruction in 1943, which set the pattern for **tripartitism**, recommended three types of school – grammar, technical, and modern – corresponding to supposed psychological categories of pupils. A Ministry pamphlet, *The New Secondary Education* (1947), claimed that it was 'impracticable to combine a system of external examinations ... with the fundamental conception of modern school education', and teachers were encouraged 'to plan the curriculum of the school on purely educational lines'. Despite this, modern schools developed sixth forms and entered pupils in growing numbers for the **General Certificate of Education** (GCE) examinations. The **Certificate of Secondary Education** (CSE) examinations were introduced in 1965 for the bulk of the modern school's population. Dissatisfaction with the different status enjoyed by the three types of school was increasingly voiced by teachers, parents and politicians. National variations in the provision of grammar school places, the questioning of the validity of **intelligence tests** as a basis of selection, and the lack of progress towards the 1944 Education Act's promise of equality of opportunity, led to the reorganisation of secondary schooling on **comprehensive** lines.

secondary school   Normally, a school providing education for children from the age of 11 years: either 11–16 or 11–18.

Secondary School Examinations Council (SSEC)   Established in 1917 as a result of the introduction of the **School Certificate**. The **Board of Education** wished to co-ordinate the work of the different university **examining boards** and to ensure parity of standards. Following the **Norwood Report**, which recommended the ending of the School Certificate, the Council was increased in size but examining boards no longer had direct representation. In 1964, the SSEC functions were transferred to the **Schools Council.**

secondment   The allocation of a teacher, on a temporary basis, to a course or another post away from his or her normal place of employment.

Secretary of State for Education (and Science)   The **Robbins Report** recommended that there should be changes in the machinery of ministerial responsibility – that the Minister of Education should be replaced by a Minister for Arts and Science. Whilst agreeing to the need for changes, the government's solution was for a single **Department of Education and Science**, the enlarged ministry to have a Secretary of State as its head. The Secretary of State had overall responsibility for the work of the Department and the formulation of general policy. He was also a member of the Cabinet. In 1992, Science was reallocated to the Duchy of Lancaster and the Department of Education and Science was replaced by the **Department for Education** (DfE). In July 1995 the DfE was merged with the Employment Department to become the **Department for Education and Employment** (DfEE). In 2001, it became the **Department for Education and Skills** (DfES).

Section 11 teacher   Section 11 of the Local Government Act (1966) empowers the Home Office to provide money to assist **local education**

authorities in the promotion of English among immigrant communities. For many years the Government paid for 75 per cent of the cost of approved schemes (most of which involved additional 'Section 11' teachers in class-rooms in schools with high proportions of non-English speaking pupils). The Grant was reduced to 57 per cent in 1993 and 50 per cent for 1994. Some Section 11 teachers are **bilingual**; others are specialists in teaching **English as a foreign language**.

Section 12 notice   When a **local education authority** intends to close a **maintained school** or change its character to a significant extent, it issues a public notice for two months to allow objections in accordance with Section 12 of the 1980 Education Act. Circular 2/80 states that local education authorities should give parents at least one term to make alternative arrange-ments and should allow at least a full 12 months between the publication of closure proposals and the date on which they come into effect. The **Secretary of State for Education** has, under the Act, to approve Section 12 notices. It should be noted that the establishment and alteration of **voluntary schools** are covered by Section 13 of the same Act.

Sector Skills Development Agency (SSDA)   The SSDA was estab-lished in 2002, having been announced by Estelle Morris, Secretary of State for Education, in October 2001. It was intended as a means of developing world-class skills for business to help the UK compete in a global economy. From April 2002 Sector Skills Councils (SSCs) brought together employ-ers, trade unions and professional bodies working with government to develop the skills that UK business needs to improve productivity. There is a Sector Skills Team, based at the **Department for Education and Skills** (DfES), working in partnership with the Scottish Executive, the National Assembly for Wales and the Northern Ireland Executive. The Agency funds and supports the network of SSCs. It is a company limited by guarantee with an employer-led Board and a Chair appointed from the world of business. (See also **Further Education Development Agency**, **Learning and Skills Council**)

secular schools   A movement begun in the 1830s by radicals and Non-conformists who were alarmed at the Church of England's growing hold on the provision of elementary education. In London, William Ellis pioneered secular schools, opening seven Birkbeck Schools with curricula that had a large social science component.

security of tenure   The contractual right of an **academic** (particularly in **universities**) to retain full-time employment until a specified retirement date. Security of tenure was normally granted only after satisfactory completion of a probationary period. In the early 1980s, the privileged position of academics with security of tenure was questioned by the Conservative Secretary of State for Education, Sir Keith Joseph, and others. Tenure for *new* appointments (or new contracts, e.g. due to promotion) was effectively removed by Sections 202–8 of the Education Reform Act (1988).

Select Committee   A Committee made up of named members of either House of Parliament with the purpose of taking evidence on a subject and reporting its findings back to the House which appointed the Committee. It has power to summon witnesses to attend, to give evidence and to produce documents. (See also **Parliamentary Papers**)

selection   The issue of selection has a long history in education in the UK. When the 1902 Education Act permitted **local education authorities** to fund **secondary schools**, it was envisaged that only a minority of 11-year-olds would be selected to attend the new **grammar schools** by virtue of their superior **intelligence**. (Others could, however, pay for a place if their parents were willing and able to find the fees.) In 1944 the Education Act instituted 'secondary education for all', but most local education authorities interpreted this to mean two or three different types of school for different kinds of ability; selection, in the form of the **eleven plus examination**, continued. During the 1960s and 1970s it became obvious that the selection process was not entirely fair and increasingly local education authorities adopted policies of **comprehensive** secondary schools. But about 160 grammar schools remained, together with selection processes. The Labour Government of 1997 was committed to a policy of 'no selection' but they carefully avoided changing the status of existing grammar schools without clear parental support for the abolition of selection. In addition, the Government created a new category of **specialist schools**, which has encouraged another form of selection: specialist schools are permitted (but not compelled) to select up to 10 per cent of their intake according to **aptitude** but not by testing for **ability**. Those who oppose selection at 11 continue to argue that it is inefficient and unjust.

selective school   A school for which pupils have to demonstrate a level of attainment or ability to gain entry, usually by means of some kind of test or examination.

self-concept, self-image   An individual's self-concept is the way an individual sees himself or herself. Some research has been based on the hypothesis that children with a negative self-image tend to be **under-achievers** at school. It has also been suggested that children from certain ethnic minorities have a negative self-image, and that this accounts for their under-achievement in school. The evidence for this is not conclusive. (See also **multicultural education, under-achiever**)

self-fulfilling prophecy   A term originally used in sociology by Robert Merton. It has become a feature of some discussions of schools and of organisational practices, such as streaming. In education, it is often associated with the term **labelling**. If a pupil is believed by his/her teacher to be bright, he or she is likely to improve; if pupils are thought to be dull, they will become dull. This is sometimes also known as the **Pygmalion effect**.

self-instruction   A method of learning in which students use programmed learning or other materials. No direct help is given by a teacher although the course would normally be laid out with very specific goals. A **correspondence course** is not, strictly speaking, a self-instructional course, because students normally submit work that has to be marked and commented on by a tutor. Some correspondence courses might, however, include self-instructional materials or units. Some textbooks have been written on a self-instructional basis, that is, the content is so devised as to provide answers for the student and alternative routes should the student make mistakes.

semester   Whereas most English schools and **universities** have academic years which are divided into three periods of work (**terms**) plus **vacations**, North American universities tend to divide the academic year into two working periods called semesters usually lasting at least 15 weeks, with longer breaks in between. Thus, many courses in American universities are organised on a semester basis rather than as a whole year. Some English universities have adopted the American pattern.

seminar   A meeting of students in a group with a **tutor** sometimes for the purpose of following up a **lecture**. Members of the group may present papers at the seminar to stimulate discussion or raise further issues. (See also **tutorial**)

semiotics (or semiology)   The study of signs and symbols – especially in the context of human communication. It is often associated with structuralism in studies of literature. At school level it has been influential in new areas of the **curriculum** such as communication studies and media studies, especially for the analysis of film and television.

SENCO   (See **Special Educational Needs Co-ordinator**)

senior management team (SMT)   This consists of major figures in a school, and may include the **headteacher, deputy head(s), assistant head, director of studies** and the **Special Educational Needs Co-ordinator** (SENCO).

Service Children's Education (SCE)   A Defence Agency providing schooling for Service personnel children and appointing teachers, mainly civilians, working outside the UK. The SCE administers 51 schools world-wide, 42 of which are primary or first schools, and six secondary schools.

setting   In the early days of **comprehensive** schools most **headteachers** organised the schools on the basis of **streaming**, i.e. they allocated pupils to classes in terms of their supposed general **ability**. Pupils remained in those streamed classes for all or most subjects. Many considered streaming to be too crude and rigid a selection process, and adopted as a compromise the process of 'setting'. This might leave pupils in **mixed-ability** groups for most of their subjects, but allocate them to ability groupings for certain subjects where more homogeneous classes were thought to be necessary. Setting is most common in such subjects as modern languages and mathematics. (See also **family grouping, labelling**)

seventeen plus examinations   During the 1960s and 1970s there was much discussion about the 'new sixth former', i.e. a student who stayed on in a **comprehensive** school after completing the five-year course, but without sufficient academic success to undertake **GCE A Level** courses. Many such students simply retook **O Level** examinations which they had earlier failed, or even repeated **CSE** examinations in order to obtain improved grades. This practice was generally thought to be undesirable educationally and various proposals for alternative examinations were put forward. One of these was the Certificate of Extended Education (CEE) which was discussed in the **Keohane Report**. Other suggestions involved vocational preparation and courses designed by bodies such as the City and Guilds. In 1986 the **National Council for Vocational Qualifications** (NCVQ) was created and given responsibility for co-ordinating all courses into a series of **levels**.

short-answer question   A free-standing question for which a complete answer can be given in one well-constructed sentence or its equivalent (e.g., a simple diagram or short calculation).

sixteen plus examinations   The **Schools Council** recommended a merger of the **General Certificate of Education** (GCE) **O Level** and the **Certificate of Secondary Education** (CSE) examinations. Eight years later, the **Waddell Report** concluded that such a system was feasible. In February 1980 a modified scheme was announced by the Conservative Government, with groupings of GCE and CSE boards, and strong **national criteria**. Four groups of examination boards were established in England. Examination boards were asked to draw up criteria for every subject, and a joint council for the **General Certificate of Secondary Education** (GCSE), establishing

16 plus national criteria, was formed by the GCE and CSE boards. The first awards for the new GCSE were made in 1988.

sixth form college   Unlike the **tertiary college** which caters for all students of 16 years and over in an area, the sixth form college accommodates the traditional sixth form intake and those requiring somewhat less academic courses. Many of the students aim to go on to **higher** and **further education**, and the college offers a range of examinations. In 1991 sixth form colleges were removed from **local education authority** control.

skill   A physical, social or mental **ability** acquired mainly as a result of practice and repetition. Skill is frequently contrasted with **knowledge**, but this is an over-simplification. It may be convenient to divide educational objectives into knowledge, skills and attitudes, but it should always be recognised that these are overlapping categories. (See also **core skills**, **competence**, **social skills**)

Skinnerian   An adjective describing the work of B. F. Skinner, an American psychologist. One meaning of Skinnerian applies to the **behaviourist** theory of **learning** and its particular application in schools; a more limited use of Skinnerian applies particularly to Skinner's work on **programmed learning**, and in this sense a Skinnerian programme is a linear programme (to be contrasted with a branching programme). (See also **behaviourism**)

Social Affairs Unit (SAU)   A right-wing pressure group founded in 1980 by Dr Digby Anderson, critical of the welfare state and the education service.

Social Science Research Council (SSRC)   The Council was set up in 1965 by Royal Charter to encourage research, to provide advice, and to disseminate knowledge concerning the social sciences. It also allocated funds for **postgraduate** students, and financed high-quality research proposals from the universities. In September 1981, the Council announced that changes needed to be made to encourage a more multidisciplinary approach to problems that were seen to be important in policy formation. The SSRC suffered a cut of about 20 per cent in real resources between 1978 and 1982. In October 1982 following the recommendation of the Rothschild Report on the SSRC, the Secretary of State decided to continue the Council, but Sir Keith Joseph insisted on a change of title to **Economic and Social Research Council** (ESRC).

social skills   The ability to communicate effectively with people in social and work situations. Many schools and colleges offer courses in this area, for example, preparation for interviews. In a wider context, it may be seen as one aspect of **personal and social education** (PSE), an umbrella term covering a number of curriculum areas concerned with values and personal developmental processes. (See also **skill**)

Society of Education Officers (SEO)   A professional association for educational administrators of local authorities in England, Wales and Northern Ireland, formed in 1971. The Scottish counterpart is the Association of Directors of Education in Scotland. Its main objectives are to confer on matters relating to education for the benefit of members and through them of their authorities, and to make representations to government departments and other bodies. (See also **chief education officer**)

Society of Headmasters and Headmistresses of Independent Schools (SHMIS)   This Society was founded in 1901 and is an association of headteachers which represents the needs and views of smaller **independent schools**. The 95 schools that are members consist of both day and boarding establishments, co-educational and separate boys' and girls' schools. As with other linked organisations, it serves as a forum for discussing policy and represents their views at all levels. The SHMIS is one of the constituent bodies of the **Independent Schools Council** and its schools are subject to review by the **Independent Schools Inspectorate** every six years.

Society of Teachers Opposed to Physical Punishment (STOPP)   A **pressure group**, set up to abolish the use of physical punishment in schools. The Society was controlled by teachers but had parental membership. It lobbied governments, and church and teachers' organisations, and took cases to the European Court of Rights. After **corporal punishment** was banned in maintained schools in 1986, the Society was wound up. (See also **Human Rights Act** (1998))

spatial ability   The kind of reasoning which manifests itself as the **ability** to see relationships between objects in space or occupying space. Individuals possessing high spatial ability will find it easier to read maps, find their way in unfamiliar territory, or do jigsaw puzzles and other manipulative tasks. Spatial ability is measured in some tests of general **intelligence**; there are also specific tests of spatial ability sometimes used for **vocational guidance**. (See also **intelligence tests, verbal reasoning**)

special agreement school   A type of voluntary school, usually **secondary**, where the **local education authority** paid, by special agreement with a denominational interest, one-half to three-quarters of the cost of building a school or enlarging an existing one. Two-thirds of the governors were appointed by the voluntary body, the remainder by the local authority. The local education authorities controlled teaching staff and the governors were responsible for religious instruction in the school. This category of school ended with the School Standards and Framework Act (1998). (See also **religious education**, **voluntary aided school**, **voluntary controlled school**)

special educational needs The concept of special educational needs has developed since the 1944 Education Act's definition of 'disability of mind or body'. It has come to be recognised that special educational needs should be based on educational and developmental considerations rather than on purely medical ones. In 1978, the **Warnock Report** concluded that 'special educational needs' was a relative concept, a sentiment echoed in the 1981 Education Act: 'A child has "special educational needs" if he has a learning difficulty which calls for special educational provision to be made for him.' The Act recommended that assessment should include educational, psychological and medical components. Duties were placed on **local education authorities** and schools to identify a secure provision for a wide range of special educational needs. Parents were also to be consulted when decisions about their children's special needs were being taken, and on the choice of provision to meet these needs. The 1996 Education Act (Section 9 and Schedule 27), made clear that local education authorities were to meet the parents' wishes on the education of their children as far as possible. For children with special needs, LEAs were obliged to undertake a statutory assessment of those needs and name an appropriate school in a **statement**. Parental appeals are heard before the Special Educational Needs Tribunal (SENT). The Special Educational Needs and Disability Act (2001), which came into force in January 2002, amended the 1996 Act. It aimed at improving access to mainstream education for special educational needs pupils and streamlining the system of assessing needs. Heads had for the first time the same rights as parents in requesting assessment of children who may need additional assistance. Schools and LEAs are required to have plans in place in order to implement this provision.

All mainstream schools must appoint a **Special Educational Needs Co-ordinator** (SENCO), to ensure that suitable provision is made for special educational need pupils and to liaise with parents and staff. It is mandatory for maintained schools to publish their special educational needs policy in governing bodies' annual reports. An official survey published in May 2001 showed that one in five pupils (some 1,750,000 children) were on special educational needs registers in maintained schools in England and Wales. (See also **exceptional children**, **giftedness**, **integration**, **special school**)

Special Educational Needs Co-ordinator (SENCO) An experienced teacher who provides leadership in carrying out a school's **special educational needs** policy. SENCOs have some teaching duties, and are responsible for keeping special educational needs records, co-ordinating the drawing up of **individual education plans** (IEPs), and liaising with outside agencies and parents.

special measures   Where the **Department for Education and Skills** (DfES) and the **Office for Standards in Education** (OFSTED) identify schools that are at risk of failing, certain steps are taken. Such schools are warned that they have two years to improve or be closed down. In December 2000 almost 400 schools were on special measures. Since 1997, 650 schools have overcome their difficulties, 100 have been closed, and 25 have been given a **Fresh Start**.

Special Place system   Lord Irwin, President of the Board of Education, issued Circular 1421 in 1932 introducing a means test for all entrants to **secondary schools**. Remission of fees was to be available according to family circumstances. Open competition replaced the existing condition that candidates should have been previously attending a public **elementary school**. The name of the award was changed from **Free Place** to Special Place. This continued until the 1944 Education Act.

special school   Special schools are provided by **local education authorities** and voluntary organisations for groups of children who have **special educational needs**. Until the 1981 Education Act, children were classified into categories and special schools provided a response to one type of categorised child. The size of teaching group, pupil–teacher ratios and curriculum styles are some of the special requirements prescribed for special schools as outlined in regulations and circulars from the **Department for Education and Skills**. In 2001, there were over 90,000 pupils in special schools in England, 4,000 in Wales, and 9,400 in Scotland, despite the moves to integrate these pupils into mainstream schools. None of these schools had more than 400 pupils. (See also **assessment**, **Down's syndrome**, **educationally subnormal**, **school psychological service**)

specialist school   Evolving from the model for the **city technology college**, specialist schools, with private sector sponsorship and Government funding, are **secondary schools** with their own choice of specialisms. They aim to improve standards at a faster rate than non-specialist schools and provide their pupils with skills for employment and **higher education**. From 1994, **maintained schools** could apply for specialist school status in modern languages, design and technology, and mathematics. The programme was expanded two years later to include sports and the arts. The Green Paper, *Schools: Building on Success* (2001), proposed three further specialisms: engineering, science, and business and enterprise. Schools applying for specialist status must produce a four-year development plan, raise £50,000 by private sector sponsorship, and produce quantified performance targets. There were 181 such schools in 1997 and 650 in 2001, and the Government intends to more than double that number by 2005. One concern that has been expressed is the increasingly privileged nature of the intake of students, though **local education authority** specialist schools, which are increasing at a rapid rate, are less open to this charge. In January 2001 it was claimed that specialist schools were achieving about 27 per cent better results than other comprehensives. Specialist schools are allowed to select 10 per cent of their intake, by aptitude but not by ability. Critics of the scheme dislike selection and also the possibility that those **comprehensive schools** that do not become specialist schools may be regarded as inferior.

spelling   Another controversial issue in the **English curriculum**. The dispute centres around two issues: first, how spelling should be taught; second, what is appropriate at various ages. M. Gentry, in an article in *Reading Teacher* (1982), identified a number of stages that teachers need to recognise. Learning to spell is a process gradually acquired, perhaps over a period of several years. Some children experience little difficulty in acquiring good spelling on their own, others have to be carefully taught. (See also **dyslexia**)

Spens Report   The Report of the Consultative Committee of the Board of Education on Secondary Education with Special Reference to Grammar Schools and Technical High Schools (1938) dealt with their reorganisation and interrelation. Basing its findings on the psychological evidence then available, the Committee stated that the **tripartite** division (**grammar**, **technical** and **modern schools**) corresponded to pupils' abilities and aptitudes and that expansion should take place on that basis. The **multilateral school** was not favoured. (See also **Norwood Report**)

spiral curriculum   (See **curriculum, spiral**)

split site   A school or college that is situated on more than one site.

sports day   A tradition still carried on in many schools in the summer term when a morning or an afternoon is devoted to a number of sporting events, attended by parents. Formerly, these occasions were for the whole school but are now often organised on a year-by-year basis. The ethos has also changed from one where competition between able athletes was the norm to a situation where as many pupils as possible can join in.

staff meeting   A meeting of the staff or department of an educational institution to discuss matters concerned with the activities of the department or institution, such as **curriculum planning** and **timetabling**. The frequency of such meetings and the length of the agenda varies from place to place. (See also **head of department**)

staff–student ratio (SSR)   The ratio between the number of teachers and the number of students in a **university**, college or **school**. (See also **pupil–teacher ratio**)

standard(s)   There are two very different educational meanings for the term 'standard'. (1) After the Revised Code of 1862, the work of **elementary schools** was divided into six Standards. Pupils began Standard 1 roughly at the age of six and, given normal attainment, passed through the other five Standards year by year. Before progressing from Standard 1 to Standard 2, pupils would be tested (on a narrow and rigid curriculum) to ensure that the required knowledge had been satisfactorily mastered. Later, in 1882, Standard 7 was introduced. (2) All educational institutions have 'standards' in the sense of a level of quality of work below which they do not wish to fall, and would probably wish to raise. In **secondary schools**, standards are maintained partly by means of external or **public examinations**. Individual institutions can be compared according to national examination standards. In **universities**, standards are maintained by a combination of examinations (local not national) which are **moderated** in terms of standards by the system of **external examiners**. Doubts about standards in schools was one of the reasons given for the introduction of the **national curriculum** (with national assessment) in 1988.

Standard Assessment Task (SAT)   Standard Assessment Tasks are part of the **national curriculum** assessment procedures. Originally conceived as normal classroom assignments with built-in assessment, they have become largely pencil and paper tests. Since 1990 Standard Assessment Tasks have been renamed Standard Tests or Standard Tasks (STs). But they are still widely referred to as SATs.

standard deviation (SD)   A term used in statistics to indicate a measure of variability among the values of a frequency distribution. For example, when indicating the range or scatter of scores from the mean or average, it is sometimes convenient to express the extent of scatter in terms of standard deviations. When discussing a range of scores it is rarely sufficient to know only the average or mean score; it is also important to know the standard deviation or 'scatter' of marks. (See also **standardised**, **z-scores**)

standard English   Many experts in linguistics and the teaching of English doubt its existence, but the term is very widely used to indicate what is accepted as correct English by educated people. It is the kind of English usually used in print and normally taught in schools and to those learning **English as a foreign language**. Standard English as a concept is made more difficult by the fact that, however defined, it changes over time. It also has many sub-divisions: e.g. standard scientific English is different from standard business English. Standard spoken English is also different from standard written English. It is not the same as **received pronunciation**.

standard spending assessment (SSA)   Throughout the 1980s and 1990s the Government was anxious to restrain local authority spending – including spending on education. The two mechanisms employed were by 'capping' – i.e. enforcing a limit on local rates (later council tax); the second was by specifying how money should be allocated, by means of the SSA. The SSA for education is determined by complex formulae and broken down into five spending categories (primary, secondary, post-16, under-5 and 'other'). (See also **Local Government Acts**)

standardisation   A procedure for bringing teachers, examiners or moderators into line with agreed standards of marking.

standardised   (1) 'Standardised' marks or scores in a test mean that they have been adjusted in such a way as to make them comparable with scores from a different test, perhaps by reference to a given mean and **standard deviation**, or by use of **z-scores**. (2) A standardised test is one that has been systematically piloted and then modified in order to ensure that it has both **validity** and **reliability**. Standardised tests would have norms that have been carefully established. It would also be standardised in the sense of having unambiguous written procedures.

Standards and Effectiveness Unit (SEU)   This Unit, located within the **Department for Education and Skills** (DfES), is charged with implementing government policies for raising standards of education in schools in England. The Director of the Unit is supported by a team working in separate divisions: Unit Pupil Standards; Local Standards; School Improvement; and Excellence and School Diversity. The Unit also has 22 Education Advisors with considerable educational experience, who are recruited from schools and **local education authorities**. The Unit's work has included: launching the **numeracy** strategy; expanding the number of **education action zones**; undertaking **beacon** and **specialist schools'** initiatives; and implementing the **Excellence in Cities** programme.

Standards Fund   The DfES targets funds towards national educational priorities by means of the Standards Fund, which finances such initiatives as the **National Grid for Learning**, **Excellence in Cities**, and capital grants for schools. Since April 2001, the Standards Fund grant has been simplified by preset allocation of monies rather than relying on the receipt of claims. Schools also now have the freedom to determine spending priorities between individual grants, and allocate monies accordingly.

Standards Task Force (STF)   Formed in 1997 by the **Secretary of State for Education** to survey the needs of the education service in the quest to raise educational standards. It consists of teachers, education advisers, and business representatives, and meets not less than four times a year. The Force is responsible for shaping policies in such initiatives as **beacon schools, education action zones** and the **Teacher Training Agency** (TTA).

Standing Advisory Council on Religious Education (SACRE) **Local education authorities** are required under the **Education Reform Act** (1988) to set up a SACRE to advise on religious education and worship.

Standing Conference for Studies in Education (SCSE)   An organisation open to professional educationists but especially those in **higher education**. Its aim is to promote studies in the **disciplines of education**. It organises an annual conference on some aspect of educational theory, and is responsible for the *British Journal of Educational Studies*, which is probably the most important of the educational journals in the UK.

State school   Strictly speaking, there are no State schools in the UK because schools are owned by **local education authorities**, church organisations or trustees. **Maintained schools** are, however, often popularly referred to as State schools.

statement   The 1981 Education Act provided a legal appeal system for children with **special educational needs**. All local authorities have a general duty to identify those children whose special needs call for the authority to determine the special educational provision that should be made for them. The process of identifying and assessing special needs is left to **local education authorities** who decide on the appropriate provision. This decision to accept or reject responsibility is known as making a statement. Head teachers must carry out an annual review to check the pupil's progress, arrange an annual review meeting, and submit the subsequent report to the local education authority. There are procedures for parents to appeal against the local authority's decision. A Special Educational Needs Tribunal, a non-departmental independent body consisting of a Chair and two lay people, was established in 1994; it operates in accordance with Sections 333–6 of the 1996 Education Act to settle disputes between parents and local education authorities. (See also **remedial education**, **school psychological service**, **special school**)

statement of attainment   The scheme of assessment adopted for the 1988 **national curriculum** divided subjects into **attainment targets**, which were further sub-divided into ten **levels of attainment**. Each level of attainment was defined by several statements of attainment. Statements of attainment were abolished after the **Dearing Review** and replaced by **level descriptions**.

statement of competence   A specification of requirements in a given **National Vocational Qualification** (NVQ) area – the units of competence, elements of competence and performance criteria.

statutory instrument   A form of delegated legislation, under an Order or regulation by the Queen in Council or one of her ministers, which has the force of an Act of Parliament. Statutory instruments must be laid before Parliament before coming into operation. (See also **Parliamentary Papers**)

Steiner Waldorf schools   These schools are based on the philosophy of the Austrian educationist, Rudolph Steiner (1861–1925), which he developed at the Free Waldorf School, Stuttgart, from 1919. In his view, the school **curriculum** should be based on spiritual insights, a love of nature and the nature of children. Steiner education is divided into three phases: birth to seven, with little emphasis on academic attainment; 7–14, when children accept authority and have a sole teacher during these years; and 14–21, when 'the astral body is drawn into the physical body', causing puberty. There is emphasis on all the arts, especially eurhythmy, an art of movement expressing the inner forms and gestures of language and music. The best-known aspect of Steiner Waldorf schools is the instruction of mentally and physical handicapped children. The first school in England was opened in 1925. There are now 27 schools and 12 independent **kindergarten** schools in the UK and Ireland.

streaming   The assigning of pupils to classes on the basis of general **ability**. The number of streams depends on the size of the year group. Streamed classes usually stay together for the majority of subjects. It has been shown that streaming affects teachers' judgments of children's abilities and brings about a **self-fulfilling prophecy**. The **National Foundation for Educational Research** survey found that 50 per cent of large primary schools used streaming in 1963 but only 2 per cent employed this form of organisation in 1980. There is some evidence that a form of streaming for the basic subjects is becoming more prevalent in **primary schools**. (See also **family grouping**, **labelling**, **mixed-ability grouping**, **setting**, **unstreaming**)

structured question   An examination question containing connected parts on which a candidate is given some guidance as to the kind of responses required, the length of answers expected, and the way credit is to be allocated.

student   (1) Formerly a term reserved for those pursuing a course of study in an institution of **further** or **higher education**, e.g. at a **university** or college. It is now often used interchangeably in schools with the term '**pupil**'. (2) The non-ecclesiastical equivalent of **fellow** at Christ Church, Oxford; also for those holding endowed studentships at either Oxford or Cambridge.

student loans   (See **loans, student**)

Students' Union   A society formed by students of a college or other institution to promote social activities and provide recreational facilities. In many colleges, representatives of the Union serve on official committees which are concerned with **academic** affairs. At Oxford and Cambridge, the Union is a club with well-known debating societies. (See also **National Union of Students**)

study leave   A period of leave, usually with pay, made available to teachers in schools or in **further** or **higher education** to attend professional or **academic** courses. One of the ideas behind **recurrent education** has been the extension of this privilege to the whole population – hence 'paid study leave' as an area of negotiation for trades unions, especially within the **European Community**. (See also **sabbatical**)

study skills   Ways in which students can become more effective in their studies by becoming aware of the learning processes involved. Courses in study skills often aim to encourage independent learning by presenting information, in a workshop situation and/or by lectures, on some of the following: note-taking; drafting; problem solving; contributing to group discussion; systematic revision for examinations; and ways of finding out information. Study skills are now being taught in schools and places of **further** and **higher education** and are particularly important for those involved in **distance learning**. (See also **correspondence course, Open University**)

sub-culture   Every society has a culture. By definition all members of a society will share in some of the aspects of its culture. But within the whole society there may be groups who are identifiable by possessing distinctly different values, beliefs and behaviour patterns. In such cases it would be appropriate to talk of a sub-culture. In the UK it is possible to identify, e.g. working-class sub-cultures and the sub-cultures of certain **ethnic minorities**. (See also **multicultural education**)

subject co-ordinator   Teacher in a **primary school** with responsibility for a particular curriculum area throughout the school. Alternative titles are subject leader and subject manager.

subject working groups   Groups of specialists and others set up by the Secretary of State for Education to write (or re-write) **Attainment Targets** and **Programmes of Study** for **foundation subjects** in the **national curriculum**.

summative assessment   The kind of assessment given at the end of a course, as a final judgment. (See also **formative assessment**)

summative evaluation   (See **formative evaluation/summative evaluation**)

summer schools   Informal non-examination courses held during the school holidays, on a voluntary basis, for children of all ages. These schools vary greatly in their aims and content. In 2001, the **Department for Education and Skills** (DfES) allocated £22 million for 2,200 summer schools, specifically targeting the primary phase and pupils who failed their Level 4 assessment in **literacy** or **numeracy**. Others, such as the series being hosted by 14 **local education authorities** in Norfolk, in partnership with the **University of the First Age**, consist of week-long courses presenting a series of active challenges, both physical and mental. A third category is a broader one, where children are offered a range of artistic and sporting activities. The **Open University** also provides summer schools for its students.

Sunday schools   The Sunday school movement is usually associated with Robert Raikes of Gloucester who, from 1780, established classes for children of the poor who were in employment during the rest of the week. The movement, which saw its task as the inculcation of religion and the elimination of radical ideologies, quickly spread and was eagerly taken up by religious organisations. A century after the movement began over five-and-three-quarter million children in England were attending these schools.

Super Heads   In March 2001, the **Department for Education and Skills** announced the creation of a pilot scheme of ten Super Heads who would support groups of schools that were struggling or failing, deemed to be under **special measures**. They would work in co-operation with existing school management and would be given extra resources to gain improvements. Individual heads of schools in the Super Head pilot scheme remain responsible for the day-to-day running of their schools.

supply teachers   A teacher employed to cover the work of an absent member of staff. Formerly these were recruited by **local education authorities** but there are now many private supply agencies which have sprung up in recent years. Supply teachers who are at a school for one term must undertake **induction**.

Sure Start programme   The **Department for Education and Skills** has established Sure Start programmes in deprived areas to provide support for families with children under four in order to tackle child poverty and **exclusion**. The programmes include advice on nutrition, the provision of health services and early learning facilities. All parents are visited in the first two months after a child is born. By 2001, there were 128 programmes and by 2004 the aim is to have 400. The age range is being extended to include four-year-olds.

Swann Report   A committee was set up under the chairmanship of Sir Michael Swann in December 1965 to investigate the shortage of science and engineering graduates. The Report, published in 1968, showed that the best science and engineering graduates tended to remain at university rather than embark upon a career in industry. The Report was also concerned with the lack of good science graduates entering school teaching. It recommended some new kinds of **postgraduate** training, emphasising links between the academic world and the world of industry. Suggestions were also made about encouraging scientists to make contributions to the work of schools.

syllabus   An outline, more or less detailed, of the ground to be covered in a **course**. The distinction between syllabus and **curriculum** is not always clear, but the following distinctions might be helpful. The lowest unit in terms of curriculum planning would be an individual **lesson**; this would be part of a **scheme of work** covering several lessons (perhaps half a term or a term's work); this would be related to a syllabus (perhaps a whole year's work), and a syllabus would be related to the whole curriculum. In the **national curriculum** (1988) there are two closely related but distinct specifications: **Attainment Targets** (sub-divided into ten **levels** of achievement), and **Programmes of Study** for each subject setting out the content to be covered. The Programmes of Study are closer to the traditional concept of syllabus.

T

target   Since 1998 governing bodies of all **maintained primary** and **secondary schools** must set targets each autumn for improving pupil performance at **Key Stage** 2 in primary schools or Key Stage 4 in secondary schools. Governing bodies must publish the targets and actual performance in their annual report to parents. (See also **assessment of pupils**)

tariff questions   Where an examination paper consists of different questions pitched at different levels of difficulty, each with different mark values. Candidates can select those questions that they consider will gain them the most marks.

task   An **element** or combination of elements of work by means of which a specific result is achieved. In training assessment is likely to be by task rather than by written tests.

Task Group on Assessment and Testing (TGAT)   TGAT was appointed by Kenneth Baker, then Secretary of State for Education, in 1987, to advise him on **national curriculum assessment**. It was chaired by Professor Paul Black and produced the TGAT Model. It was at first accepted by Government but in many respects has been watered down by later events. (See also **Dearing Reports/Reviews**)

taught time   In 1993 the Secretary of State for Education asked the **Office for Standards in Education** (OFSTED) to investigate the 'relationship between the amount of taught time and the quality and standards of pupils' work, including examination results'. OFSTED produced an Interim Report in January 1994 and Final Report in July 1994, *Taught Time*. The conclusion was that neither inspection evidence nor statistical analysis revealed any relationship between the length of taught time and pupils' achievements which would support an increase in the recommended minima for the length of taught time in schools. An adequate amount of teaching time for a given subject is a necessary but not a sufficient condition for producing work of quality.

Taunton Report   As a result of two Royal Commissions (**Newcastle** and **Clarendon**) the Taunton Commission was appointed in 1864 to examine the schools not within the scope of the two Commissions. Investigations were carried out into about 800 endowed schools, as well as private and **proprietary schools**. The Commissioners revealed widespread inefficiency and misappropriation of funds. The Report (1868) recommended that a system of efficient secondary schools corresponding to the three grades of society should be created. The first grade should prepare boys for university, with a curriculum of Classics, modern languages, mathematics and natural sciences. The leaving age should be 18. Second grade schools would cater for boys preparing for the professions, business and the Army. Latin was included in the curriculum but most of the time would be devoted to 'modern subjects'. Boys would leave at about 16. The third grade was considered most urgent because there were large numbers of pupils, the sons of small tenant farmers, tradesmen and superior artisans. Third grade schools would have a leaving age of 14 and would concentrate on the basics of 'very good reading, very good writing, very good arithmetic' as well as some practical subjects. No recommendations were made about girls. It was also suggested that a 'scholarship ladder' should be established for needy pupils; that an independent Examinations Council should be established; and that there should be inspection of the three grades of schools with a central authority for secondary education.

taxonomy   Classification, especially in relation to general laws or principles of classification. In education, the word is most usually associated with the work of B. S. Bloom and his *Taxonomy of Educational Objectives* (1956).

Taylor Report   A Committee of Enquiry chaired by Mr Tom Taylor was set up in 1975 to review the management and government of **primary** and **secondary schools** in England and Wales. Its Report was published in 1977 and recommended that **governors** should have more involvement in the school curriculum, and that governing bodies should consist of four equal elements: **local education authority**, **teachers**, parents and local community representatives.

teacher   Many changes in the training, appointment and conditions of service of teachers have occurred in recent years. There are a number of different entry routes into the profession – **Professional Graduate Certificate of Education** (PGCE), **Bachelor of Education degree** (BEd), **Fast Track**, **Graduate and Registered Teacher Programme**, **Overseas Trained Teacher** Scheme – and the training is largely school-based. (See also **initial teacher training, Teacher Training Agency, teacher tutor, teachers' centres, teachers' salaries, teachers' unions, teaching assistant**)

teacher appraisal   Teachers' professional organisations have tended to oppose teacher appraisal when it is linked to salaries but not if appraisal is part of a process of **professional development**. Since 1997, New Labour has vigorously pursued a policy of **performance related pay**, which includes evidence partly based on teacher appraisal. In 1999, a compromise solution was reluctantly accepted by teachers' unions, and most teachers who applied to pass beyond the threshold of competence received a sufficiently good appraisal to be granted the additional salary.

teacher assessment (TA)   As part of their normal teaching, teachers are required to assess attainments defined in the National Curriculum Orders. Since 1994 TA judgments have been reported to parents together with the pupil's results on standard tests.

teacher support staff This may take the form, depending on the type of school, of administrative help, such as secretaries or classroom help, nursery nurses or helpers. Included under this heading are schoolkeepers, cleaners and kitchen staff. (See also **teachers' aides**)

Teacher Training Agency (TTA) This Agency was established in September 1994 under the Education Act (1994), replacing the **Council for Accreditation of Teacher Education** (CATE). Its duties include improving the quality and efficiency of all routes into the teaching profession, including **initial teacher training** (ITT); promoting more flexible **postgraduate** courses for entry into the profession; regulating the national **skills tests** for trainee teachers; facilitating the involvement of schools in ITT; and promoting teaching as a career.

teacher training skills tests The Green Paper, *Teachers: Meeting the Challenge of Change* (2000), proposed the introduction of new national **skills tests** for all trainee teachers to ensure they possessed high-level skills in **numeracy, literacy** and **information and communications technology** (ICT). The tests are computerised and were introduced for trainee teachers completing their courses between 1 May 2001 and 30 April 2002. The tests then became part of the process leading to the award of **qualified teacher status** (QTS).

teacher tutor Institutions concerned with **initial teacher training** involve practising teachers in the work of trainees, especially for professional aspects of the course and school **teaching practice**. These part-time tutors, often referred to as teacher tutors, are normally senior and experienced members of staff. (See also **mentor**)

teachers' aides A term used in the **Plowden Report** on **primary schools** (1967) to describe a person without formal teaching qualifications who is employed in infant or primary classes. Aides assist teachers in classroom work and supervision. (See also **dilution**, **teaching assistant**)

teachers' centres Centres run by **local education authorities** to promote professional development in the education service from the primary to the tertiary sectors. They are general purpose institutions but provide a focus for **In-service Education of Teachers** (INSET) programmes and house resources for consultation by teachers. Many teachers' centres provide the base for the activities of advisory and support staff, though in some authorities such staff may be located in the local education authority offices. Only a few authorities still offer specialist teachers' centres, e.g. for service teaching. The head of a teachers' centre may have a title such as centre manager, warden, or centre leader. There is an association for professional development in education, which issues a newsletter for leaders and also arranges conferences. The provision of teachers' centres is not mandatory and the number of centres is diminishing.

teachers' pay and conditions   Arrangements and regulations governing teachers' pay are set out in the School Teachers' Pay and Conditions Document which is revised annually by the **Secretary of State for Education**. The Document states that the duties and working time of teachers are 1,265 hours per year. It was announced in October 2002 that teachers' contracts were to be changed from 2004 in order to pass responsibility for 25 administrative tasks to clerical staff, and to allow primary school teachers guaranteed planning and preparation time. The School Teachers' Review Body (STRB) was established by the School Teachers Pay and Condition Act (1991). It makes recommendations to the Secretary of State for teachers' pay and conditions in England and Wales. After consultation with interested parties, including **local education authorities** and teachers' representatives, the Secretary of State sets out the decisions in the Document.

There is a single pay spine, ranging from unqualified teachers to those with **qualified teacher status**, and **advanced skills teachers**; and a leadership spine for heads, deputies, and those with substantial managerial responsibilities. Additional allowances are available for a wide range of duties, including recruitment and selection and **special educational needs**.

An extra **London Allowance** is awarded, graded into Inner London, Outer London, and fringe bands. Extra money in the form of **performance related pay** is also available on the basis of appraisal by senior managers. With increasing autonomy being given by the **Department for Education and Skills**, especially to secondary schools, many schools are able to alter teachers' pay and conditions.

teachers' unions   Bodies organised on a national scale to safeguard the interests, salaries, working conditions and welfare of their members. They also promote views on educational issues and consult with national and local government and other organisations; they are represented by many bodies concerned with formulating educational policies.

There are a number of different bodies which represent the teaching profession in the UK. For schools, there is the **National Union of Teachers** (NUT), the largest union; the **National Association of Schoolmasters/ Union of Women Teachers** (NAS/UWT); the **Association of Teachers and Lecturers** (ATL); and the **Professional Association of Teachers** (PAT). Headteachers are represented separately by the **National Association of Headteachers** (NAHT); and the **Secondary Heads Association** (SHA). In further and higher education, there is the **National Association of Teachers** in **Further and Higher Education** (NATFHE); and the **Association of University Teachers** (AUT). In Scotland, 80 per cent of all teachers from nursery to further education belong to the **Educational Institute of Scotland** (EIS). Recent attempts to explore mergers between unions have not been successful.

With the reorganisation of educational institutions at both school and higher education levels, unions are widening their range of membership. The former Assistant Masters and Mistresses Association is now called the Association of Teachers and Lecturers (ATL), to cater for the staff in the independent **sixth form** and **tertiary colleges**.

teaching assistant   A term that covers classroom assistants, integration assistants, learning support assistants, advanced teaching assistants and others who assist a teacher in the classroom. In 2001, there were about 95,000 assistants in schools. Pay and conditions vary from local authority to local authority and there are no national requirements for qualifications, which may vary from modest achievements to PhDs. Teaching assistants, also called classroom assistants, were required to meet uniform training standards from 2002. The new National Standards have been developed by the Local Government Training Organisation, with **National Vocational Qualifications** (NVQ) accredited by the **Quality and Curriculum Authority** (QCA) from 2001. In October 2002, the Secretary of State for Education announced the creation of a new class of advanced teaching assistants who would take lessons and mark pupils' work in certain circumstances, thus reducing teachers' workloads.

teaching methods   Approaches to teaching methods vary between subjects and phases of education. For instance, it was long accepted that for younger children, the **child-centred** approach was most appropriate, emphasising discovery learning and the use of project work. Since the introduction of national testing and the questioning of standards in the basic subjects, there has been a tendency to concentrate more on effective methods of teaching, as in **reading**. New developments in teaching methods can arise from **curriculum development projects** such as the Schools History Project. (See also **child-centred education, teaching style**)

teaching practice   A period of time when trainees are placed in schools during their training programme. The term 'teaching practice' is often replaced by terms such as 'school experience' or 'practical teaching experience'.

teaching quality assessment (TQA)   A project designed by the **Quality Assurance Agency** (QAA) to evaluate the quality of teaching in every UK **higher education** (HE) institution. The project began in 1991, and has been much criticised for wasting time and money. In 2001, the project was reduced in terms of frequency of inspections and the amount of paperwork involved.

teaching style The ways in which teachers differ in presenting materials to their pupils, in particular, the kind of social relationship established within the classroom. Teaching styles may be categorised in a number of different ways: e.g., formal, informal; authoritarian, democratic; didactic, enquiry-based; child-centred, subject-centred. (See also **teaching methods**)

team teaching A method of teaching where a team of teachers works together with a large number of children. This form of organisation is often used where a **project** or a **topic** is being pursued, with individual teachers taking responsibility for particular aspects of the work. (See also **teaching methods**)

Technical and Vocational Education Initiative (TVEI) An initiative introduced in 1983 for 14- to 18-year-olds in full-time education which emphasised **vocational** and **technical education** and preparation for working life. This project, under the auspices of the **Manpower Services Commission** (MSC), was financed by the Department of Employment, by-passing the then **Department of Education and Science** in order to circumvent the legal restrictions of the 1944 Education Act.

technical education The impetus for providing technical education came in the last quarter of the nineteenth century. Reports from the **Devonshire** and **Samuelson Commissions**, and legislation – the Technical Instruction Act (1889), and the Local Taxation (Customs and Excise) Act (1890) – led to the founding of many **polytechnics** or technical institutes. After 1902, **local education authorities** became responsible for most of this work. The 1944 Education Act also made them responsible for **further education**. The **Percy Report** (1945) recommended a number of changes. Circular 305/1956 classified technical colleges into: Colleges of Advanced Technology (CATS), Regional Colleges, Area Colleges and Local Colleges. The **Robbins Report** (1963) transferred CATS to the university sector. A White Paper (1966) recommended the creation of 30 polytechnics.

Technician Education Council (TEC) Created in 1973 as a result of the **Haslegrave Report**, the TEC was responsible for the design, validation, examination and provision of programmes below degree level in technician education in England and Wales. It was later merged with the **Business Education Council** to become the **Business and Technology Education Council** (BTEC).

technical high and secondary technical school The **Spens Report** 1938 recommended a new type of higher school of technical character, distinct from the traditional **grammar school**, offering a broadly based general course combined with specialised studies having a vocational significance.

Entrance was to be by selective examination. After the 1944 Education Act, a number of **local education authorities** built secondary technical schools but they failed to achieve parity with grammar schools (in the eyes of parents) and most disappeared with comprehensive reorganisation.

Technical Instruction Act (1889)   The decline in British industrial supremacy, which was observed at the 1867 Paris Exhibition, was attributed to the lack of a good system of industrial education. The report of the **Samuelson Commission** led to the passing of the Technical Instruction Act 1889. This allowed county and county borough councils to levy a penny rate for **technical education**. Further income became available in 1890 with 'whisky money' (the proceeds of increased duty on beer and spirits).

Technological Baccalaureate   A new examination with a four-part curriculum structure starting at 16 plus: A – exploration and development of individual potential; B – a common curriculum within a technological and commercial context; C – an elective curriculum related to aesthetic or performing arts, the humanities or recreation; D – an extension curriculum suited to the individual student's post-qualification intentions. Three certificates are offered: the Technological Baccalaureate; with credit; with distinction. (See also **Baccalauréat**, **International Baccalaureate**)

technology   Technology may be defined as 'the application of scientific knowledge to the solution of practical problems'. In education the term is used in two very different ways:

1. A 'new' subject introduced into the **national curriculum** in 1989, it combines art, craft, design and technology (CDT), home economics, business studies and **information and communications technology** (ICT). The aim of technology is to develop technical skills, knowledge and understanding through working with materials and systems. It is often carried out through projects or topics.

2. Educational technology often means no more than **visual aids**, but it should refer to the techniques and understanding of the whole process of learning as well as the hardware.

tenure   The existence of tenure, particularly at universities, has long been seen as a prerequisite for academic freedom. Good reason for dismissal has to be shown by the employing body and the findings challenged in a court of law. The Education Reform Act (1988) provided for a revision of university statutes to weaken rights of tenure. There are great variations already between universities, varying from strong tenure to no tenure. In all institutions, new members of staff are increasingly offered short-term contracts.

term   The academic year of schools and colleges in the UK is normally divided into three periods: autumn, spring and summer, though some universities still use older names (e.g. the Oxford terms are Michaelmas, Hilary and Trinity). The length of both school and college terms vary, though the former are usually of longer duration. Some institutions are now working in **semesters** rather than terms. Many educationists now believe that a six-term school year would make for more efficient curriculum planning and better timing of **A Level** and **General Certificate of Secondary Education** examinations. In December 2001, the Independent Commission on the Organisation of the School Year, set up by the **Local Government Association**, recommended a change to a six-term school year by 2005.

terminal examination   An examination taken after the completion of a course of study. An external terminal examination is a requirement for each **General Certificate of Secondary Education** (GCSE) subject assessment.

tertiary college   A college catering for all students aged 16–19, full- and part-time, in a particular area. It brings under one roof both the range of courses found in normal sixth forms in schools and the **vocational** and **technical** courses offered in **further education**.

testing   Evaluation of a student's understanding of a lesson, module or course. The new requirements of the **national curriculum** for testing at 7, 11, 14 and 16 has produced the claim that such tests impose much strain, especially on the younger age groups. National testing is becoming more popular as countries become more interested in ways of raising educational achievement.

TGAT   (See **Task Group on Assessment and Testing** (TGAT))

thesis   A treatise, based on research, submitted for an award or qualification, such as a Master of Arts (MA) or Doctor of Philosophy (PhD). It is similar to a **dissertation**, though a thesis may be considered as contributing original knowledge to a **discipline**. (See also **graduate**, **postgraduate**, **viva**)

Thompson Report   The Thompson Committee was set up by the Government in January 1981 to review the provision of the **Youth Service** in England and to consider whether the existing resources could be employed more effectively. The chairman was Mr Alan Thompson, formerly a **Department of Education and Science** official. The Report, issued in October 1982, was critical of the Service in terms of its unequal availability, lack of co-ordination between the statutory and the voluntary sectors, and unclear objectives. It recommended that a DES minister should co-ordinate all youth affairs; that **local education authorities** be given statutory responsibility to provide facilities for those between 11 and 21; and that the Youth Service be funded at a high level. The Report stated that the primary need in this age group was social rather than for recreational facilities, and that the youth service should co-operate with schools in devising an appropriate curriculum for adolescents. (See also **Albemarle Report, McNair Report**)

three Rs   The Revised Code of 1862 altered the system of government grants to schools. The money that had been paid to certificated teachers was now given to the **managers**, who paid the teachers according to the average attendance of pupils and their achievements at examinations conducted by **Her Majesty's Inspectorate** (HMI) – hence the title of this system **'payment by results'**. The subjects tested were the three Rs – reading, writing and arithmetic, with plain needlework for girls. This system led to greater pressure from teachers on pupils, and at the same time a narrowing of the **curriculum**. From 1867, other subjects were allowed to be offered for grant purposes and a liberalising of the Code continued until the end of the century. The term is still used to refer to these three subjects.

tiering   A method of achieving **differentiation by task** at **General Certificate of Secondary Education** (GCSE). From September 1996 tiering was a requirement for all subjects. For most subjects there is a foundation tier covering Grades G–C and a higher tier covering Grades D–A*. (This is an example of overlapping tiering.) For mathematics a three-tier structure operates: a foundation tier, Grades G–D; an intermediate tier, Grades E–B; and a higher tier for Grades C–A*. Art, music, history and PE are allowed to do without tiers – instead **differentiation by outcome** operates.

timetabling   Refers to the groupings of pupils, the **curriculum** and the allocation of teachers in an institution. Traditionally, timetables explained *when* things happened rather than reflecting the aims of the organisation. A more analytical approach to planning in schools and resource allocation is now favoured which takes into account types of pupil grouping and curriculum philosophy.

topic work   A method of teaching, particularly in **primary schools**, which aims at developing children's conceptual development through a study of a particular topic over a period of days or weeks. Some topics may attempt to cover the whole **curriculum**, but many are confined to subjects such as history, geography and social studies. (See also **assignment, project**)

trainee   Term used by the **Teacher Training Agency** for those training to be teachers.

training   The provision of learning experiences enabling learners to develop specified skills or competence.

Training and Enterprise Councils (TECs)   The 82 locally based TECs, established in 1991, took over many of the functions of the former **Manpower Services Commission** (MSC). Members of TEC boards consisted of leading businessmen in the area, who dispensed a government-funded budget to finance courses for **youth training** in **further education colleges**, participated in **vocational** and **technical** initiatives in schools, and took a close interest in local authorities, many TECs having representatives from this constituency on their boards. The objective of TECs was to offer every young person the opportunity to attend vocational education courses, to gain relevant qualifications, and to improve their work skills. In Scotland the equivalent was carried on by 22 Local Enterprise Companies (LECs). TECs ceased to exist when the **Learning and Skills Council** took over their functions in April 2001. (See also **training credits**)

training college   Dating from the nineteenth century, the training college provided courses of training for teachers, mainly for those intending to work in primary schools, with some offering courses for secondary school teaching. They were provided either by **local education authorities** or **voluntary bodies**. Courses were of two years' duration, until 1960, when they were increased to three. The **Robbins Report** recommended a change of name to **colleges of education**.

training credits   An initiative launched by government in 1990 whereby 16- and 17-year-olds who have left full-time education are given training credits or **vouchers** to buy the training of their choice under the **Training and Enterprise Councils'** scheme.

training school   Secondary schools that can develop new initiatives in **initial teacher training**, along with their **higher education** providers, spread good practice, train **mentors** and undertake research. The scheme, described in the Green Paper, *Teachers: Meeting the Challenge of Change* (1998), started in 2000. Most training schools are existing partnership schools and receive funding through the **Standards Fund**. Successful schools can receive up to £100,000 a year extra. Eighty-two schools were named in the first batch.

transition from primary to secondary school   In most, but not all **local education authorities** there is a transition at the age of 11 from **primary school** to **secondary school** for the majority of pupils. This can create problems of two kinds. First, there is, in many authorities, a lack of continuity between the **curriculum** of the primary school and the curriculum of the secondary school; second, the regime of the secondary school is likely to be much more formal and puzzling for the 11-year-old than the regime of the primary school, where the pupil probably had only one teacher for all subjects rather than a different teacher for six or seven periods every day. Partly to counteract the difficulties of this transition, **middle schools** were set up in some authorities and, at one stage, it was suggested that primary and secondary schools should pay attention to the 'middle years' so that greater continuity would be achieved. (See also '**Great Debate**', **Plowden Report**)

triangulation   A research technique, particularly associated with the work of John Elliott, in which evaluation is carried out by means of a threefold process. The teacher has a view of what he/she wants to do (and of how successfully he/she has achieved it); this may be different from the view or views of **pupils**; in addition, an independent, neutral observer may have yet further views. The hypothesis is that by open discussion of these three points of view the teacher's performance and competence may be improved. Triangulation in this sense is part of the 'teacher as researcher' model. (See also **participant observation**)

tripartite system   Refers to the threefold classification of secondary schools postulated by the **Spens Report** (1938): i.e. **grammar**, **technical** and **modern** schools. Later, in 1943, the **Norwood Report**, basing its findings on psychological evidence, claimed that there were three types of minds corresponding to the schools: the **academic**, the applied scientific, and those with the ability to handle concrete things rather than ideas. No mention of types of schools was made in the 1944 Education Act; but **local education authorities** were allowed to establish various kinds of secondary schools with **selection** tests determining pupil allocation. The system was largely replaced by **comprehensive schools**. With the advent of the **grant maintained school**, **city technology colleges** and a revival of the **grammar school**, there is once more diversity in the structure of secondary education.

tripos   An honours **degree** course of study at the University of Cambridge. The name is derived from the three-legged stool on which medieval undergraduates used to sit. A student must pass two tripos examinations to qualify for a Bachelor of Arts (BA). The majority of triposes are in two parts: it is possible for the student to take both parts of the same tripos or one tripos followed by part 1 or 2 of a different tripos.

trivium   Three of the seven liberal arts – grammar, logic and rhetoric – in the school curriculum of the Middle Ages. The remaining four formed the **quadrivium**.

truancy   A problem of long standing, in fact since **compulsory education** was introduced in the last century. Truancy is often associated with low levels

of **literacy** and **numeracy** as well as boredom. The **Children Act** (1989) introduced a system which gave **education welfare officers** responsibility for
working with parents to ensure that their children return to school. Another
approach that is being adopted is for a local authority to co-operate with
industry in providing part-time work where the pupils receive basic **skills**
lessons and **counselling**. It was estimated in October 2000 that some 50,000
pupils truant from schools in England every day. Measures to reduce this
figure since have included: an increase in the number of education welfare
officers being employed in inner city schools; targets being set for improvement for schools with poor records; and 'truancy buster' awards of up to
£10,000 for those showing the greatest improvement. The **Department for
Education and Skills** has given extra funds for local projects to reduce
truancy, and has increased the number of **Learning Support Units** (LSUs).
Courts can now impose fines of up to £2,500 on parents for their children's
persistent truancy, or three months in jail.

truant school   From the time of the Industrial Schools Act (1857) truants
could be sent to **industrial schools**, but persistent truants would go to
truant schools. These were administered by both lay and denominational
bodies. Military drill featured prominently, and the regime was deliberately
harsh. Children attended for a short period and were then returned to their
schools.

tutor   There are several kinds of tutors. In **higher** and **further education**
it is the person responsible for the supervision of students' **academic** work,
often operating through **tutorials**. A tutor may be designated as an **adviser**
to students, acting as a counsellor. In schools, tutors may be in charge of a
tutor group which encourages pupils to become integrated into the school
community as well as to achieve their own academic and personal potential.
Finally, there is the private tutor, employed to **coach** an individual to achieve
success in an examination or to remedy weakness in a subject. **Tutorial colleges**
exist for the same purpose.

tutorial   A meeting between a **tutor** and one or more students, frequently
based on a paper or essay submitted by a student. Such meetings normally
take place throughout the student's course. Tutorials are very common in
institutions of **further** and **higher education**, though with the large expansion
of student numbers, it has been argued that other more economical teaching
methods should be used.

tutorial college   (See **crammers**)

TVEI   (See **Technical and Vocational Education Initiative**)

U

under-achiever A pupil whose performance at school is identifiably below what would be expected from his or her known **ability**. Under-achievers probably fall into at least two main groups: first, individual pupils whose achievement does not come up to their performance on **intelligence quotient** (IQ) tests; second, groups of students (e.g. working-class pupils or children from ethnic **minorities**) whose work is generally below average when there is no reason to believe that their **intelligence** level is below average. (See also **intelligence test**, **multicultural education**, **self-concept/self-image**)

undergraduate A student following a course leading to a first degree. (See also **graduate**, **postgraduate**, **university entry requirements**)

Undergraduate Teacher Training Scheme (UTTS) A scheme introduced in 2001 which allows second- and third-year **undergraduates** to obtain teacher training experience alongside their degree studies. They are expected to spend ten days in total in a **secondary school**, to observe lessons, assist class teachers, and work with small groups of pupils. In addition, they attend a Saturday induction day and four 'twilight sessions' where they explore key teaching issues. On successful completion of the course students receive £400 and 10 per cent credit towards **qualified teacher status**. The pilot scheme, which is Government funded, was, at the time of writing, being conducted by six teacher training institutions.

uniform, school Often justified on the ground that it demonstrates a school's corporate identity and helps in the enforcement of discipline. School uniform is generally compulsory in the older **independent schools**, such as Eton and Harrow, though less so in State schools. Heads and governors decide on the wearing of uniforms, their design, and up to what age they should be worn, though under Section 130 of the 1996 Education Act, the governors are ultimately responsible. Schools are expected to consult parents wherever possible on school uniform matters. It has been calculated that parents spend one billion pounds a year on uniforms. Nearly one-third of **local education authorities** provide no help for families on low incomes.

unit A sub-division of the **National Vocational Qualification** (NVQ) **statement of competence**. A unit is made up of elements of competence. In **General National Vocational Qualifications** (GNVQs) a unit is a sub-division of the outcome statement.

United Nations Educational, Social and Cultural Organisation (UNESCO)   One of the sub-divisions of the United Nations, founded in 1946 to promote international, cultural and educational co-operation. It has its own constitution and budget. Its permanent headquarters are in Paris. It is administered by a Director-General and an international Civil Service of about 800. Member states are required to establish national citizen commissions, to advise UNESCO on policy, and to encourage participation in activities that flow from UNESCO programmes. UNESCO-sponsored activities can be classified as follows: (1) emergency aid and reconstruction; (2) advancement of knowledge; (3) promotion of human welfare; and (4) the encouragement of international understanding. In the early-1980s there was some criticism that certain UNESCO activities were becoming 'political'; in 1984 the USA (which contributed 25 per cent of the UNESCO budget) withdrew from membership, and the UK followed in 1985, but rejoined in 1997.

Universities and Colleges Admissions Service (UCAS)   The clearing house for admissions to **higher education** which was formed in 1992 from a merger of the **Universities Central Council on Admissions** (UCCA) and the Polytechnics Central Admissions System (PCAS). UCAS is also responsible to **Universities UK** for public relations about admissions. UCAS deals with some 450,000 applications in the UK each year. It has also taken over the work of the **Graduate Teacher Training Registry** (GTTR).

universities, history of   The oldest universities in the UK are Oxford and Cambridge, both founded in the thirteenth century. Scotland established three universities (Aberdeen, St Andrew's and Glasgow) in the fifteenth century, and one at Edinburgh a hundred years later. Durham was the first of the universities to be built in the nineteenth century (1832), closely following the Oxbridge pattern. At almost the same time in London, a secular institution, University College, was founded; also an Anglican rival, King's College, which stressed religious instruction. The University of London was established in 1836 as a degree-awarding body to affiliated colleges in various parts of the kingdom, including University College and King's College.

The provincial civic universities of the second half of the century were often the result of local benefactors (who favoured a science-based curriculum) and the **university extension** movement. Owens College, Manchester, was the first, opened in 1851. Between 1874 and 1902, university colleges were founded at Birmingham, Bristol, Exeter, Leeds, Liverpool, Nottingham, Reading, Sheffield and Southampton. All were eventually granted full university status. During this period, the University of Wales, a federal body, came into existence. Between the two World Wars, only two new colleges were founded – at Hull and Leicester.

After 1945, there was a dramatic expansion of university provision. The University College of North Staffordshire was the first in 1949, followed by East Anglia, Essex, Kent, Lancaster, Sussex, Warwick and York in the years 1961–65. In 1963, Newcastle became a university in its own right (it had formerly been associated with Durham). The final phase of expansion followed the **Robbins Report** (1963) recommendation that the nine **Colleges of Advanced Technology** – Aston, Bath, Bradford, Brunel, Chelsea, City, Loughborough, Salford and Surrey – should became full universities. At the same time Strathclyde, Dundee and Heriot-Watt were founded in Scotland. Northern Ireland has Queen's, Belfast, and the University of Ulster at Coleraine. The **Open University**, established in 1966 for mature students, has more students than any other UK university. The only private university in the UK is the University College of Buckingham; established in 1976, it offers courses for two-year honours degrees.

In 1992, the **binary** line distinction between **polytechnics** and universities was abolished, thus adding considerably to the total number of universities and university places in the UK. Some adopted the name of a region, such as the University of Northumbria and the University of West of England; others chose to be named after a county, such as the University of Glamorgan, the University of Hertfordshire, and Staffordshire University. A third category took their name from the city in which the university was situated, such as the University of Portsmouth and the University of Wolverhampton. In London, the 'new' universities have such names as the University of North London, University of East London, London Guildhall University, University of Westminster and the South Bank University. In 2001 the first new university to be created for eight years was the University of Gloucestershire, formerly the Cheltenham and Gloucester College of Higher Education.

Universities Funding Council   (See **University Grants Committee**)

Universities UK   (See **Committee of Vice-Chancellors and Vice-Principals**)

University Central Council on Admissions (UCCA)   The Council was set up in 1961 as a clearing house to handle all applications for entrance to universities in England (except the **Open University** and Buckingham), Scotland, Wales and Northern Ireland. The Council played no part in the selection of students but forwarded candidates' application forms to universities. Up to five universities could be named on the form. An unsuccessful candidate might take advantage of either the continuing applications procedure, which provided for further chances, or the clearing scheme, which operated every September in a final attempt to place candidates. The UCCA

scheme did not cover **postgraduate** applicants, who applied direct to universities. In 1992, UCCA was replaced by the **Universities and Colleges Admissions Service** (UCAS). (See also **clearing house, entry qualifications, open admission, Open College, undergraduate, university entry requirements**)

university college   A college of **university** rank that is unable to award its own degrees. Most of the civic universities were at one time university colleges, but they have since achieved full university status. (See also **federal university, universities, history of**)

university day training college   One of the recommendations of the Cross Commission (1888) was that day training colleges should be established in connection with local universities or university colleges. The Education Department's Code for 1890 sanctioned this arrangement for training elementary school teachers, and 14 day training departments were opened; the course was to be of three years' duration.

university department of education (UDE)   A university department, specialising in teacher education. UDEs grew out of **university day training colleges**, which were established in 1890 to enable student-teachers to follow a three-year course and take a **degree** if they wished. They were at first called university training departments (UTD), but after the Second World War most had assumed this nomenclature. Many are now called **Schools of Education**. (See also **in-service education of teachers, teacher tutor**)

university entrance requirements   The normal (minimum) entrance requirement for admission to a **university** is the possession of two **GCE A Level** passes. Individual departments may stipulate more detailed achievements above the minimum. Many universities also operate special entry systems for mature students as well as access courses for those without A Levels. The **Open University** accepts students without formal qualifications. (See also **entry qualification, open admission, undergraduate**)

university extension   A movement that began in the second half of the nineteenth century – instigated mainly by James Stuart, then a Fellow at Cambridge – which attempted to set up a 'peripatetic university' in towns where none existed. Following the success of his lectures on gravitation in a number of northern towns in 1867, he persuaded Cambridge to found a range of courses in 1873 in the region surrounding the University. Three years later, the University of London followed and, in 1878, so did Oxford. The success of the movement led to the establishment of university colleges such as Sheffield and Nottingham; it also brought into prominence the lack of university education provision for women. Today's **extramural departments** of universities are another outcome. (See also **universities, history of**)

University for Industry (UfI)   A 'virtual' university, launched in 1999, offering open and **distance learning**, which caters for basic skills, information technology skills, management of small and medium-sized businesses and skills needed in specific industries and services. A private–public partnership, the UfI works with courses supplied by universities, **colleges of higher education** and other institutions. Advice for companies and individuals is available by telephone, letter, fax or email or at UfI enquiry desks located in supermarkets, shops and colleges. UfI's learning services are delivered through learndirect, which provides 80 per cent of courses on line. There are more than 1,000 learning centres, situated in libraries and shopping centres, where people can access UfI courses and materials. A prospectus drawn up by experts in skills, marketing and finance was published in spring 2002.

University Grants Committee (UGC)   Established in 1919, the Committee's main terms of reference were to 'enquire into the financial needs of university education in the UK and to advise the government as to the application of any grants that may be made by parliament towards meeting them'. After 1964, on the recommendation of the **Robbins Report**, the UGC became the responsibility of the **Secretary of State for Education and Science**. One of the provisions of the Education Reform Act (1988) was to abolish the UGC and replace it by a **Universities Funding Council** (UFC). The UFC was in turn replaced by the **Higher Education Funding Council** (HEFC) in 1992 following the recommendations of the White Paper, *Higher Education: A New Framework* (May 1991), and the 1992 Act.

University of the First Age   This initiative was proposed in 1995 by Professor Tim Brighouse, Chief Education Officer for Birmingham. The aim was to provide pupils from all types of schools the opportunity to extend their skills, knowledge and understanding in areas such as science or the arts, or sports, mathematics, and foreign languages. They pursued that interest in a week or a fortnight on courses organised after the end of the normal spring and summer terms in Birmingham City's network of schools, universities and colleges. The aim was to accelerate learning without the normal social disadvantages that might be inevitable in the normal school timetable. The courses in these spring and summer weeks are planned and provided by groups of volunteer teachers drawn from the City of Birmingham schools. In addition to the chosen subject there are lessons in citizenship and development of thinking skills. Pupils are able to consolidate and extend their learning when they return to the classroom by means of **distance learning**, making considerable use of **information and communication technology**. The University of the First Age is staffed by professors and lecturers working with the **secondary schools** taking part. The experiment is regarded as a considerable success and it is planned to continue indefinitely. (See also **summer schools**)

University of the Third Age (U3A)   The first *Université du Troisieme Age* was founded in Toulouse in 1972 as a **summer school** for retired people; the university staff did the teaching. The English version began in 1982 and was different from the French inasmuch as the teachers were not necessarily professionals and received no fee. The main aim of U3A is to provide educational opportunities for older members of society (the over-50s) to enable them to have a better quality of life.

university training department (UTD)   (See **university department of education**)

unstreaming   This is the product of a diametrically opposite philosophy to **streaming**: pupils are randomly assigned for teaching purposes without reference to **ability**, or are deliberately placed in **mixed-ability groups**. (See also **labelling, setting**)

upper school   Originally, a term reserved for the top forms of a **public school** or **grammar school**, it now generally refers to **comprehensive schools** with feeders from middle or lower schools.

V

vacation   A period of time when an educational institution is not in session. The major breaks in the UK are at Easter, in the summer, and at Christmas. Formerly, the term was used mainly in connection with universities. (See also **semester, term**)

validation   Universities are empowered by their charters to award **degrees**. This privilege includes the right to validate degrees in other institutions – e.g., in **colleges of higher education**. The validation procedure normally consists of the formal submission of plans and syllabuses, visits to the site, and ensuring that the teaching staff are adequately qualified. The university would also monitor the **standards** of the awards.

validity   An intelligence test or examination rarely measures exactly what it is intended to measure. For example, a test of **creativity** might give results that are superficially plausible but which, on further investigation, turn out to be no more than a test of **intelligence**. The validity of many tests of attitude is often called into question: asking students to say what they would do may not be a valid measure of what they would actually do in real life. (See also **reliability**)

value added   Part of the result of some policies of the 1980s encouraging parental choice of school has been the attempt to find ways of providing evidence of school quality. One obvious, but unsatisfactory, practice is to publish the examination results of schools, and the results of **national curriculum** tests in **league table** form. An objection to this practice is that such 'raw scores' do not give an accurate picture of school quality. To avoid this trap, some assessment experts have advocated that examination results should be published in a 'value-added' form – i.e. measuring the difference that the schools have made by comparing, e.g., the results of schools with very similar intakes. (See also **benchmarking**)

verbal reasoning   One aspect of general **intelligence**. Verbal reasoning tests (often used for **eleven plus selection** procedures for **grammar schools**) focused upon this aspect of intelligence rather than **spatial ability**. It is the aspect of intelligence which is most difficult to separate from environmental factors.

verification   The process of monitoring by a vocational awarding body to make sure that assessment is conducted according to procedures.

verifier   An 'examiner' appointed by a vocational awarding body to carry out processes of **verification**.

vertical age grouping   (See **family grouping**)

vice-chancellor   The vice-chancellor is the chief academic and administrative officer of a university. He is often the chairman of many important university committees and an *ex officio* member of all of them. He is involved in the appointment of senior university posts and is the channel of communication with bodies such as the **Committee of Vice-Chancellors and Principals** (now **Universities UK**). Vice-chancellors vary in their style of leadership. It should be noted that in the University of London, the vice-chancellor is assisted by a **principal**, who shares the administrative load. (See also **chancellor**)

Vice-President of the Committee of Council   A post created in 1856 when the **Education Department** was established. The Vice-President, who was always an MP, acted as spokesman for the Department in the House of Commons, as the **Lord President** did in the Lords. The post disappeared in 1900, and was replaced by the **President of the Board of Education**.

village college   The brain-child of Henry Morris, County Education Secretary (Chief Education Officer), for Cambridgeshire (1922–54), the village college was envisaged as a community centre of a neighbourhood. Its aim was to 'provide for the whole man, and abolish the duality of education and ordinary life'. Thus Morris's first college, opened at Sawston in 1930, contained a school, an **adult education** centre and a community centre. Morris had hoped that 12 such colleges would be built for the county though in fact only five – at Sawston, Linton, Bottisham, Impington and Bassingbourn – were completed. After the Second World War, this notion was revived in the form of the **community college** or school. (See also **adult education**, **community education**)

village schools   Characterised by their smallness, village schools have come under pressure in recent years. A **Department of Education and Science** Report, *Better Schools* (1985), pointed out the need for a school to be large enough to offer a full curriculum to its pupils and for classes to be of economic size. Since then, the advent of the **national curriculum** and **local management of schools** (LMS) has presented further problems. Although village schools are popular with the community, administrative and financial considerations are becoming increasingly important in determining their survival. (See also **falling rolls**)

virement   The power to transfer money from one budget heading to another.

viva   Short for *viva voce*. An oral examination most frequently used in connection with the award of higher **degrees** but also applies now to many other different examinations.

Vocational A Level   One of the **Dearing Report**'s (1996) recommendations for the 16–19 age group was that the distinction between academic and vocational qualifications should be blurred, giving qualifications such as the **General National Vocational Qualifications** (GNVQs) greater parity of esteem. One outcome was that, from 2002, GNVQ Level 3 was renamed as a Vocational A Level or the Vocational Certificate of Education, with assessment being somewhat closer to academic **A Level** requirements. Vocational **AS Levels** will be available from 2004.

vocational awarding bodies   Vocational qualifications tended to develop in a very haphazard way over many years so that by the 1980s there were more than 500 vocational awarding bodies for about 6,000 qualifications. The Government saw the need for rationalisation, and in 1986 the **National Council for Vocational Qualifications** (NCVQ) was established to co-ordinate vocational awards and ensure that they adhered to national standards. Following the **Dearing** recommendation in 1997, attempts were made to bring vocational and academic awards closer together. The NCVQ merged with the **Schools Curriculum and Assessment Authority** (SCAA) to form the **Qualifications and Curriculum Authority** (QCA).

Vocational Certificate of Education   (See **Vocational A Level**)

vocational education   Education designed to prepare people for work in a particular occupation or groups of occupations. (See **further education** and **higher education**).

vocational education and training (See **National Vocational Qualification**)

vocational guidance   Giving advice to young people and adults about the occupations most suitable to their aptitudes and personality. **Aptitude** tests are extensively used in the diagnosis of special abilities and inclinations.

vocational preparation   (See **National Vocational Qualification**)

voluntary aided school   Until the School Standards and Framework Act (1998), this was a type of voluntary school where the governors controlled the admission of pupils and the type of religious education given, though parents had the right for their children to be taught according to the **agreed syllabus**. The church authority concerned appointed two-thirds of the governing body, which was responsible for the capital expenditure on alterations or enlargement of a school, but the **Secretary of State for Education** made a contribution of 85 per cent towards the expenditure. The **local education authority** maintained such schools and paid the salaries of the teachers. Approximately one-half of the total of voluntary schools in England are of this type and some 2,300 of the 5,000 in this category are Church of England. Arrangements under the 1998 Act are similar to those previously existing. (See also **special agreement school**, **voluntary controlled school**)

voluntary controlled school   Until the School Standards and Framework Act (1998), this was a type of voluntary school, where the **local education authority** was responsible for the total expenditure and maintenance of the building. It appointed two-thirds of its governing body and the teaching staff, though governors were consulted on the appointment of heads and on teachers giving denominational religious instruction. Most controlled schools belong to the Church of England. Arrangements made under the 1998 Act are similar to those previously existing. (See also **religious education**, **special agreement school**, **voluntary aided school**)

voluntary body   An organisation, usually religious, that is responsible for **voluntary schools**.

voluntary school   Originally owned by voluntary bodies, usually religious, but now in receipt of public funds. They may be of two kinds: **voluntary aided** and **voluntary controlled**, as distinct from those schools that are entirely within the province of the **local education authority**. Approximately 30 per cent of **maintained schools** in England are voluntary schools. (See also **religious education**)

Voluntary Service Overseas (VSO)   An organisation established in 1958 and dedicated to assisting development in the world's poor countries. Each year around 700 men and women set out to work on projects in more than 40 developing countries. The average age of a volunteer is 33, with the youngest in their early twenties and the oldest in their late sixties. The range of skills sought and requested includes: agriculture and natural resources; education; technical trades and engineering; social development; and business and commercial development. Volunteers are normally paid the equivalent amount of someone who does the same job in that country on a permanent basis.

Waddell Report   In 1970, the **Schools Council** recommended a single system of examining at 16 plus and, after some experimenting, repeated its belief in such a system in 1976. The then **Secretary of State for Education**, Shirley Williams, agreed that a Steering Committee should be formed to make an intensive study of 'outstanding problems'. The Committee, under the chairmanship of Sir James Waddell, reported in July 1978. Entitled *School Examinations*, the Report concluded that a common examination was educationally feasible and could be introduced without causing major difficulties. It recommended a seven-point grading system, with the first three grades representing the **General Certificate of Education** (GCE) **O Level** pass grades of A, B, and C and the other four representing **Certificate of Secondary Education** (CSE) grades 2, 3, 4 and 5. An ungraded category was to be included for those who did not gain a certificate. An important organisational change was that GCE and CSE boards were to be regionally grouped, four in England and one in Wales. Schools were not to be limited in their choice of examining board by regional considerations. **General Certificate of Secondary Education** courses began in 1986 with the first examinations taken in 1988. (See also **examination boards**, **national criteria**, **sixteen plus examination**)

Warnock Report   The Committee of Enquiry into the education of handicapped children and young people, chaired by Mary Warnock, was set up in 1973 and reported in 1978. It recommended that the **Department of Education and Science**'s statutory categories should be abolished, that services should be planned on the assumption that one in six children at any time attending schools would need help, and that intellectually impaired children and children with remedial problems should be referred to as **children with learning difficulties**. Attention was drawn to the need for more parental involvement in children's education and for greater opportunities for young people aged between 16 and 19 years. **Special educational needs** were an essential element in **initial teacher training** and in-service training courses. Although the issue of **integration** of children with special needs into ordinary schools was fundamental to the work of the Warnock Committee, the Report did not make specific proposals as to how this should be achieved. A Government White Paper, *Special Needs in Education* (1980), accepted the proposal to abolish categories of handicap as a basis for planning services. This was implemented in the 1981 Education Act, but no concessions were made on the running down of **special schools** or the redistribution of resources to help develop ordinary school-based provision. Special schools were to remain. (See also **integration**, **remedial education**)

Weaver Report   A Study Group, headed by T. R. Weaver, Deputy Secretary at the **Department of Education and Science**, published its Report, *The Government of Colleges of Education*, in 1966. One of its major recommendations was that each **college of education** should have an academic board, responsible for academic work, the selection of students, and other college business. The Board was to be responsible for electing members of the teaching staff, other than the Principal, who would serve on the governing body. Legislation was also introduced, requiring **local education authorities** to make instruments of government for the constitution of college governing bodies. Up to this time, many had been sub-committees of local education authorities.

weighting   The contribution that an examination component makes to the distribution of candidates' results. If the scores for one examination component are more widely spread (i.e. have a greater **standard deviation**) than that for a second component, the first will exercise a greater influence on the overall attainment order of candidates, even if both components have the same mark allocations. Its *actual* weighting will be higher than its *intended* weighting.

welfare assistant   Often employed by **local education authorities** to help teachers with children who have **special educational needs**. Welfare assistants have no teaching qualifications and, as the title indicates, are especially concerned with the pupil's physical needs.

Welsh Baccalaureate (WelshBac)   The WelshBac being developed by the **Welsh Joint Education Committee** and the **Welsh Language Board** is intended to replace **A Levels** with a broad curriculum more in line with other European countries. The proposed curriculum aims at parity of esteem between vocational and academic studies, and at encouraging an international outlook with a distinctive Welsh dimension. Trials of the pilot six-subject WelshBac were held in schools throughout Wales in 2001–2.

Welsh Joint Education Committee (WJEC)   The WJEC was established in 1948. It was originally a consortium of LEAs, but it has developed into the main provider of educational services in Wales, and is owned and controlled by the 22 unitary authorities. The educational services include examinations: the WJEC operates as an **examination board**, subject to the **Qualifications and Curriculum Authority** (QCA) and ACCAC (Qualifications and Assessment Authority for Wales) **codes of practice**. As well as **General Certificate of Secondary Education** (GCSE) and **A Level** examinations, the WJEC has particular responsibility for examinations in Welsh, including tests for adults learning Welsh as a second language, in association with the **Welsh Language Board** (WLB).

Welsh Language Board (WLB)   The WLB is a statutory body, established following the Welsh Language Act (1993). Its main purpose is to promote and facilitate the use of the Welsh language. It is directly responsible to the **National Assembly for Wales**. In 2001 a partnership was agreed with the **Welsh Joint Education Committee** to develop a Welsh for Adults examinations system. (See also **Qualifications and Curriculum Authority for Wales**)

Welsh Office   Until 1970, the **Department of Education and Science** (DES) was responsible for education in Wales. In that year, primary and secondary education transferred to the Education Department of the Welsh Office, and in 1978 non-university institutions and public libraries were also transferred. In 1998, the **Government of Wales Act** abolished the Welsh Office when it established the **National Assembly for Wales** from 1999.

White Paper The name given to the majority of government discussion documents, derived from the colour of the publication. A White Paper describes official policy towards an issue and is often a prelude to legislation, e.g. the White Paper, *Choice and Diversity* (1992). (See also **Parliamentary Papers**)

William Tyndale School An Islington primary school that became the subject of an official inquiry by the **Inner London Education Authority** in 1975. (See also **Auld Report, accountability**)

women's studies Courses at any level of education (**secondary school, undergraduate** or **postgraduate**) that are intended to emphasise the contributions made – e.g. in history, English literature or philosophy – by women. (See also **girls' education**)

Woodard schools Founded by the Revd Nathaniel Woodard in the mid-nineteenth century, the schools were to provide a good, cheap Christian education for the middle and upper working classes. The money for the schools was raised by private subscription. The first at Shoreham in 1848 was followed by Hurstpierpoint 1850 and Lancing in 1857. Revd Woodard anticipated the **Taunton Report** by creating grades of school according to social rank.

work experience Placement of a student or trainee with a company or organisation to give experience of the working environment. (See also **sandwich course**)

workcards Cards, often devised by the teacher, giving information on a particular subject or **topic**, with follow-up arising out of it. Workcards are used as a means of individualising instruction, as, for example, in a **mixed-ability** setting. (See also **individual learning, teaching methods**)

Workers' Educational Association (WEA) Founded in 1903 by Albert Mansbridge as a means of developing the intellectual capacity of working men [*sic*], the WEA was an alliance between universities, trade unions and the Co-operative Society. Up until 1945 the WEA provided courses for many thousands of workers and was associated with the Labour Party. After the Second World War, the WEA became identified with middle-class leisure pursuits, but efforts have been made to return to the original purpose, e.g. the day release courses for shop stewards in aspects of trade unionism run in association with the Trades Union Congress.

By 1992 WEA activities were subsidised by direct government grants amounting to about £2 million, with another £1 million being received via the **local education authorities**. From April 1993, however, government grants were channelled through the **Further Education Funding Council** (FEFC), and the Association has to compete for funds rather than having amounts earmarked as was previously the case. In addition, local education authorities are unlikely to be able to continue their previous level of support. The long-term future of WEA courses (like many other kinds of **adult education**) seems doubtful.

workhouse schools   The first Report of the Poor Law Commissioners for 1834 revealed the neglect of 90,000 children in workhouses. Most received little or no instruction and lived in an unsuitable environment. Dr Kay, then an Assistant Poor Law Commissioner, recommended that small workhouse schools be replaced by large district schools where children would be taught by qualified staff outside the workhouse.

World Class Tests   In 2000–1 tests were introduced, on a voluntary basis, for pupils up to age 9, and again at age 13, in mathematics and problem-solving. Pupils take the tests when they are ready rather than at a specific age. The tests are in line with the idea that differential rates of progression should operate for groups of pupils able to maintain a faster pace of learning, with deeper understanding. (See also **Curriculum Online**)

World Education Fellowship   (See **New Education Fellowship**)

Y

Yellow Book   A confidential report on standards in education compiled by civil servants in the **Department of Education and Science** in 1975 for the then Prime Minister, James Callaghan. It voiced many criticisms of primary and secondary schools which were reflected in Callaghan's **Ruskin College** speech in October 1976. It proved to be the basis for the subsequent 'Great Debate', which included, amongst other things, discussion on the need for a **national curriculum**.

Youth Opportunities Programme (YOP)   The **Manpower Service Commission** (MSC) organised a number of schemes under the YOP for 16- to 19-year-olds who were unemployed. It was replaced in September 1983 by the **Youth Training** Scheme. (See also **national traineeships, new deal**)

Youth Service   The 1944 Education Act placed the responsibility upon **local education authorities** to provide adequate facilities for recreation, and social and cultural activities for young people between the ages of 11 and 25. In the same year, the **McNair Report** made recommendations for the supply, recruitment and training of youth leaders. Other reports, such as **Albemarle** (1960) and **Thompson** (1982), have pointed out the inadequacies of the service. Although the Youth Service was always somewhat neglected in the days of full employment of young people, some effort was made to make available leisure and education programmes for those who had left school at 15 or 16. During the 1980s and 1990s, youth unemployment became a major problem and the priority shifted away from leisure pursuits for the young to **training** of the kind that would enable school-leavers to get and keep a worthwhile job. That was part of the purpose of the **Manpower Services Commission** (MSC), set up in 1974, and also of the Training Agency, which replaced MSC in 1988, and of the **Training and Enterprise Councils** (TECs) from 1991. This shift in emphasis towards training for work was maintained by the Labour Governments after 1997 but LEAs retain a responsibility for leisure services for young people as well as some educational services such as providing information about drugs. The work of LEAs and government is co-ordinated nationally by the **National Youth Agency** (NYA). The NYA is intended to advance youth work and to promote the personal and social development of young people. An attempt was made to update policy in 2001 with the publication of *Transforming Youth Work*, which emphasised the importance of the Youth Service in preventing disaffection and social exclusion. (See also **Connexions**)

Youth Training (YT)   In December 1981, the Government issued a White Paper, *A New Training Initiative: A Programme for Action*, which proposed radical reform of training. YT offered places on a vocational programme of up to two years for 16–18-year-olds not involved in work or in **further education**. Such schemes have been superseded by **national traineeships** or by opportunities provided by the **Learning and Skills Council** (LSC).

Z

zeitgeist   Literally 'spirit of the time' (German). The dominant ideas of a particular period – e.g. the 1920s or the 1980s – reflected in politics, philosophy, literature, art and architecture, even education and the curriculum.

zero-based budgeting   A budget that is prepared by ignoring previous spending priorities and begins with a completely clean slate to decide a school's requirement.

z-scores   A form of **standardised** score on a test which is obtained by expressing the raw score (actual score) in terms of the relationship of that score to the mean or average score. The difference is expressed in units of the **standard deviation**. For example, a raw score that was above the mean score by one standard deviation would have a z-score of +1; a raw score below average would have a minus z-score.

SECTION THREE

Historical Background

Landmarks in the Development of English Education since 1800

1802   *Health and Morals of Apprentices Act.* Apprentices to receive some instruction in the three Rs.

1816–18   Select Committee on the Lower Orders (Brougham). Inquiry into the educational provision for the poor.

1833   First Government grant for education: £20,000 for elementary schools.
              Factory Act. Children at work aged between 9 and 13 to attend school two hours a day.

1839   Committee of the Privy Council on Education established. The beginning of a national policy and the appointment of the first two HMIs.

1840   *Grammar Schools Act.* Allowed grammar schools to teach subjects other than Latin and Greek.

1853   Science and Art Department formed at South Kensington to encourage scientific and technical instruction for the industrial classes.

1856   The Education Department, with a Minister responsible for education, superseded the Committee of the Privy Council on Education.

1861   *Report of Royal Commission into the State of Popular Education in England* (Newcastle Report) advocated sound and cheap elementary education for the poor.

1862   *Revised Code.* 'Payment by Results'.

1864   *Report of the Royal Commission on the Public Schools* (Clarendon). An investigation into the endowments, finances, methods, subjects and teaching of nine leading schools.

1868   *Report of the Schools Inquiry Commission* (Taunton). An examination of 800 endowed grammar schools. Recommended that they should be divided into three grades according to social class.

1870   *Elementary Education Act* (Forster). To provide efficient elementary schools in England and Wales for all children. The beginning of the dual system.

1872–5   *Report of Royal Commission on Scientific Instruction and the Advancement of Science* (Devonshire). Urged the development of science teaching at university and schools.

1880   *Education Act* (Mundella). Education obligatory for the majority of children until aged ten.

1882–4   *Report of Royal Commission on Technical Instruction* (Samuelson). Promoted technical education in elementary and secondary schools and highlighted the need for technical colleges.

1888   *Report of Royal Commission on Elementary Education Acts* (Cross). Commissioners were divided in their views.

1889   *Technical Instruction Act*. Allowed county and county borough councils to levy a penny rate for technical education.

1891   *Elementary Education Act*. Made the great majority of public elementary schools free.

1895   Ending of 'Payment by Results'.
              Report of Royal Commission on Secondary Education (Bryce). Called for system of secondary education in England with one central authority.

1899   *Board of Education Act*. A central body, the Board of Education, was set up in the following year with three branches – elementary, secondary and technical – headed by a President.

1902   *Education Act* (Balfour). Created local education authorities to promote all forms of education. Many county secondary schools and training colleges established.

1905   *Handbook of Suggestions for Teachers*. Centralised control of the curriculum by regulations supplemented by the *Handbook* suggesting approaches to teaching.

1907   *Free Places in Secondary Schools*. Twenty-five per cent of secondary school places to be free.

1911   *Report of Consultative Committee on Examinations in Secondary Schools*. Supported a system of public examinations at 16.

1917   Secondary School Examinations Council set up. An advisory body to co-ordinate standards and methods. School Certificate introduced.

1918   *Education Act* (Fisher). Proposed raising school leaving age to 15 and compulsory part-time education to 18.

1923   *Report of Consultative Committee on Differentiation of Curriculum for Boys and Girls*. Exposed the differences in opportunities available to boys and girls in secondary education.

1926   *Report of Consultative Committee on the Education of the Adolescent* (Hadow). Recommended the separation of primary and secondary education at 11. Two types of secondary school – grammar and modern.

1931   *Report of Consultative Committee on the Primary School* (Hadow). Proposed a progressive curriculum for the junior part of the primary school.

1933   *Report of Consultative Committee on Infant and Nursery Schools* (Hadow). Recommended separate infant schools and the provision of a national system of nursery schools.

1938   *Report of Consultative Committee on Grammar and Technical High Schools* (Spens). Recommended a tripartite system of secondary schools – grammar, technical and modern – each with appropriate curriculum.

1943   *Report of Consultative Committee on the Secondary School Examinations Council* (Norwood). Reinforced Spens' views on tripartism: suggested replacement of the School Certificate.

1944   *Report of Committee on Supply, Recruitment and Training of Teachers and Youth Leaders* (McNair). To raise the status of teachers, suggested increasing teachers' salaries and proposed three years' training.
             Education Act (Butler). Provision for raising the school leaving age to 15; education organised in three stages – primary, secondary and further.

1945   *Report of Special Committee on Higher Technological Education* (Percy). Recommended upgrading some technical colleges to Colleges of Advanced Technology.
             Ministry of Education replaced the Board of Education.

1951   General Certificate of Education introduced.

1959   *Report of Central Advisory Council, 15–18* (Crowther). Recommended raising school leaving age to 16 and condemned over-specialisation in sixth forms.

1960   *Report of Departmental Committee on the Youth Service* (Albemarle).
             Report of Committee on Secondary School Examinations (Beloe). Recommended the Certificate of Secondary Education (CSE).

1963   *Report of Central Advisory Council: Half Our Future* (Newsom).
             Report of Committee on Higher Education (Robbins). Recommended expansion of Higher Education.

1964   Ministry of Education replaced by Department of Education and Science (DES).
             DES Report of Working Party on Schools' Curricula and Examinations (Lockwood). Led to Schools Council for the Curriculum and Examinations, which took over the work of Secondary School Examinations Council.

1965	DES Circular 10/65: *The Organisation of Secondary Education.* Six ways in which local education authorities could reorganise for comprehensive education.
1966	White Paper: *A Plan for the Polytechnics and Other Colleges.*
1967	*Report of Central Advisory Council: Children and Their Primary Schools* (Plowden). Recommended positive discrimination and expansion of nursery education.
1968	*Report of Committee of Enquiry into Flow of Candidates in Science and Technology into Higher Education* (Dainton).
1970	DES Circular 10/70: *The Organisation of Secondary Education.* The Conservatives cancelled 10/65 and allowed local education authorities' discretion.
1972	*Report of Committee of Enquiry into Teacher Education and Training* (James). Recommended reorganisation of ITT into three cycles. DipHE introduced.
	DES White Paper: *A Framework for Expansion.* Colleges of Education encouraged to become more diverse.
1974	APU set up by DES for assessing and monitoring achievement.
1975	*Report of Committee of Inquiry: A Language for Life* (Bullock). Language across the curriculum.
	Sex Discrimination Act. Equal Opportunities Commission set up.
1976	*Education Act.* Local education authorities required to submit comprehensive schemes; direct grant schools to join maintained system or become independent.
1977	*Report of Committee of Enquiry: A New Partnership for Our Schools* (Taylor). Recommended widening powers and representation of governing bodies.
	Green Paper: *Education in Schools: A Consultative Document.*
1978	*Report of Committee of Enquiry into the Education of Handicapped Children and Young People* (Warnock). Recommended integration.
	Report of Steering Committee to Consider Proposals for Replacing GCE O Level and CSE by a Common System of Examining (Waddell).
1979	*Education Act.* Repealed 1976 Act.
1980	*Education Act.* 'Parents' Charter'.
1981	*Education Act.* Implementation of Warnock Report.
	Department of Employment White Paper: *A New Training Initiative – A Programme for Action.* A year's training for all 16–17-year-old school leavers.
1982	School Curriculum Development Committee (SCDC) and a

	Secondary Examinations Council (SEC) replace Schools Council.

1983 White Paper: *Teaching Quality.*

1984 *Education (Grants and Awards) Act.* Tighter central control of allocation of monies to local education authorities.

1985 *Report of Committee of Enquiry: Education for All* (Swann). Investigated under-achievement in ethnic minority groups and made proposals for teaching of all children.
White Paper: *Better Schools.*

1986 *Education Act.* Required all maintained schools to have a governing body with increased parental representation. Corporal punishment prohibited from 1987.

1987 *Teachers' Pay and Conditions Act.* Secretary of State appointed interim advisory committee to impose teachers' pay and conditions.

1988 *Education Reform Act.* National Curriculum 5–16. SEC and SCDC replaced by School Examinations and Assessment Council (SEAC) and a National Curriculum Council (NCC). General Certificate of Secondary Education introduced.
Report of the Committee of Inquiry into the Teaching of English Language (Kingman). Proposed a model for the teaching of English.

1989 *Report of Committee of Inquiry: Discipline in Schools* (Elton). Recommended measures to secure orderly atmosphere for teaching and learning.

1990 *Education (Student Loans) Act.*

1991 *School Teachers' Pay and Conditions Act.* Superseded 1987 legislation.
White Paper: *Higher Education: A New Framework.*

1992 White Paper: *Choice and Diversity: A Framework for Schools.*
Education (Schools) Act. New arrangements for school inspection. OFSTED.
Further and Higher Education Act. Unification of funding of higher education with a Higher Education Funding Council (HEFC) for England and a separate one for Wales. CNAA disbanded; polytechnics to become universities by December 1993. Further education colleges to be independent of local education authorities.

1993 Department of Education and Science becomes Department for Education (DfE).
Education Act. NCC and SEAC replaced by School Curriculum and Assessment Authority (SCAA). Unsatisfactory schools

to be subject to tighter supervision.

Funding Agency for Schools (FAS).

National Commission on Education published *Learning to Succeed*.

1994 White Paper: *Competitiveness – Helping Business to Win*.

Report on the National Curriculum and its Assessment (Dearing). Proposals to reduce the content of the national curriculum and to simplify assessment arrangements.

Education Act. Established a Teacher Training Agency (TTA) for England and Wales to fund teacher training courses and to involve schools in initial training partnerships with higher education institutions.

1995 White Paper: *Competitiveness – Forging Ahead*.

Department for Education merged with Employment Department to become Department for Education and Employment (DfEE).

Sir Ron Dearing's *Review of 16–19 Qualifications: Interim Report*.

1995 Office for Standards in Education (OFSTED) Review of Inspection Framework.

Further Education Development Agency (FEDA) established to replace Further Education Unit and Further Education Staff College.

Launch of *Improving Schools Programme*.

1996 A busy year for education: five Education Acts:

Education (Student Loans) Act.

Education (Scotland) Act.

Nursery Education and Grant Maintained Schools Act.

Education Act. Consolidated or repealed earlier legislation, including some aspects of the 1944 Education Act.

School Inspections Act.

Dearing Report: *Review of Qualifications for 16–19-year-olds*.

White Paper: *Learning to Compete*.

1997 *Education Act*. The last Act before the General Election: miscellaneous provisions, including on school discipline.

The Archbishop of Canterbury supported School Curriculum and Assessment Authority (SCAA) on teaching about values in schools.

May: General Election – 'Education, Education, Education' was Labour Party slogan.

White Paper: *Excellence in Schools*.

Education (Schools) Act. Abolished Assisted Places Scheme.

The School Curriculum and Assessment Authority merged with the National Council for Vocational Qualifications to become the Qualifications and Curriculum Authority (QCA).

Kennedy Report: *Learning Works.* A Committee chaired by Helena Kennedy, was set up by the Further Education Funding Council (FEFC) to make recommendations about improving participation in further education (FE). One major conclusion was that FE should not be left to market forces.

1998 *Education Act: School Standards and Framework.*

Teaching and Higher Education Act. A General Teaching Council to be established from 2000; OFSTED functions for initial teacher training (ITT) clarified.

Government of Wales Act. A National Assembly for Wales from 1999; some education functions transferred to the National Assembly.

Northern Ireland Act. A Northern Ireland assembly established taking over some education functions.

Scotland Act. Scottish Parliament established from 1999.

Reorganisation of County boundaries.

National Literacy Strategy introduced.

Department for Education and Employment (DfEE) Action Programme: *Meeting Special Educational Needs.*

Beacon Schools Initiative.

Green Paper: *Teachers Meeting the Challenge of Change.*

DfEE Circular 4/98: a compulsory curriculum for ITT.

1999 *Further and Higher Education Act.*

Moser Report: *A Fresh Start – Improving Literacy and Numeracy.*

Learning to Succeed: A New Framework for Post-16 Learning.

National Numeracy Strategy introduced.

2000 Review of Circular 4/98, a response to criticisms of too much detailed prescription in the ITT curriculum.

David Blunkett, Secretary of State for Education, announced plans for a new two-year Foundation Degree, to start in 2001–2.

General Teaching Council (GTC) England established.

Hay McBer Report on effective teaching.

White Paper: *Enterprise Skills and Innovation: Opportunity for All in a World of Change.*

Education Act. Learning and Skills Council (LSC) to replace the Further Education and Funding Council (FEFC) and Training Enterprise Boards.

2001   Green Paper: *Schools: Building on Success.*
DfEE Consultation Document on Continuing Professional Development.
June: General Election. Return of Labour Government.
Department for Education and Employment becomes Department for Education and Skills (DfES).
July: Publication of Consultation Document on Revision of Circular 4/98 (together with OFSTED *Arrangements for Inspection*). New system to start in September 2002.
White Paper: *Schools: Achieving Success.*
Special Educational Needs and Disability Act.

2002   Green Paper: *14–19: Extending Opportunities, Raising Standards.* Several moves in the direction of improving the quality of vocational education and access to further studies.
Education Act. Concerned with raising standards: more flexibility in the curriculum, organisation and financial arrangements, particularly regarding faith schools and specialist schools.

SECTION FOUR

Political Leaders

The Central Authority in Education: Political Leaders

Vice-Presidents of the Committee of Council on Education

W. F. Cowper	2 February 1857–5 April 1858
C. B. Adderley	6 April 1858–5 July 1859
Robert Lowe	6 July 1859–25 April 1864
H. A. Bruce	26 April 1864–25 July 1866
T. L. Corry	26 July 1866–18 March 1867
Lord Robert Montagu	19 March 1867–8 December 1868
W. E. Forster	9 December 1868–1 March 1874
Viscount Sandon	2 March 1874–3 April 1878
Lord George Hamilton	4 April 1878–2 May 1880
A. J. Mundella	3 May 1880–23 June 1885
Hon. E. Stanhope	24 June 1885–16 September 1885
Sir Henry Holland	17 September 1885–5 February 1886
Sir Lyon Playfair	6 February 1886–2 August 1886
Sir Henry Holland	3 August 1886–24 January 1887
Sir William Hart Dyke	25 January 1887–17 August 1892
A. H. D. Acland	18 August 1892–3 July 1895
Sir John Gorst	4 July 1895–8 August 1902

Presidents of the Board of Education

Duke of Devonshire	1 January 1900–7 August 1902
Marquess of Londonderry	8 August 1902–9 December 1905
Augustine Birrell	10 December 1905–22 January 1907
Reginald McKenna	23 January 1907–11 April 1908
Walter Runciman	12 April 1908–22 October 1911
Joseph Pease	23 October 1911–24 May 1915
Arthur Henderson	25 May 1915–17 August 1916
Marquess of Crewe	18 August 1916–9 December 1916
Herbert Fisher	10 December 1916–23 October 1922
Edward Wood (later Lord Irwin)	24 October 1922–21 January 1924
Charles (later Sir Charles) Trevelyan	22 January 1924–5 November 1924
Lord Eustace Percy	6 November 1924–6 June 1929
Sir Charles Trevelyan	7 June 1929–1 March 1931

Hastings Lees-Smith	2 March 1931–24 August 1931
Sir David Maclean	25 August 1931–14 June 1932
Lord Irwin	15 June 1932–6 June 1935
(later Viscount Halifax)	
Oliver Stanley	7 June 1935–27 May 1937
Earl Stanhope	28 May 1937–26 October 1938
Earl De La Warr	27 October 1938–2 April 1940
Herewald Ramsbotham	3 April 1940–19 July 1941
R. A. Butler	20 July 1941–2 August 1944

Ministers of Education

R. A. Butler	3 August 1944–24 May 1945
Richard Law	25 May 1945–2 August 1945
Ellen Wilkinson	3 August 1945–9 February 1947
George Tomlinson	10 February 1947–1 November 1951
Florence Horsbrugh	2 November 1951–17 October 1954
Sir David Eccles	18 October 1954–13 January 1957
Viscount Hailsham	14 January 1957–16 September 1957
Geoffrey Lloyd	17 September 1957–13 October 1959
Sir David Eccles	14 October 1959–16 July 1962
Sir Edward Boyle	17 July 1962–31 March 1964

Secretaries of State for Education and Science

Quintin Hogg	1 April 1964–16 October 1964
(later Viscount Hailsham)	
Michael Stewart	19 October 1964–23 January 1965
Anthony Crosland	24 January 1965–30 August 1967
Patrick Gordon-Walker	31 August 1967–5 April 1968
Edward Short	8 April 1968–19 June 1970
Margaret Thatcher	20 June 1970–4 March 1974
Reginald Prentice	5 March 1974–10 June 1975
Frederick Mulley	11 June 1975–10 September 1976
Shirley William	11 September 1976–7 May 1979
Mark Carlisle	8 May 1979–13 September 1981
Sir Keith Joseph	14 September 1981–20 May 1986
Kenneth Baker	21 May 1986–25 July 1989
John MacGregor	26 July 1989–1 November 1990
Kenneth Clarke	2 November 1990–10 April 1992
John Patten	11 April 1992–5 July 1993

Secretaries of State for Education

John Patten	6 July 1993–19 July 1994
Gillian Shephard	20 July 1994–4 July 1995

Secretaries of State for Education and Employment

Gillian Shephard	5 July 1995–1 May 1997
David Blunkett	2 May 1997–8 June 2001

Secretaries of State for Education and Skills

Estelle Morris	9 June 2001–23 October 2002
Charles Clarke	24 October 2002–

SECTION FIVE

Acronyms and Abbreviations

A Level	Advanced Level Examination (GCE)
AACTE	American Association of Colleges of Education
AAU	Academic Audit Unit
ACAC	Awdurdod Cwricwlwm ac Asesu Cymru (Curriculum and Assessment Authority for Wales)
ACACE	Advisory Council for Adult and Continuing Education
ACC	Association of County Councils
ACCAC	Awdurdod Cymwysterau, Cwricwlwm ac Asesu Cymru (Qualifications, Curriculum and Assessment Authority, Wales)
ACE	Advisory Centre for Education
ACFHE	Association of Colleges for Further and Higher Education
ACRG	Access Course Recognition Group
ACS	Average Class Size
ACSET	Advisory Committee for the Supply and Education of Teachers
ACT	Association of Career Teachers
ACU	Association of Commonwealth Universities
AE	Adult Education
AEB	Associated Examining Board
AEF	Aggregated External Finance
AERA	American Educational Research Association
AFC	Association for Colleges
AFE	Advanced Further Education
AHGMS	Association of Heads of Grant Maintained Schools
ALBSU	Adult Literacy and Basic Skills Unit
A Level	Advanced Level Examination (GCE)
ALI	Adult Learning Inspectorate
ALL	Association for Language Learning
AMA	Association of Metropolitan Authorities
AMG	Annual Maintenance Grant
AMMA	Assistant Masters and Mistresses Association
AoC	Association of Colleges
APA	Annual Performance Agreement
APC	Association of Principals of Colleges
APG	Annual Per Capita Grant
APL	Accreditation of Prior Learning
APR	Age Participation Rate
APS	Assisted Places Scheme
APT	Association of Polytechnic Teachers
APU	Assessment of Performance Unit

APVIC	Association of Principals in Sixth Form Colleges
AQ	Achievement Quotient
ARELS	Association of Recognised English Language Schools
AS	Advanced Supplementary Level Examination (now Advanced Subsidiary)
ASB	Aggregated Schools Budget
ASE	Association for Science Education
ASLIB	Association of Special Libraries and Information Bureaux
AST	Advanced Skills Teacher
AT	Articled Teacher
AT	Attainment Target (National Curriculum)
ATD	Art Teachers Diploma
ATL	Association of Teachers and Lecturers (formerly AMMA)
ATO	Area Training Organisation
AUR	Alternative Use of Resources
AUT	Association of University Teachers
AVA	Audio-Visual Aids
AVA	Authorised Validating Agencies
AWPU	Age-Weighted Pupil Unit
BA	Bachelor of Arts
BD	Bachelor of Divinity
BAAS	British Association for the Advancement of Science
BAC	British Accreditation Council for Independent Further and Higher Education
BACIE	British Association for Commercial and Industrial Education
BCIES	British Comparative and International Education Society
BD	Bachelor of Divinity
BEC	Business Education Council
BEd	Bachelor of Education
BEI	British Education Index
BEMAS	British Educational Management and Administration Society
BERA	British Educational Research Association
BIAE	British Institute of Adult Education
BL	British Library
BLitt	Bachelor of Letters
BMus	Bachelor of Music

BPhil	Bachelor of Philosophy
BPS	British Psychological Society
BSA	Boarding Schools Association
BSA	Basic Skills Agency (formerly Adult Literacy and Basic Skills Unit)
BSc	Bachelor of Science
BTEC	Business and Technology Education Council (formerly Business Education Council and Technician Education Council)
CACE	Central Advisory Council for Education
CAI	Computer Assisted Instruction
CAL	Computer Assisted Learning
CAS	Careers Advisory Service
CASE	Campaign for (the Advancement of) State Education
CAT	Computer Assisted Teaching
CATE	Council for the Accreditation of Teacher Education
CATS	Consortium for Assessment and Testing in Schools
CATS	Credit Accumulation and Transfer Scheme
CBET	Competency-Based Education and Training
CBI	Confederation of British Industry
CBT	Competency-Based Teaching
CBTE	Competency-Based Teacher Education
CBVE	Central Bureau for Educational Visits and Exchanges
CCEA	Council for Curriculum Examinations and Assessment (Northern Ireland)
CCT	Compulsory Competitive Tendering
CCT	Cross Curriculum Themes
CCTV	Closed Circuit Television
CCW	Curriculum Council for Wales
CDC	Council for Disabled Children
CD-ROM	Compact Disc-Read Only Memory
CDT	Craft Design and Technology
CE	Common Entrance
CEA	Conservative Education Association
CEDEFOP	Centre Européen pour le Développement de la Formation Professionelle
CEE	Certificate of Extended Education
CEE	Common Entrance Examination
CEF	Colleges Employers Forum
CEG	Careers Education and Guidance

CEO	Chief Education Officer
CEP	Career Entry Profile
CERI	Centre for Educational Research and Innovation (OECD)
CertEd	Certificate in Education
CET	Council for Educational Technology
CET	Continuing Education and Training
CEWC	Council for Education in World Citizenship
CFE	College of Further Education
CFF	Common Funding Formula
CFHE	College of Further and Higher Education
CGC	Child Guidance Clinic
CGLI	City and Guilds of London Institute
CHE	College of Higher Education
CI	Chief Inspector (of Schools)
CIHE	Council for Industry and Higher Education
CILT	Centre for Information on Language Teaching and Research
CIPFA	Chartered Institute of Public Finance and Accountancy
CLC	City Learning Centre
CLEA	Council of Local Education Authorities
CLS	Curriculum Led Staffing
CNAA	Council for National Academic Awards
COPE	Committee on Primary Education (Scotland)
COPERNICUS	Co-operation Programme in Europe for Research on Nature and Industry through Co-ordinated University Studies
COSE	Committee on Secondary Education (Scotland)
CP	College of Preceptors
CPD	Continuing Professional Development
CPS	Centre for Policy Studies
CPVE	Certificate of Pre-Vocational Education
CRAC	Careers Research and Advisory Centre
CRE	Campaign for Real Education
CRE	Commission for Racial Equality
CSA	Classroom Support Assistant
CSCFC	Conference of Scottish Centrally Funded Colleges
CSE	Certificate of Secondary Education
CSR	Continuous Student Record
CSV	Community Service Volunteers
CTC	City Technology College
CU	Course Unit

CVCP	Committee of Vice-Chancellors and Principals
D&T	Design and Technology
DD	Doctor of Divinity
DE	Department of Employment
DEd	Doctor of Education
DENI	Department of Education Northern Ireland
DEO	Divisional Education Officer
DES	Department of Education and Science
DfE	Department for Education
DfEE	Department for Education and Employment
DfEL	Department for Employment and Learning (Northern Ireland)
DfES	Department for Education and Skills
DHFETE	Department for Higher and Further Education, Training and Employment (Northern Ireland)
DipEd	Diploma in Education
DipHE	Diploma in Higher Education
DLitt	Doctor of Letters
DPhil	Doctor of Philosophy
DSc	Doctor of Science
DRTF	Disability Rights Task Force
DVE	Diploma of Vocational Education
EA	Education Association
EAL	English as an Additional Language
EAZ	Education Action Zone
EBD	Emotional and Behavioural Difficulties
EBP	Education-Business Partnership
EC	European Community
ECCTIS	Education Counselling and Credit Transfer Information Service
EdD	Doctor of Education
EDP	Education Development Plan
EEC	Early Excellence Centre
EFL	English as a Foreign Language
EHE	Enterprise in Higher Education
EiC	Excellence in Cities
EIS	Educational Institute of Scotland
EIU	Economic and Industrial Understanding
ELWa	Education and Learning (Wales)

EMIE	Education Management Information Exchange
ENTO	Employment National Training Organisation
EO	Education Otherwise
EOC	Equal Opportunities Commission
EPA	Education Priority Areas
EPC	Educational Publishers Council
ERA	Education Reform Act (1988)
ERASMUS	European Action Scheme for the Mobility of University Students
ERIC	Educational Resources Information Centre (USA)
ES	Employment Service
ESCALATE	Education Subject Centre: Advancing Learning and Technology in Education
ESF	European Social Fund
ESG	Education Support Grant
ESL	English as a Second Language
ESN	Educationally Sub-Normal
ESRC	Economic and Social Research Council
ESS	Education Standards Spending, England
ESTYN	Her Majesty's Inspectorate for Wales
ESW	Educational Social Worker
ESYN	Directorate for Early Education (Wales)
ET	Employment Training
ETG	Education and Training Group, British Council
ETI	Education and Training Inspectorate (Northern Ireland)
ETS	Educational Testing Service (USA)
ETV	Educational Television
EU	European Union
EurBac	European Baccalaureate
EUREKA	European Research Co-ordinating Agency
EWO	Education Welfare Officer
EWS	Educational Welfare Service
EYD	Early Years Directorate
EYDCP	Early Years Development and Child Care Partnership
FAS	Funding Agency for Schools
FE	Further Education
FEDA	Further Education Development Agency (formerly FEU)
FEFC	Further Education Funding Council for England
FEFWC	Further Education Funding Council, Wales
FENTO	Further Education National Training Organisation

FEU	Further Education Unit
FHE	Further and Higher Education
FLA	Foreign Language Assistant
FTE	Full-Time Equivalent
FTET	Full-Time Education and Training
GA	Graded Assessment
GBA	Governing Bodies Association of Boys' Schools
GBGSA	Governing Bodies of Girls' Schools Association
GCE	General Certificate of Education
GCSE	General Certificate of Secondary Education
GDST	Girls' Day School Trust (formerly Girls' Public Day School Trust)
GED	General Education Diploma
GERBIL	Great Education Reform Bill (Education Reform Bill, 1987–88)
GEST	Grants for Education Support and Training
GLC	Greater London Council
GM	Grant Maintained
GNVQ	General National Vocational Qualification
GO	Government Office for the Regions
GRC	Grant Related Criteria (GCSE)
GRE	Grant Related Expenditure
GRIDS	Guidelines for Review and Internal Development in Schools
GRIST	Grant-Related In-Service Training
GRTP	Graduate Registered Teachers' Programme
GS	Grammar School
GSA	Girls' School Association
GSVQ	General Scottish Vocational Qualification
GTC	General Teaching Council
GTCS	General Teaching Council (Scotland)
GTCW	General Teaching Council (Wales)
GTP	Graduate Teacher Programme
GTP	Gifted and Talented Programme
GTTR	Graduate Teacher Training Registry
HA	Historical Association
HE	Higher Education
HEA	Health Education Authority
HEADLAMP	Head Teachers Leadership and Management Programme

HEC	Health Education Council
HEFC	Higher Education Funding Council
HEFCNI	Higher Education Funding Council (Northern Ireland)
HEFCS	Higher Education Funding Council for Scotland
HEFCW	Higher Education Funding Council for Wales
HEI	Higher Education Institution
HEQC	Higher Education Qualifications Council
HM	Head Master /Mistress
HMC	Headmasters' and Headmistresses' Conference
HMCI	Her Majesty's Chief Inspector of Schools (England)
HMI	Her Majesty's Inspectorate
HMIE	Her Majesty's Inspector of Education for Scotland
HMSO	Her Majesty's Stationery Office
HNC	Higher National Certificate
HND	Higher National Diploma
HOD	Head of Department
HOY	Head of Year
HSC	Higher School Certificate
IAASE	Independent Appeals Authority for School Examinations
IAEP	International Assessment of Educational Progress
IAPS	Incorporated Association of Preparatory Schools
IB	International Baccalaureate
IBE	International Bureau of Education
ICET	International Council for Educational and Training Technology
ICS	Institute of Citizenship Studies
ICT	Information and Communications Technology
IDS	Inter-Disciplinary Studies
IE	Instrumental Enrichment
IEA	Institute of Economic Affairs
IEA	International Association for the Evaluation of Educational Achievement
IHE	Institute of Higher Education
IIEP	International Institute for Educational Planning
ILB	Industry Lead Body
ILEA	Inner London Education Authority
ILP	Independent Learning Programme
ILT	Institute of Learning and Teaching
INSET	In-Service Education of Teachers
IPPR	Institute for Public Policy Research

IPS	Independent Parent Support
IQ	Intelligence Quotient
ISC	Independent Schools Council
ISI	Independent Schools Inspectorate
ISCIS	Independent Schools Council Information Service (formerly Independent Schools Information Service)
ISR	Individualised Student Record
ISCED	International Standard Classification of Education
IT	Information Technology
ITA	Initial Teaching Alphabet
ITE	Initial Teacher Education
ITT	Initial Teacher Training
JCGCSE	Joint Council for the General Certification of Secondary Education
JCGQ	Joint Council for General Qualifications
JCNVAB	Joint Council of National Vocational Awarding Bodies
KAL	Knowledge About Language
KS	Key Stage (of national curriculum)
LA	Library Association
LAPP	Lower Attaining Pupil Programme
LCCI	London Chamber of Commerce and Industry
LEA	Local Education Authority
LEATGS	Local Education Authority Training Grants Scheme
LEC	Local Enterprise Companies (Scotland)
LGA	Local Government Association
LINC	Language in the National Curriculum
LISE	Librarians of Institutes and Schools of Education
LLB	Bachelor of Laws
LLD	Doctor of Laws
LMS	Local Management of Schools
LPSH	Leadership Programme for Serving Headteachers
LSA	Learning Support Assistant
LSDA	Learning and Skills Development Agency
LSC	Learning and Skills Council
LSU	Learning Support Unit
MA	Master of Arts
MA	Modern Apprenticeship

MACOS	Man – A Course of Study
MBA	Master of Business Administration
MEd	Master of Education
MFL	Modern Foreign Language
MIS	Management Information System
MLA	Modern Language Association
MLD	Moderate Learning Difficulties
MLitt	Master of Letters
MPhil	Master of Philosophy
MSc	Master of Science
MSC	Manpower Services Commission
NAB	National Advisory Body
NACEIC	National Advisory Council on Education for Industry and Commerce
NACETT	National Advisory Council for Education and Training Targets
NACGT	National Association of Careers Guidance Teachers
NAEIAC	National Association of Educational Inspectors, Advisers and Consultants (formerly National Association of Inspectors and Educational Advisers)
NAFE	Non-Advanced Further Education
NAGC	National Association for Gifted Children
NAGM	National Association of Governors and Managers
NAHT	National Association of Head Teachers
NAIEA	National Association of Inspectors and Educational Advisers
NALI	National Association of Lay Inspectors
NAME	National Anti-Racist Movement in Education
NAPE	National Anti-Racist Movement in Education
NAS/UWT	National Association of Schoolmasters/Union of Women Teachers
NASN	National Association for Special Needs
NAT	New Attainment Target
NATE	National Association for the Teaching of English
NATFHE	National Association of Teachers in Further and Higher Education
NAW	National Assembly for Wales
NC	National Curriculum
NCA	National Curriculum Assessment
NCB	National Children's Bureau

NCC	National Curriculum Council
NCDS	National Child Development Study
NCE	National Commission on Education
NCET	National Council for Educational Technology
NCPTA	National Confederation of Parent–Teacher Associations
NCS	National Childcare Strategy
NCSL	National College for School Leadership
NCVQ	National Council for Vocational Qualifications
NEAB	Northern Examinations and Assessment Board
NEC	National Extension College
NEF	New Education Fellowship
NFER	National Foundation for Educational Research in England and Wales
NGC	National Governors' Council
NGfL	National Grid for Learning
NGO	Non-Governmental Organisation
NIACE	National Institute of Adult Continuing Education
NICED	Northern Ireland Council for Educational Development
NICER	Northern Ireland Council for Educational Research
NNEB	National Nursery Examination Board
NOCN	National Open College Network
NPQH	National Professional Qualification for Headship
NQT	Newly Qualified Teacher
NRA	National Record of Achievement
NTA	National Training Awards
NTET	National Targets for Education and Training
NTO	National Training Organisation
NTONC	National Training Organisation National Council
NTS	Non-Teaching Staff
NUS	National Union of Students
NUSS	National Union of School Students
NUT	National Union of Teachers
NVQ	National Vocational Qualification
NYA	National Youth Agency
O Level	Ordinary Level Examination (GCE)
OCA	OFSTED Complaints Adjudicator
OCA	Open College for the Arts
OCN	Open College Network
OCR	Oxford, Cambridge and RSA Examinations Board
OECD	Organisation for Economic Co-operation and Development

OFSTED	Office for Standards in Education
OFTOT	Early Years Directorate
OHMCI	Office of Her Majesty's Chief Inspector of Schools (Wales)
ONC	Ordinary National Certificate
OND	Ordinary National Diploma
ORACLE	Observational Research and Classroom Learning Evaluation
OTT	Overseas Trained Teacher
OU	Open University
PANDA	Performance and Assessment Reports (OFSTED)
PAT	Professional Association of Teachers
PBTE	Performance-Based Teacher Education
PC	Profile Component (National Curriculum)
PCAS	Polytechnics Central Admissions System
PCFC	Polytechnics and Colleges Funding Council
PE	Physical Education
PESC	Public Expenditure Survey Committee
PFI	Private Finance Initiative
PGCE	Postgraduate Certificate of Education
PGCE	Professional Graduate Certificate of Education
PGR	Parent-Governor Representatives
PhD	Doctor of Philosophy
PHIP	Professional Headship Induction Programme (Wales)
PI	Performance Indicator
PICKUP	Professional Industrial and Commercial Up-dating
PL	Principal Lecturer
PLA	Pre-School Learning Alliance
PLR	Public Lending Right
PoS	Programme of Study
PPA	Pre-School Playgroup Alliance
PPB	Planned Programme Budgeting
PPP	Public Private Partnership
PRF	Performance Related Funding
PRP	Performance Related Pay
PRU	Pupil Referral Unit
PSB	Potential School Budget
PSE	Personal and Social Education
PSHE	Personal, Social and Health Education
PSLA	Pre-School Learning Association
PT	Part time

PTA	Parent–Teacher Association
PTR	Pupil–Teacher Ratio
PVC	Pro Vice-Chancellor
QA	Quality Assurance
QAA	Quality Assurance Agency
QAU	Quality Audit Unit
QCA	Qualifications and Curriculum Authority, England
QCAAW	Qualifications, Curriculum and Assessment Authority, Wales
QE	Qualifying Examination
QTS	Qualified Teacher Status
QUANGO	Quasi-Autonomous Non-Governmental Organisation
R and D	Research and Development
RBL	Resource Based Learning
RDA	Regional Development Agency
RE	Religious Education
REB	Regional Examining Body
RI	Registered Inspector (OFSTED)
RIAT	Registered Inspectors Appeals Tribunal
ROA	Record of Achievement
ROM	Read Only Memory
ROSLA	Raising of the School Leaving Age
RPA	Record of Personal Achievement
RSA	Royal Society of Arts
RSG	Revenue Support Grant (formerly Rate Support Grant)
RTP	Registered Teacher Programme
S Level	Special Level (GCE) Examination
SA	Special Agreement Schools
SACRE	Standing Advisory Council on Religious Education
SAM	Skills Analysis Model
SAT	Scholastic Aptitude Test (USA)
SAT	Standard Assessment Task
SATRO	Science and Technology Regional Organisation
SAU	Social Affairs Unit
SBC	Schools Broadcasting Council
SBS	Small Business Service
SCAA	School Curriculum and Assessment Authority
SCDC	School Curriculum Development Council

SCE	Scottish Certificate of Education
SCE	Service Children's Education
SCEA	Service Children's Educational Authority
SCETT	Standing Conference for the Education and Training of Teachers
SCI	Senior Chief Inspector (HMI)
SCITT	School-Centred Initial Teacher Training
SCOP	Standing Conference of Principals
SCOTCATS	Scottish Credit Accumulation and Transfer Scheme
SCOTVEC	Scottish Vocational Educational Qualification
SCRE	Scottish Council for Research in Education
SCSE	Standing Conference for Studies in Education
SCUE	Standing Conference on University Entrance
SD	Standard Deviation
SDP	School Development Plans
SEA	Socialist Education Association
SEAC	School Examinations and Assessment Council
SEB	Scottish Examination Board
SEC	Secondary Examinations Council
SED	Scottish Education Department
SEED	Scottish Executive Education Department
SEN	Special Educational Needs
SENJIT	Special Educational Needs Joint Initiative and Training
SEO	Society of Education Officers
SEU	Social Exclusion Unit
SEU	Standards and Effectiveness Unit (DfEE)
SGCT	Scottish General Teaching Council
SHA	Secondary Heads Association
SHEFC	Scottish Higher Education Funding Council
SHMIS	Society of Headmasters and Headmistresses in Independent Schools
SI	Staff Inspector
SL	Senior Lecturer
SLA	School Library Association
SLD	Severe Learning Difficulties
SLS	School Library Services
SMF	Social Market Foundation
SMILE	Secondary Mathematics Individualised Learning Experiment
SMP	School Mathematics Project
SMSC	Spiritual, Moral, Social and Cultural (Development)

SMT	Senior Management Team
SoA	Statement of Achievement
SOC	School Organisation Committee
SOED	Scottish Office Education Department
SOEID	Scottish Office Education and Industry Department
SPG	Special Purpose Grant
SQA	Scottish Qualifications Authority
SRB	Single Regeneration Budget
SRC	Science Research Council
SRHE	Society for Research into Higher Education
SSA	Standard Spending Assessment
SSDA	Sector Skills Development Agency
SSE	School Self-Evaluation
SSEC	Secondary School Examinations Council
SSG	School Standards Grant
SSR	Staff–Student Ratio
SSRC	Social Science Research Council
SST	Special Support Teachers (SEN)
SSTA	Scottish Secondary Teachers' Association
STA	Specialist Teacher Assistant
STF	Standards Task Force
STOPP	Society of Teachers Opposed to Physical Punishment
STRB	School Teachers' Review Body
SUfI	Scottish University for Industry
SWAP	Scottish Wider Access Programme
SVQ	Scottish Vocational Qualification
TA	Teacher Assessment
TA	Teaching Assistant
T&EA	Training and Employment Agency (Northern Ireland)
TC	Technology College
TC	Training Commission
TDD	Teachers Development Day
TEC	Technician Education Council
TEC	Training and Enterprise Council
TEED	Training Enterprise and Education Department
TEFL	Teaching English as a Foreign Language
TES	Times Educational Supplement
TESL	Teaching English as a Second Language
TESOL	Teaching of English to Speakers of Other Languages
TGAT	Task Group on Assessment and Testing

TI	Training Inspectorate
TQA	Teaching Quality Assessment
TQE	Total Quality Education
TQM	Total Quality Management
TSC	Training Standards Council
TTA	Teacher Training Agency
TUC	Trades Union Congress
TVEI	Technical and Vocational Education Initiative
TWES	Training and Work Experience Scheme
UCAS	Universities and Colleges Admissions Service
UCCA	Universities Central Council on Admissions
UCET	Universities Council for the Education of Teachers
UCLES	University of Cambridge Local Examinations Syndicate
UDE	University Department of Education
UFA	University of the First Age
UFC	Universities Funding Council
UfI	University for Industry
UGC	University Grants Committee
UKRA	United Kingdom Reading Association
ULEAC	University of London Examinations and Assessment Council
UNESCO	United Nations Educational, Scientific and Cultural Organisation
UOA	Unit of Assessment
UTTS	Undergraduate Teacher Training Scheme
UUK	Universities United Kingdom
UVP	Unified Vocational Preparation
U3A	University of the Third Age
VA	Voluntary Aided
VC	Voluntary Controlled
VC	Vice-Chancellor
VCE	Vocational Certificate of Education
VET	Vocational Education and Training
VP	Vice-Principal
VS	Voluntary School
VS	Voluntary Sector
VSO	Voluntary Service Overseas

WBL	Work-Based Learning
WEA	Workers' Educational Association
WEF	World Education Fellowship
WLGA	Welsh Local Government Association
WO	Welsh Office
WRFE	Work-Related Further Education
WWW	World Wide Web
YOP	Youth Opportunities Programme
YSS	Youth Support Service
YT	Youth Training
YTS	Youth Training Scheme